MUTTS

by Patrick McDonnell

"Dog-Eared"

Andrews McMeel
Publishing

Kansas City

Other Books by Patrick McDonnell

Mutts
Cats and Dogs: Mutts II
More Shtuff: Mutts III
Yesh!: Mutts IV
Our Mutts: Five
A Little Look-See: Mutts VI
What Now: Mutts VII
I Want to Be the Kitty: Mutts No. Eight

Mutts Sundays
Mutts Sunday Mornings
Mutts Sunday Afternoons

The Mutts Little Big Book

Mutts is distributed internationally by King Features Syndicate, Inc. For information write King Features Syndicate, Inc., 888 Seventh Avenue, New York, New York 10019.

04 05 06 07 08 BBG 10 9 8 7 6 5 4 3 2 1

ISBN: 0-7407-4740-1

Library of Congress Control Number: 2004106215

"Dog-Eared" is printed on recycled paper.

Mutts can be found on the Internet at
www.muttscomics.com.

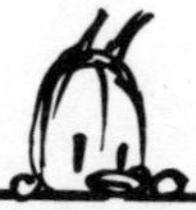

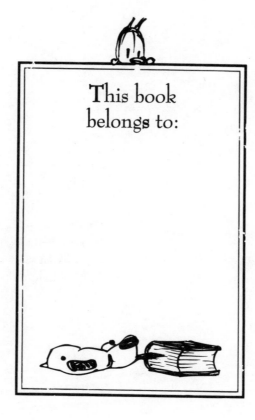

This book
belongs to:

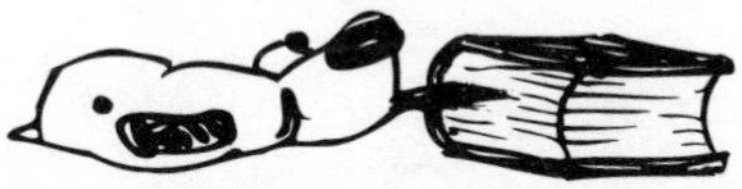

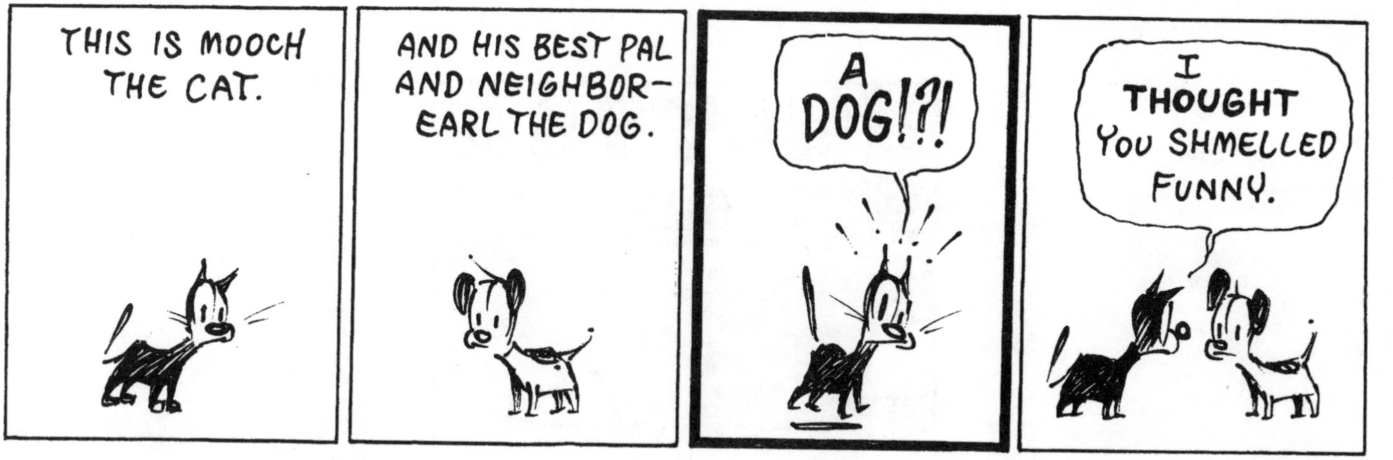
THIS IS MOOCH THE CAT.
AND HIS BEST PAL AND NEIGHBOR– EARL THE DOG.
A DOG!?!
I THOUGHT YOU SHMELLED FUNNY.

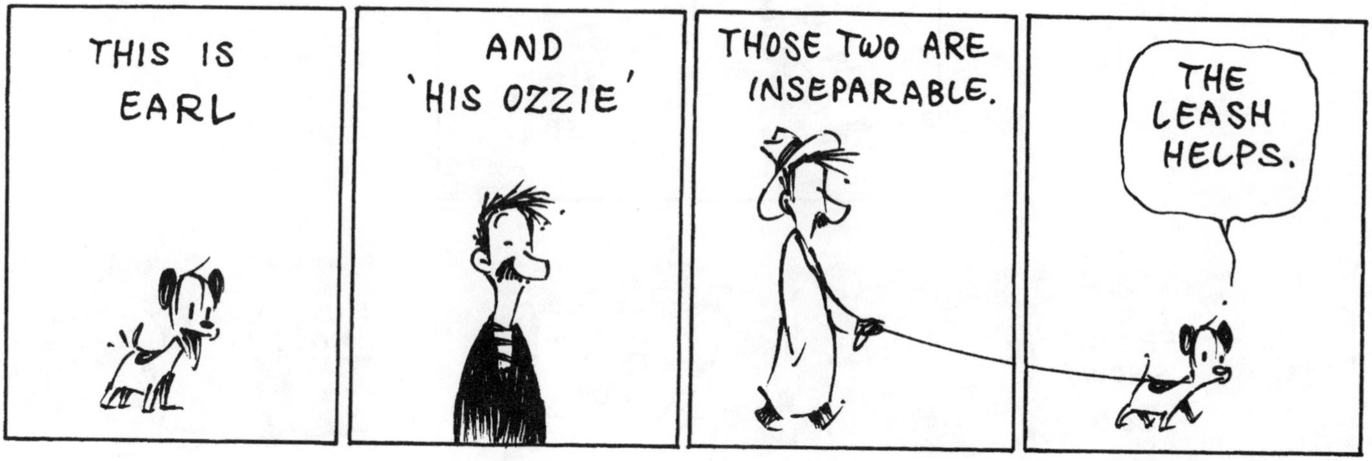
THIS IS EARL
AND 'HIS OZZIE'
THOSE TWO ARE INSEPARABLE.
THE LEASH HELPS.

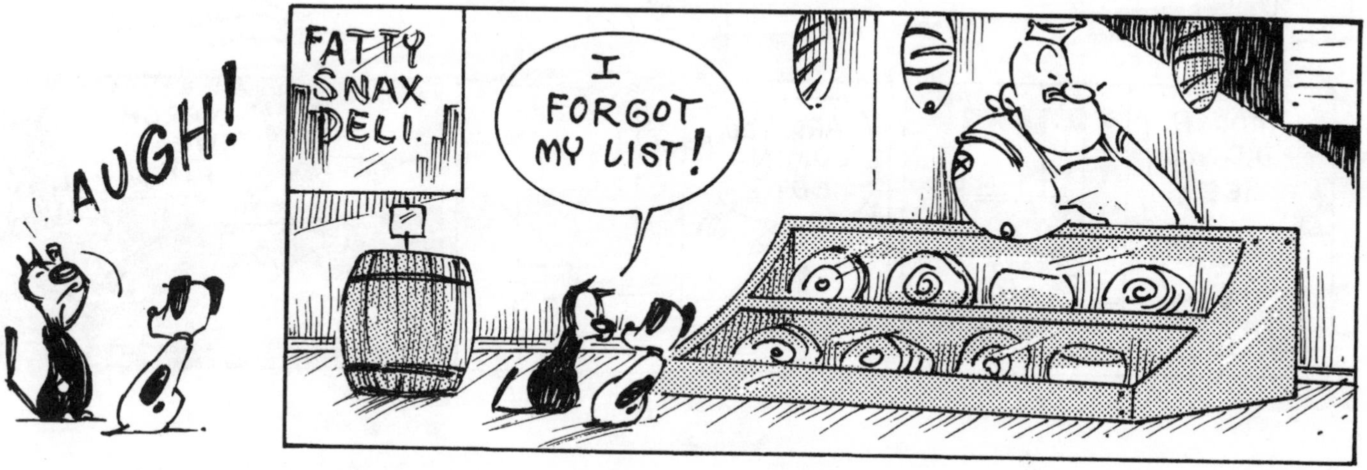
FATTY SNAX DELI.
I FORGOT MY LIST!
AUGH!

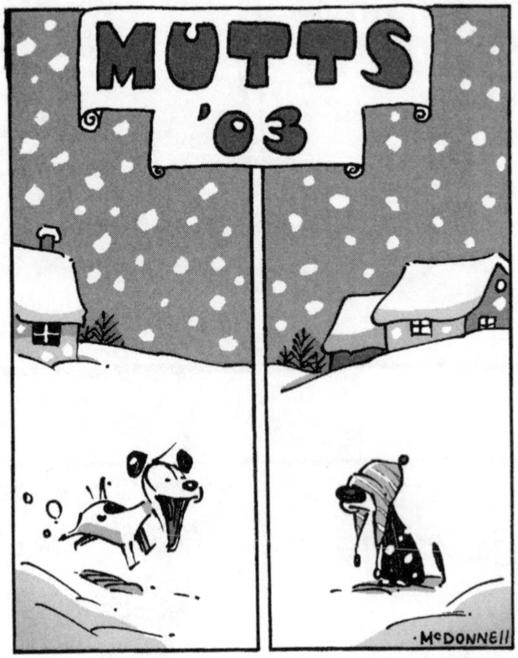
MUTTS
'03
McDONNELL

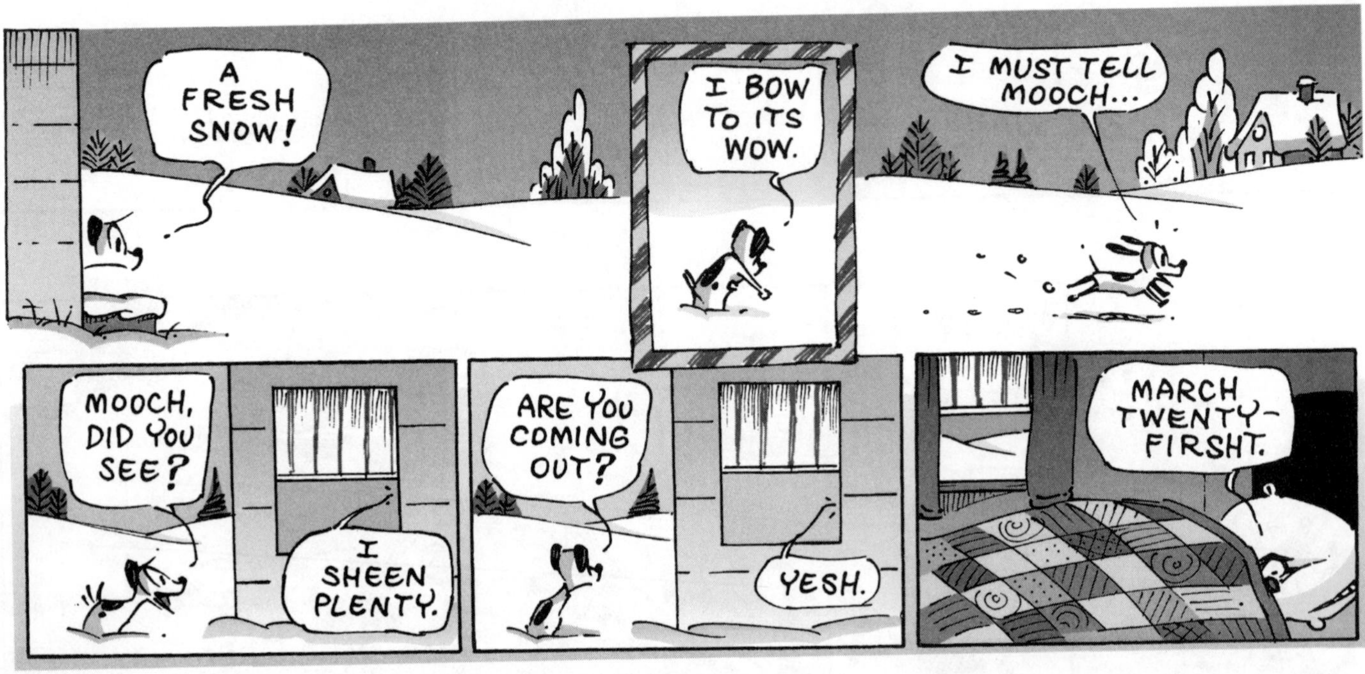
A FRESH SNOW!
I BOW TO ITS WOW.
I MUST TELL MOOCH...
MOOCH, DID YOU SEE?
I SHEEN PLENTY.
ARE YOU COMING OUT?
YESH.
MARCH TWENTY-FIRSHT.

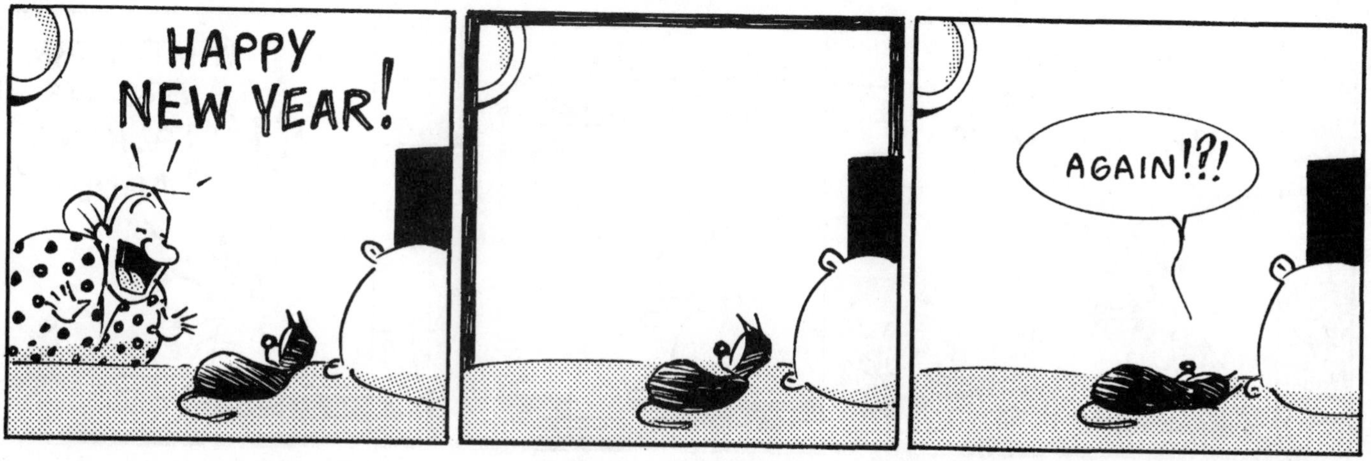
HAPPY NEW YEAR!
AGAIN!?!

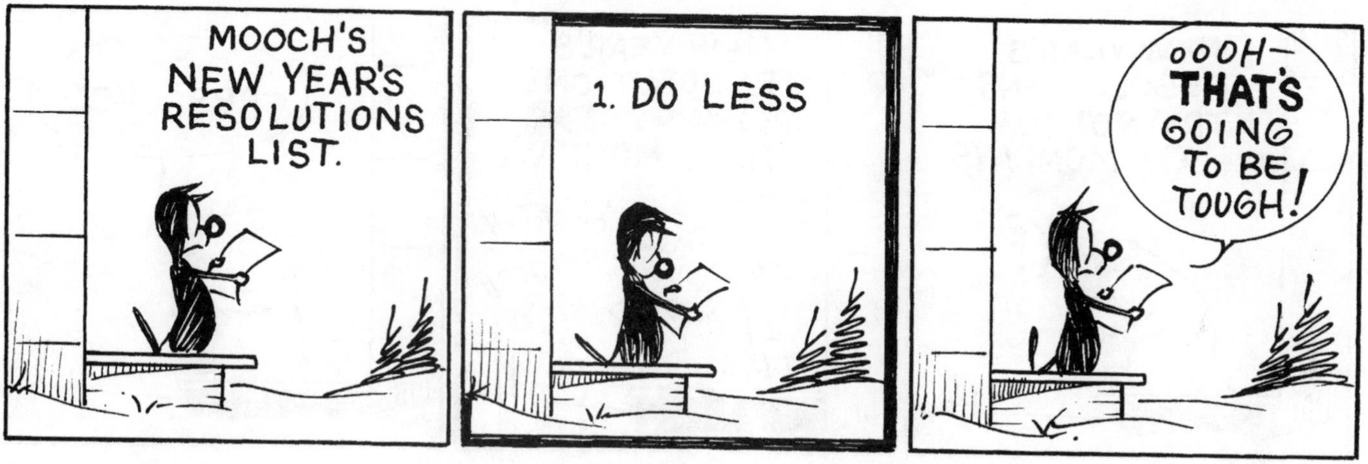
MOOCH'S NEW YEAR'S RESOLUTIONS LIST.
1. DO LESS
OOOH— THAT'S GOING TO BE TOUGH!

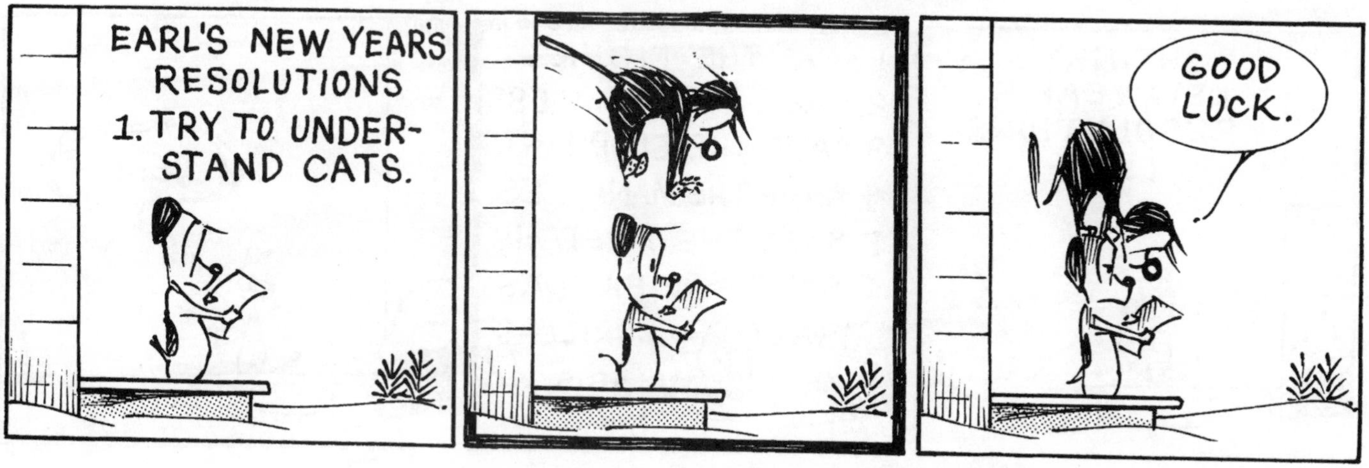
EARL'S NEW YEAR'S RESOLUTIONS
1. TRY TO UNDER-STAND CATS.
GOOD LUCK.

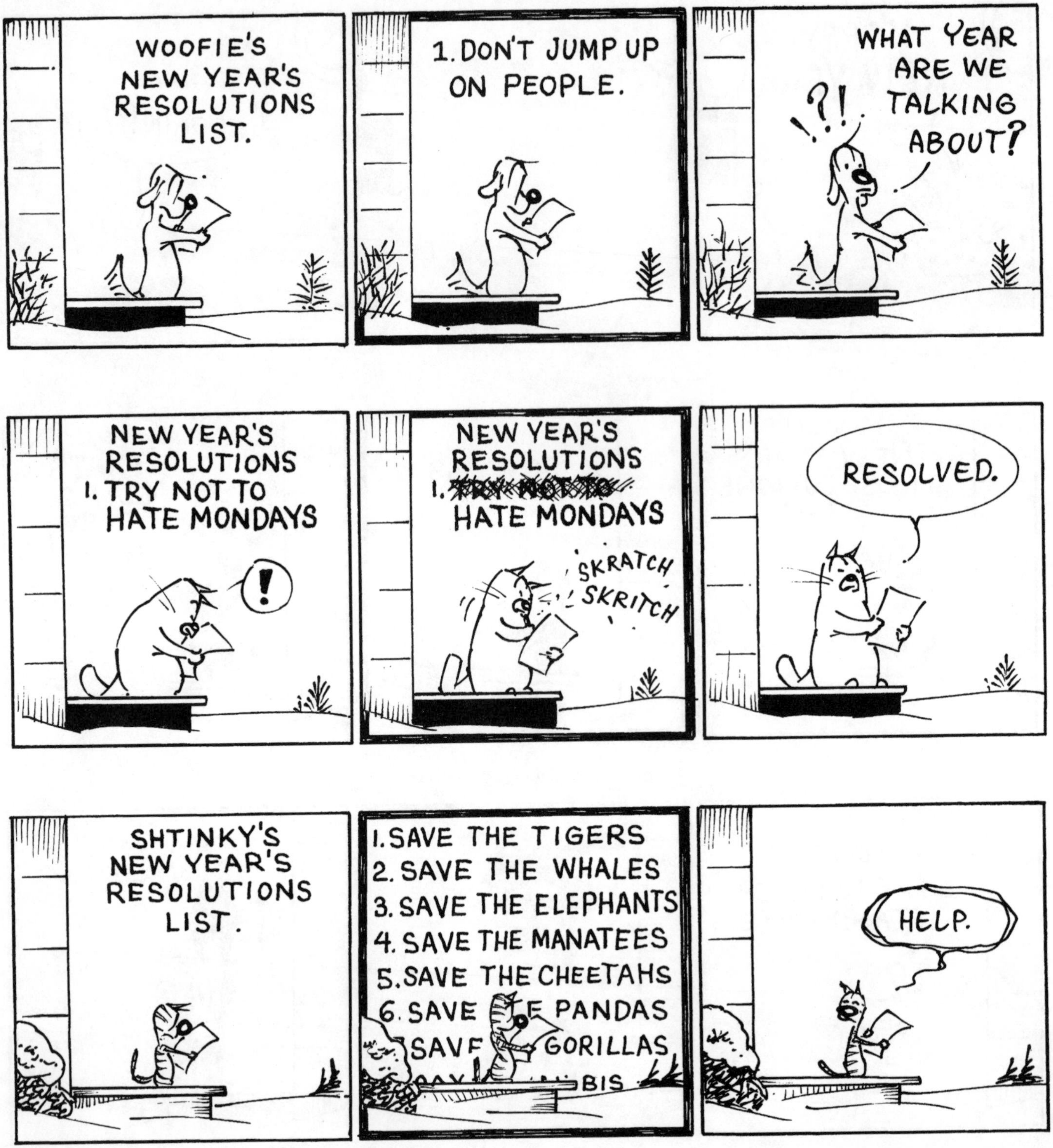

WOOFIE'S NEW YEAR'S RESOLUTIONS LIST.
1. DON'T JUMP UP ON PEOPLE.
!?!
WHAT YEAR ARE WE TALKING ABOUT?
NEW YEAR'S RESOLUTIONS
1. TRY NOT TO HATE MONDAYS
!
NEW YEAR'S RESOLUTIONS
1. ~~TRY NOT TO~~ HATE MONDAYS
SKRATCH SKRITCH
RESOLVED.
SHTINKY'S NEW YEAR'S RESOLUTIONS LIST.
1. SAVE THE TIGERS
2. SAVE THE WHALES
3. SAVE THE ELEPHANTS
4. SAVE THE MANATEES
5. SAVE THE CHEETAHS
6. SAVE
PANDAS
SAVE
GORILLAS
BIS
HELP.

mutts

COMIC ART BY
Patrick McDonnell

NEW YEAR'S RESHOLUTIONS Hmmmm...

HA! HA! THAT'S GOOD!

OOH—THAT'S **EVEN** BETTER!

DEFINITELY DO-ABLE.

YESH! YESH! **YESH!**

WHERE DO I SHTOP!?!

HERE, EARL, I'VE MADE SHOME NEW YEAR'S RESHOLUTIONS FOR **YOU!**

FOR **ME!?!** YOU'RE SUPPOSED TO MAKE NEW YEAR'S RESOLUTIONS FOR YOURSELF!

WHAT FUN IS **THAT!?!**

9

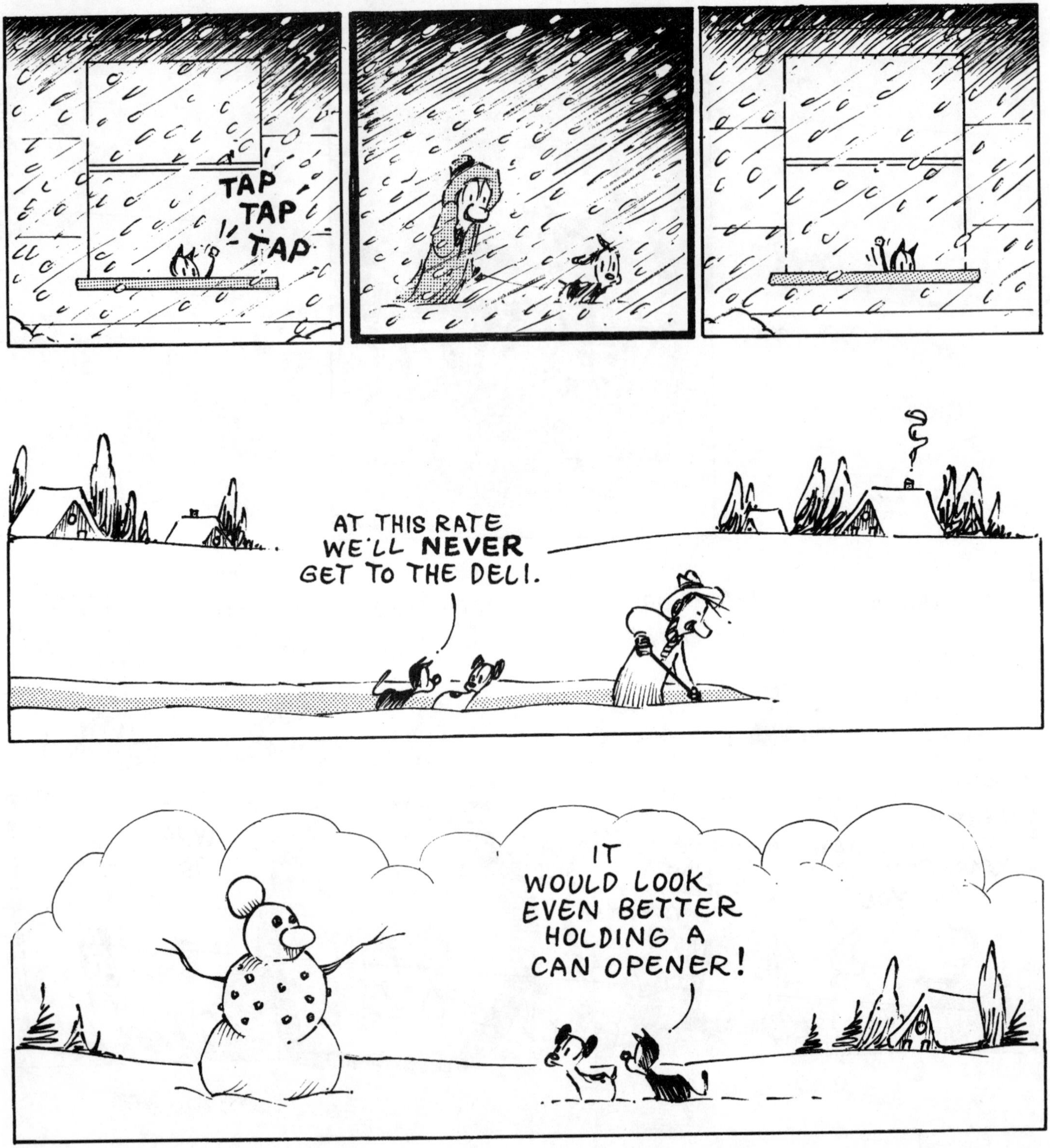
TAP
TAP
TAP
AT THIS RATE WE'LL **NEVER** GET TO THE DELI.
IT WOULD LOOK EVEN BETTER HOLDING A CAN OPENER!

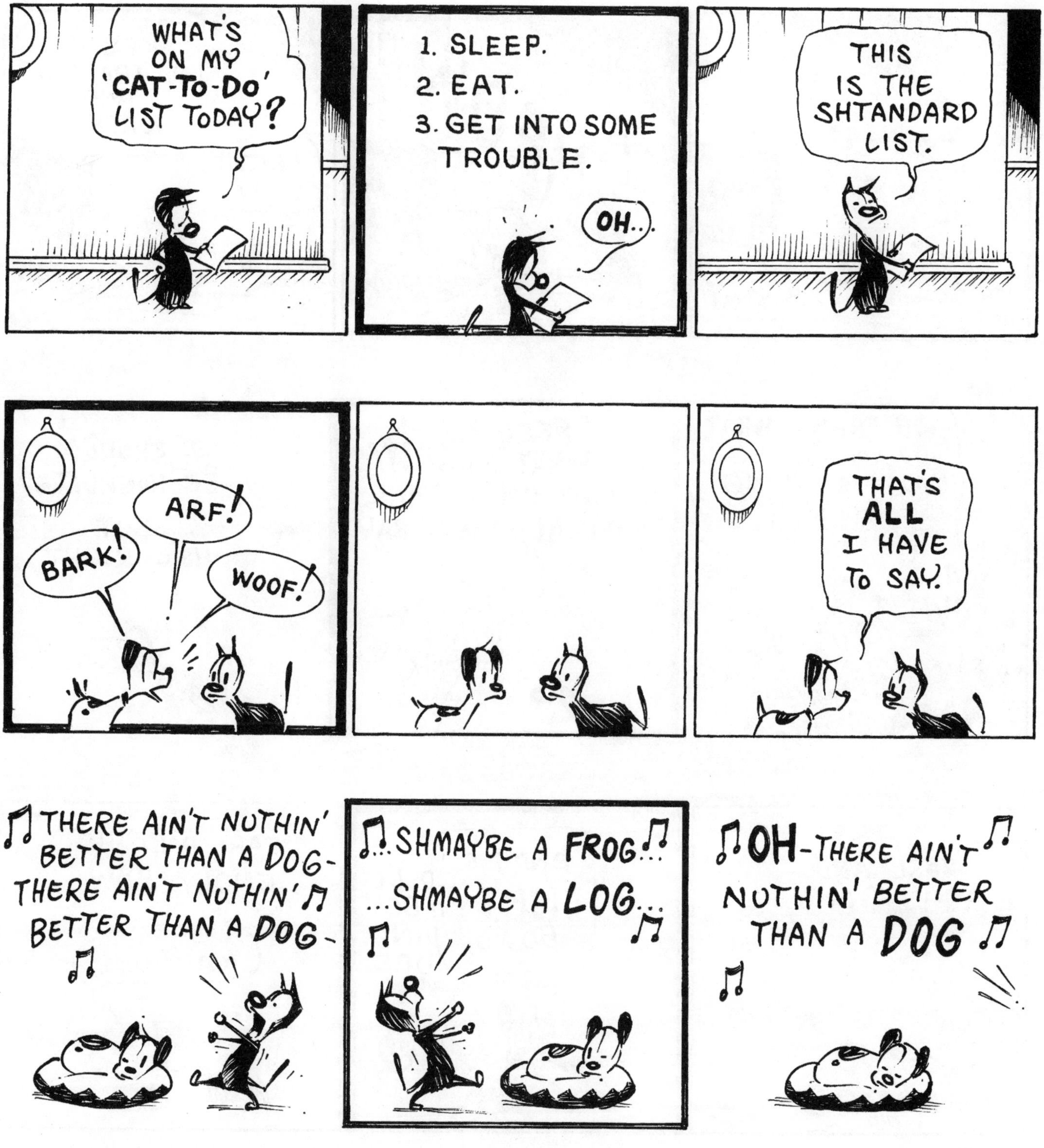
WHAT'S ON MY 'CAT-TO-DO' LIST TODAY?
1. SLEEP.
2. EAT.
3. GET INTO SOME TROUBLE.
OH...
THIS IS THE SHTANDARD LIST.
BARK!
ARF!
WOOF!
THAT'S ALL I HAVE TO SAY.
THERE AIN'T NUTHIN' BETTER THAN A DOG-
THERE AIN'T NUTHIN' BETTER THAN A DOG-
...SHMAYBE A FROG...
...SHMAYBE A LOG...
OH-THERE AIN'T NUTHIN' BETTER THAN A DOG

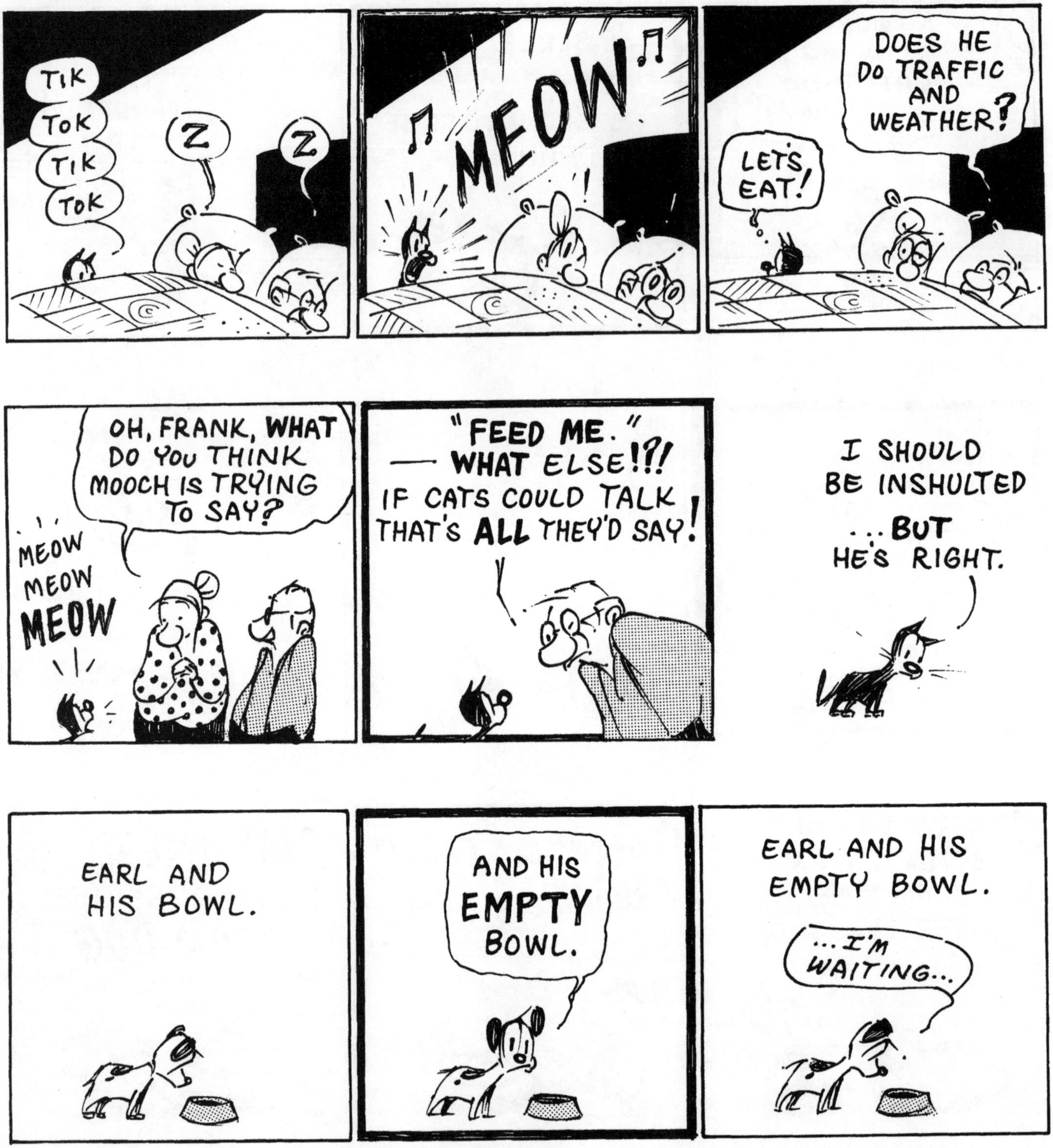
TIK
TOK
TIK
TOK
Z
Z
MEOW
DOES HE DO TRAFFIC AND WEATHER?
LET'S EAT!
OH, FRANK, WHAT DO YOU THINK MOOCH IS TRYING TO SAY?
MEOW MEOW MEOW
"FEED ME." — WHAT ELSE!?! IF CATS COULD TALK THAT'S ALL THEY'D SAY!
I SHOULD BE INSHULTED ...BUT HE'S RIGHT.
EARL AND HIS BOWL.
AND HIS EMPTY BOWL.
EARL AND HIS EMPTY BOWL.
...I'M WAITING...

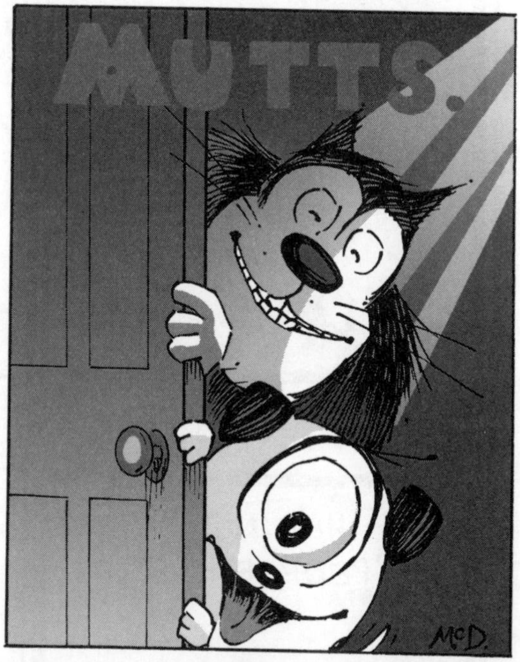
MUTTS.
McD.

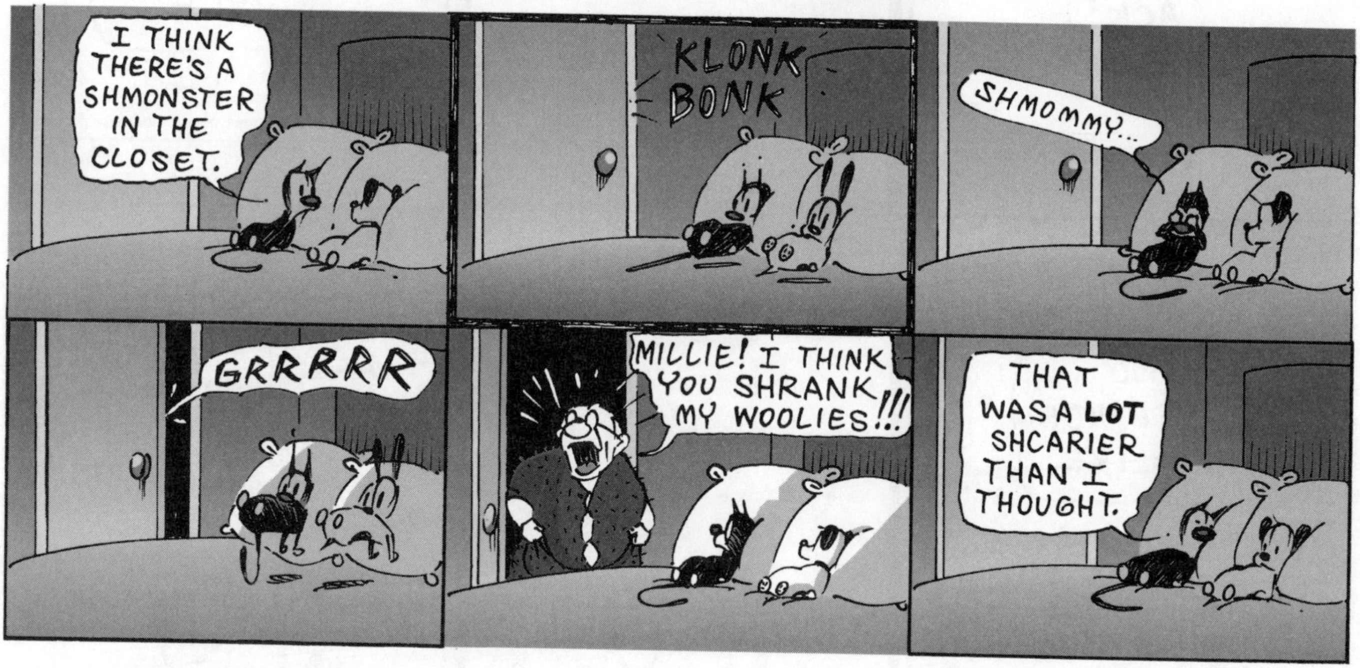
I THINK THERE'S A SHMONSTER IN THE CLOSET.
KLONK BONK
SHMOMMY...
GRRRRR
MILLIE! I THINK YOU SHRANK MY WOOLIES!!!
THAT WAS A LOT SHCARIER THAN I THOUGHT.

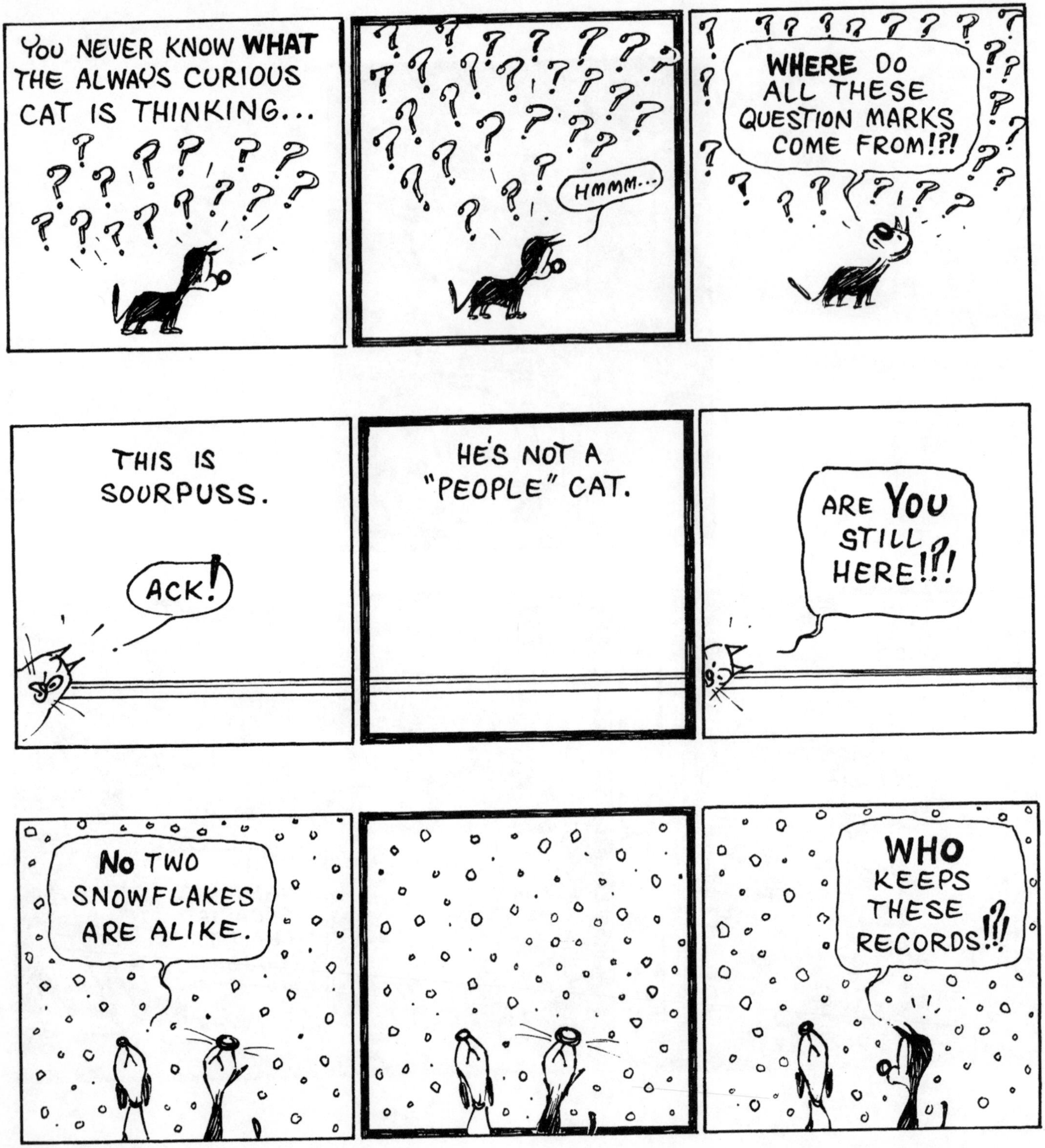

YOU NEVER KNOW WHAT THE ALWAYS CURIOUS CAT IS THINKING...
HMMM...
WHERE DO ALL THESE QUESTION MARKS COME FROM!?!
THIS IS SOURPUSS.
ACK!
HE'S NOT A "PEOPLE" CAT.
ARE YOU STILL HERE!?!
NO TWO SNOWFLAKES ARE ALIKE.
WHO KEEPS THESE RECORDS!?!

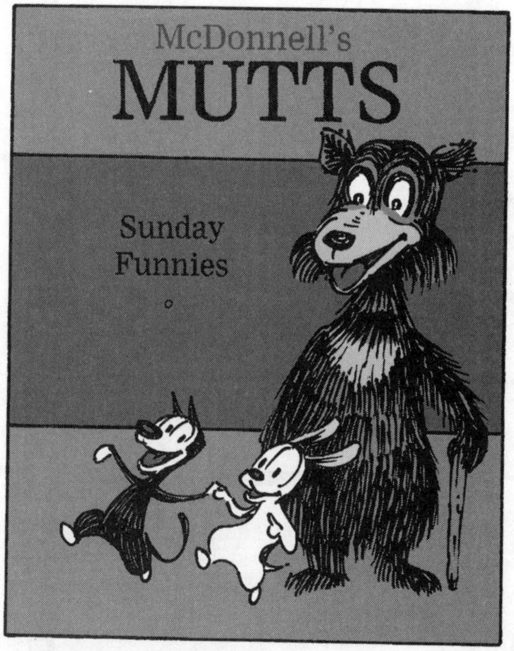
McDonnell's
MUTTS
Sunday
Funnies

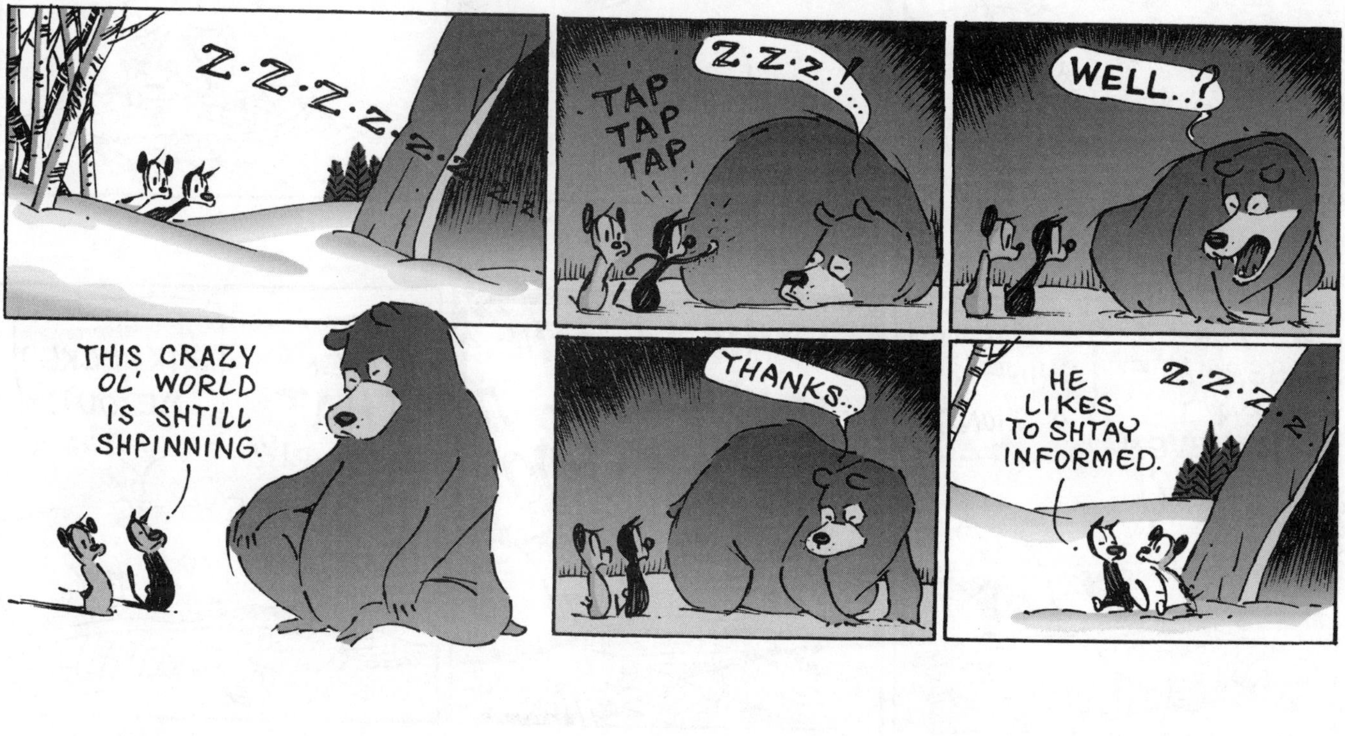
Z·Z·Z·Z·Z·Z
TAP
TAP
TAP
Z·Z·Z!...
WELL..?
THIS CRAZY OL' WORLD IS SHTILL SHPINNING.
THANKS...
HE LIKES TO SHTAY INFORMED.
Z·Z·Z·Z

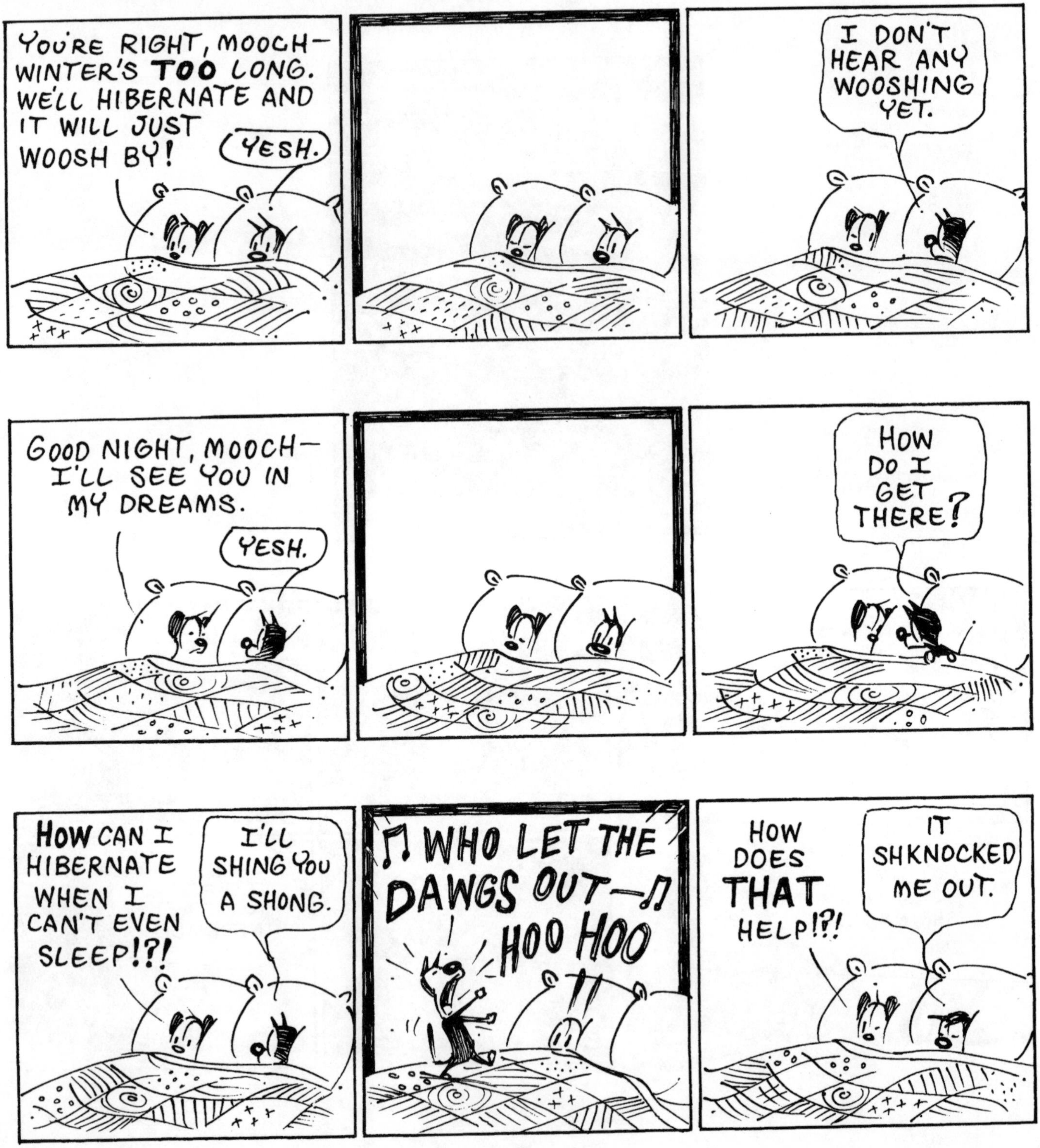
YOU'RE RIGHT, MOOCH-
WINTER'S **TOO** LONG.
WE'LL HIBERNATE AND
IT WILL JUST
WOOSH BY!
YESH.
I DON'T
HEAR ANY
WOOSHING
YET.
GOOD NIGHT, MOOCH-
I'LL SEE YOU IN
MY DREAMS.
YESH.
HOW
DO I
GET
THERE?
HOW CAN I
HIBERNATE
WHEN I
CAN'T EVEN
SLEEP!?!
I'LL
SHING YOU
A SHONG.
♫ WHO LET THE
DAWGS OUT—♫
HOO HOO
HOW
DOES
THAT
HELP!?!
IT
SHKNOCKED
ME OUT.

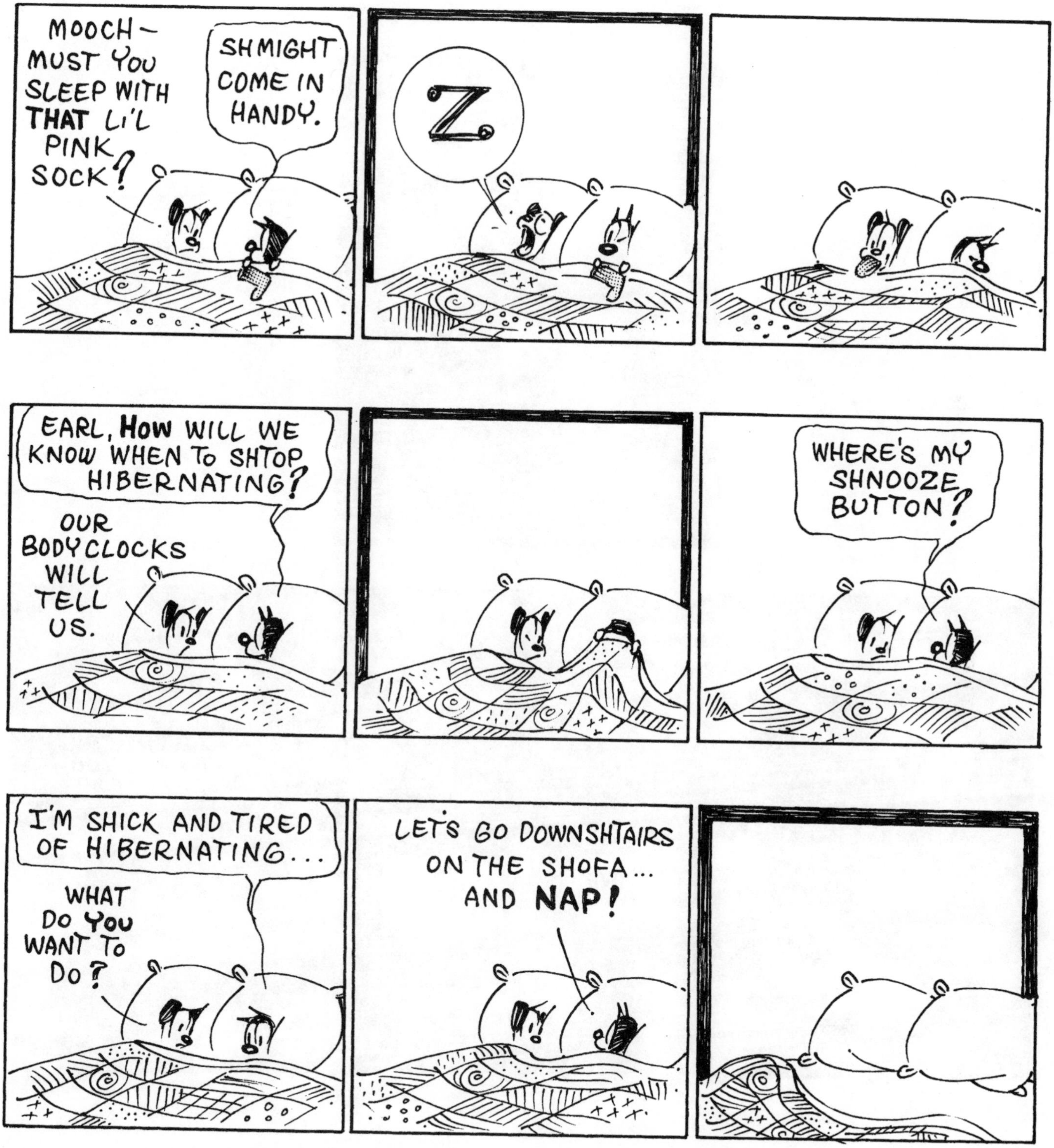
MOOCH- MUST YOU SLEEP WITH THAT LI'L PINK SOCK?
SHMIGHT COME IN HANDY.
Z
EARL, HOW WILL WE KNOW WHEN TO SHTOP HIBERNATING?
OUR BODYCLOCKS WILL TELL US.
WHERE'S MY SHNOOZE BUTTON?
I'M SHICK AND TIRED OF HIBERNATING...
WHAT DO YOU WANT TO DO?
LET'S GO DOWNSHTAIRS ON THE SHOFA... AND NAP!

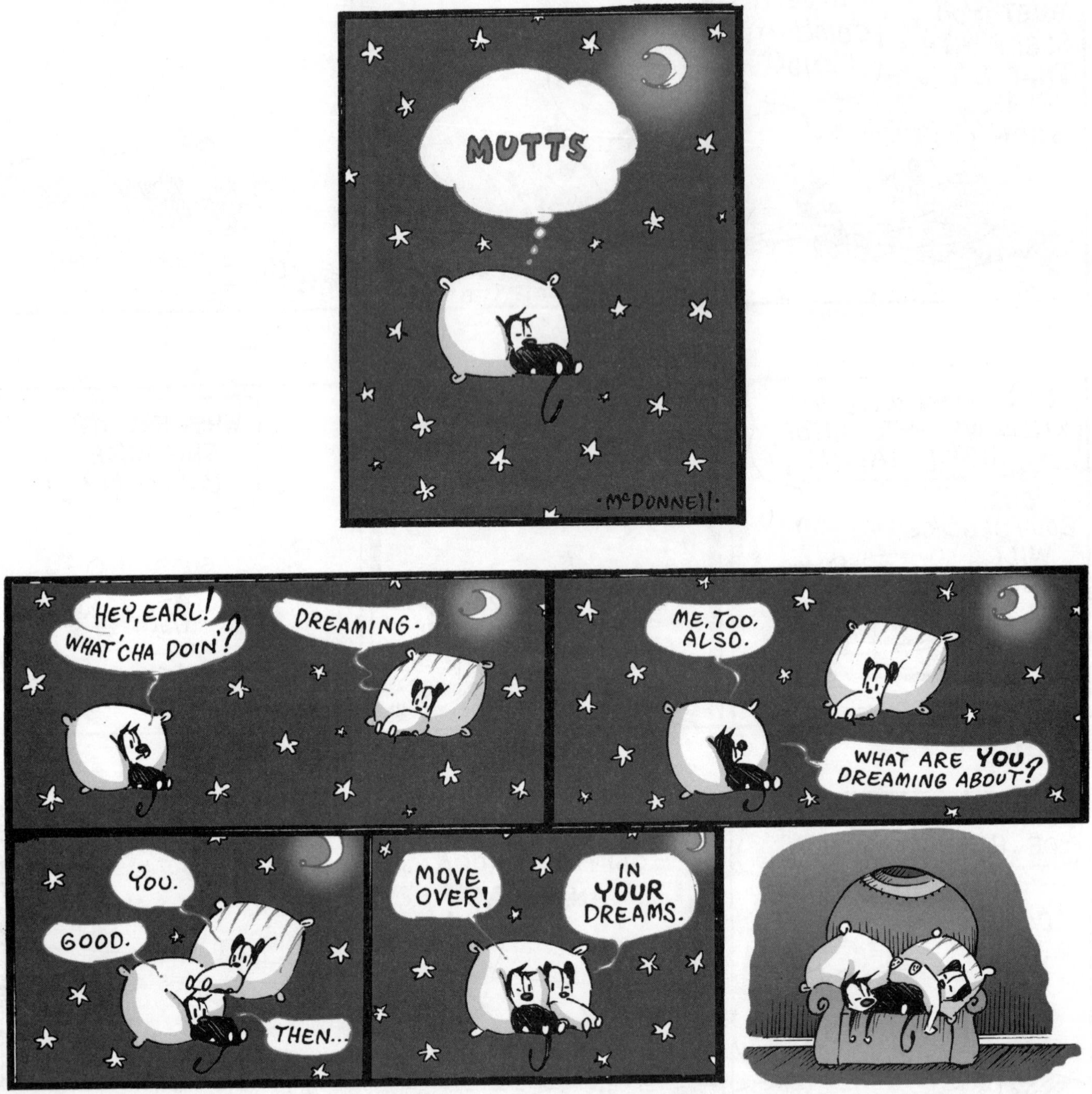
MUTTS
·McDONNELL·
HEY, EARL! WHAT'CHA DOIN'?
DREAMING.
ME, TOO. ALSO.
WHAT ARE YOU DREAMING ABOUT?
YOU.
GOOD.
THEN...
MOVE OVER!
IN YOUR DREAMS.

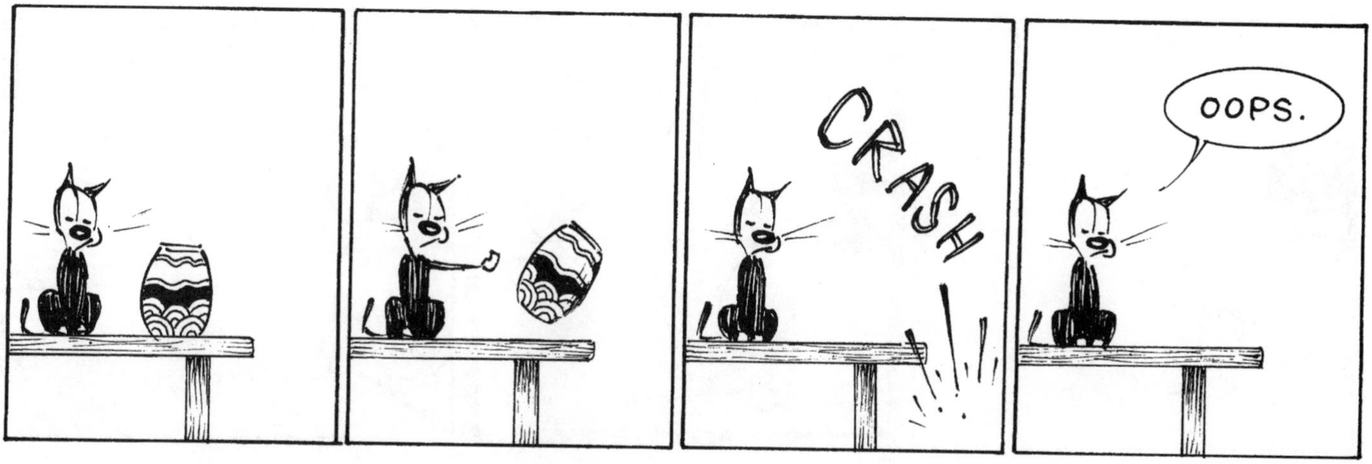
CRASH
OOPS.

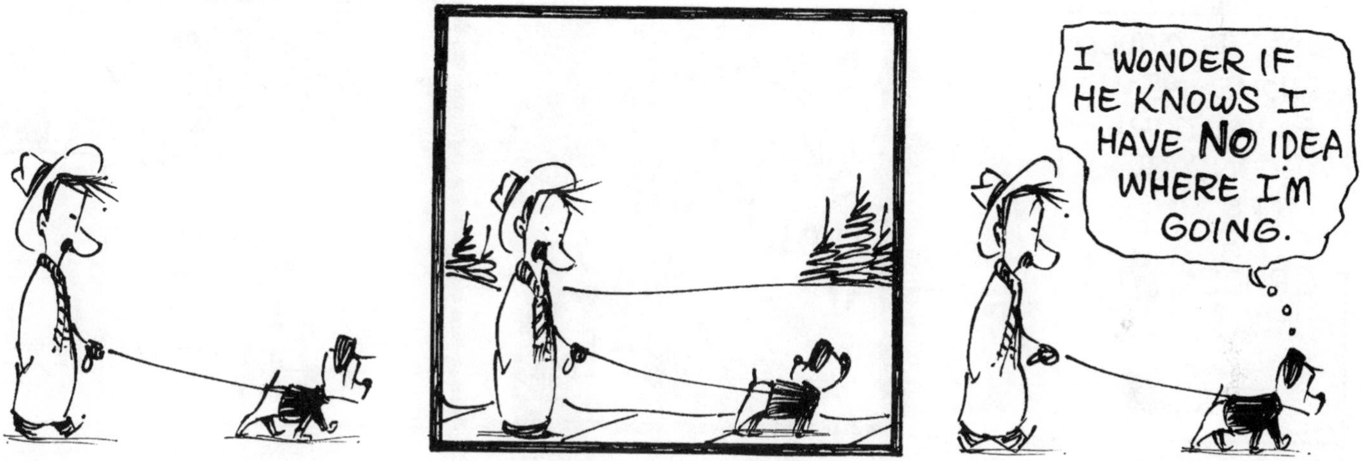
I WONDER IF HE KNOWS I HAVE NO IDEA WHERE I'M GOING.

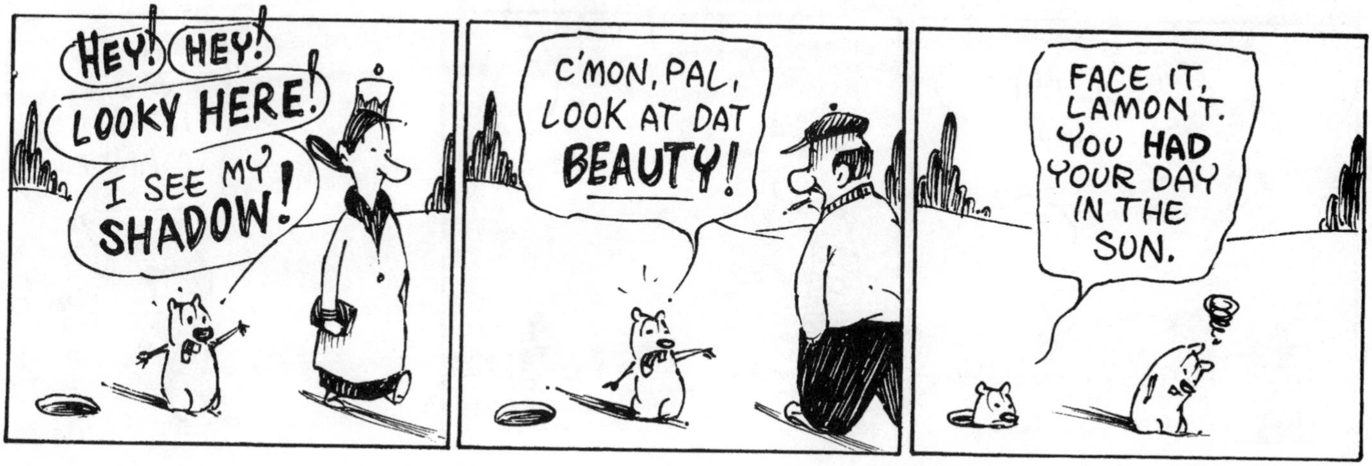
HEY! HEY!
LOOKY HERE!
I SEE MY SHADOW!
C'MON, PAL, LOOK AT DAT BEAUTY!
FACE IT, LAMONT. YOU HAD YOUR DAY IN THE SUN.

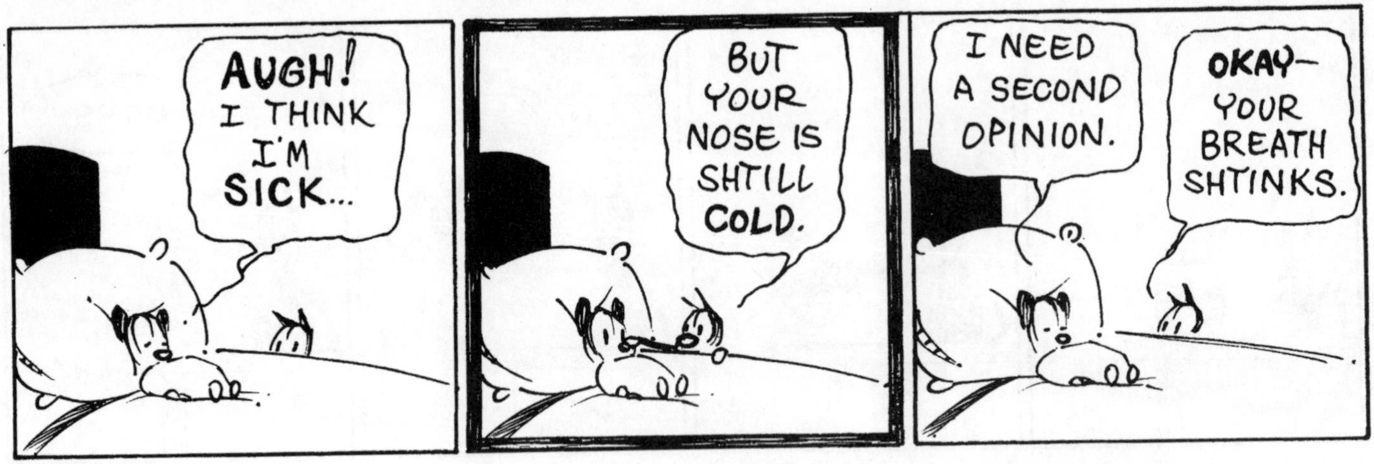
AUGH! I THINK I'M SICK...
BUT YOUR NOSE IS SHTILL COLD.
I NEED A SECOND OPINION.
OKAY— YOUR BREATH SHTINKS.

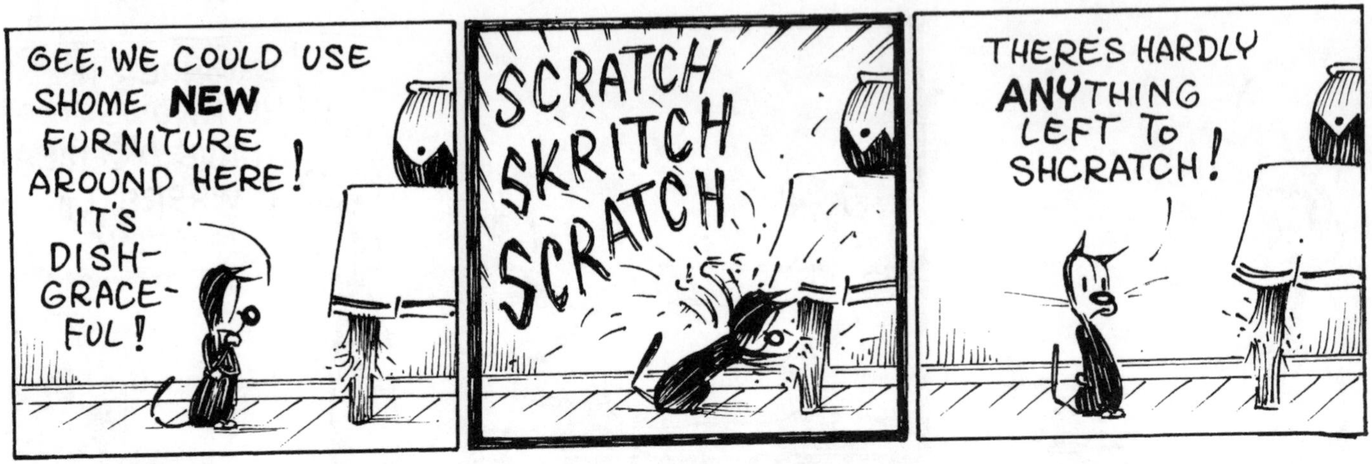
GEE, WE COULD USE SHOME NEW FURNITURE AROUND HERE! IT'S DISH-GRACE-FUL!
SCRATCH SKRITCH SCRATCH
THERE'S HARDLY ANYTHING LEFT TO SHCRATCH!

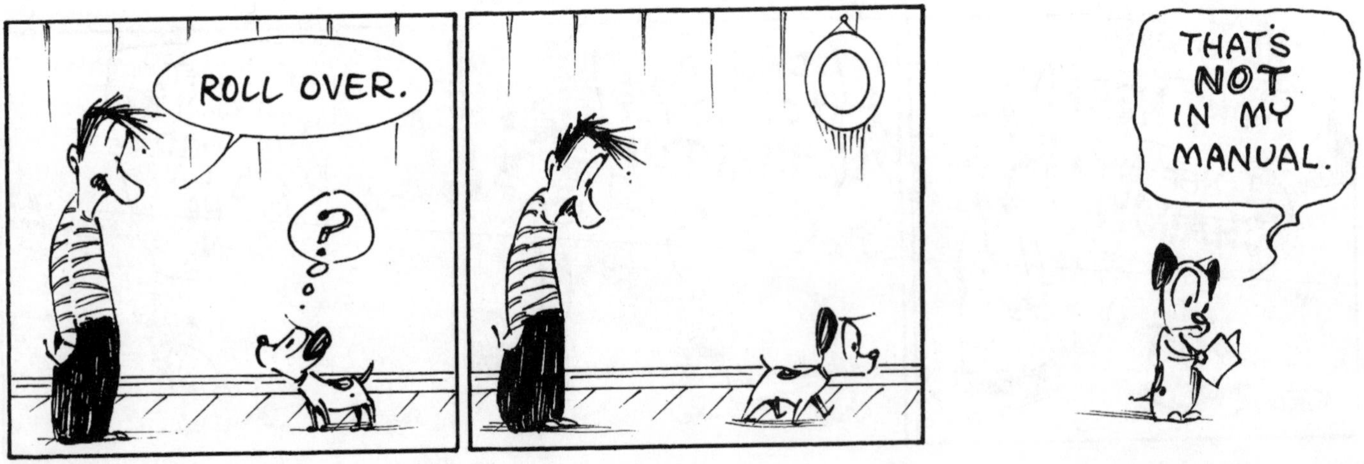
ROLL OVER.
?
THAT'S NOT IN MY MANUAL.

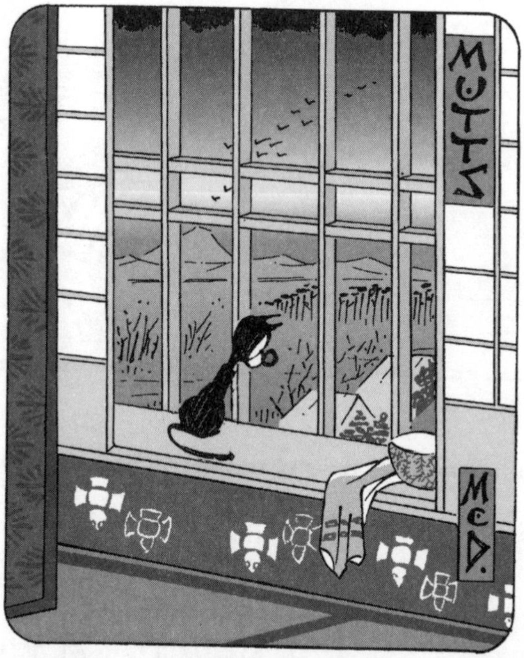
MUTTS
McD.

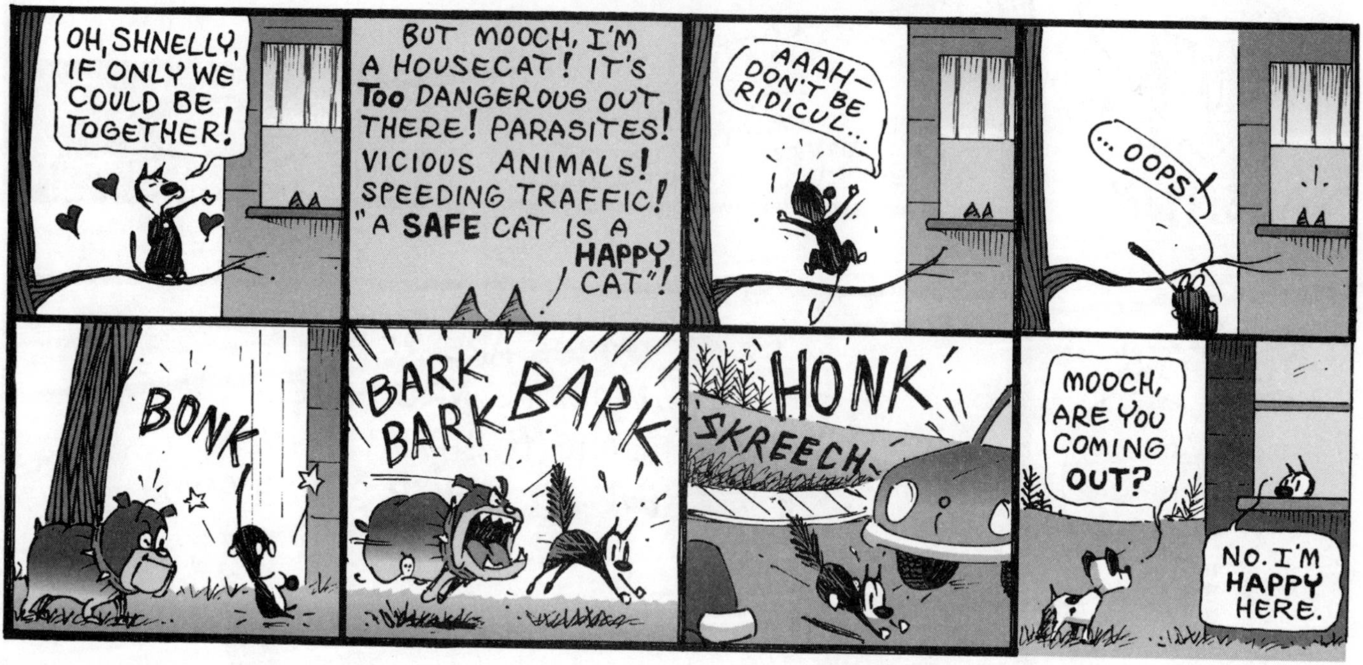
OH, SHNELLY, IF ONLY WE COULD BE TOGETHER!
BUT MOOCH, I'M A HOUSECAT! IT'S TOO DANGEROUS OUT THERE! PARASITES! VICIOUS ANIMALS! SPEEDING TRAFFIC! "A SAFE CAT IS A HAPPY CAT"!
AAAH- DON'T BE RIDICUL...
...OOPS!
BONK
BARK BARK BARK
HONK
SKREECH
MOOCH, ARE YOU COMING OUT?
NO. I'M HAPPY HERE.

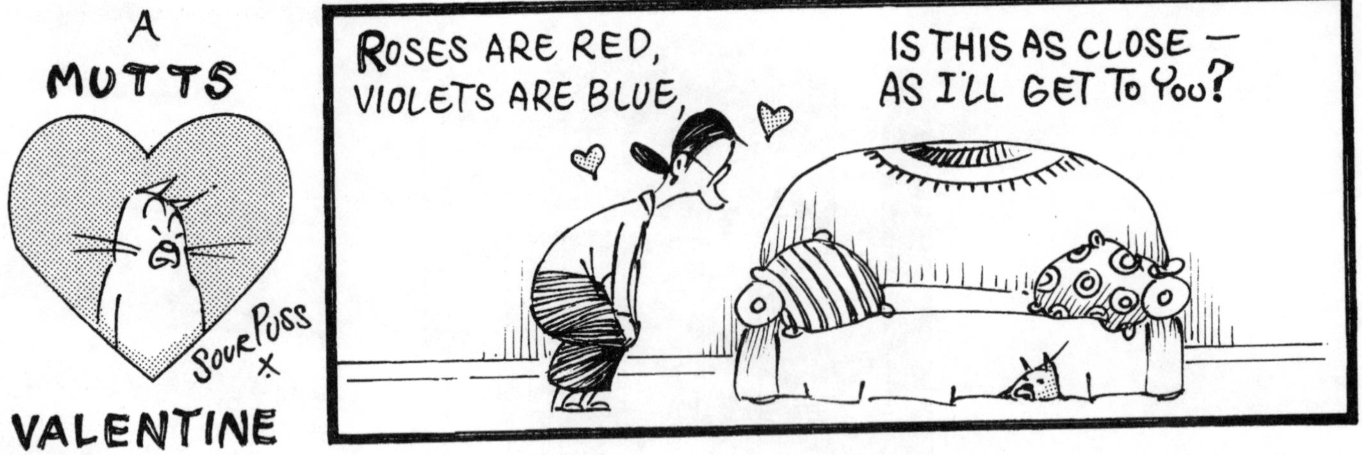
A MUTTS VALENTINE
SOURPUSS X
ROSES ARE RED, VIOLETS ARE BLUE,
IS THIS AS CLOSE — AS I'LL GET TO YOU?

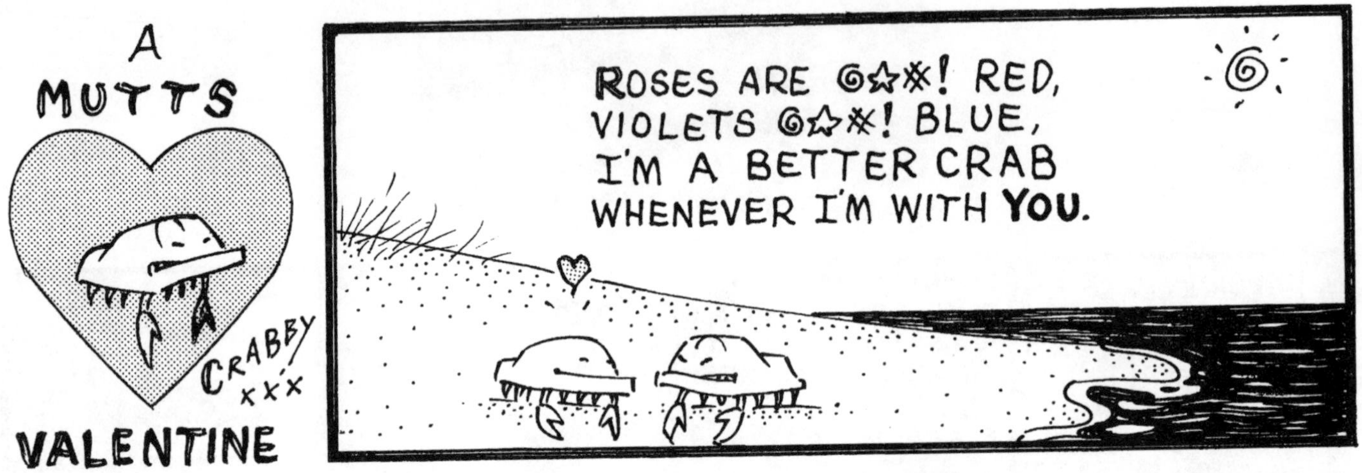
A MUTTS VALENTINE
CRABBY XXX
ROSES ARE @☆*! RED,
VIOLETS @☆*! BLUE,
I'M A BETTER CRAB
WHENEVER I'M WITH **YOU**.

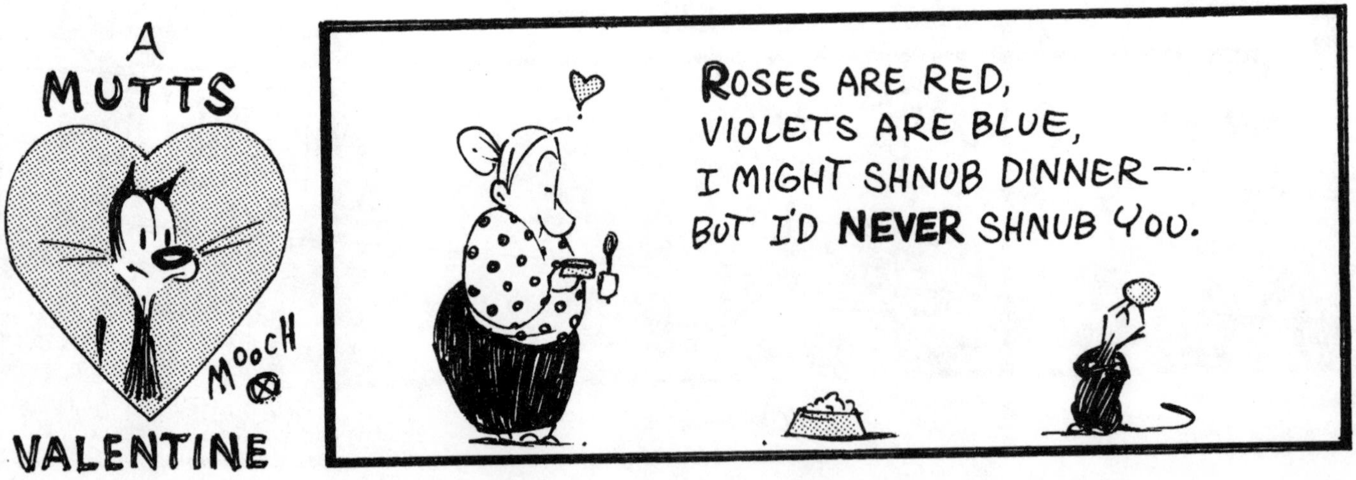
A MUTTS VALENTINE
MOOCH
ROSES ARE RED,
VIOLETS ARE BLUE,
I MIGHT SHNUB DINNER—
BUT I'D **NEVER** SHNUB YOU.

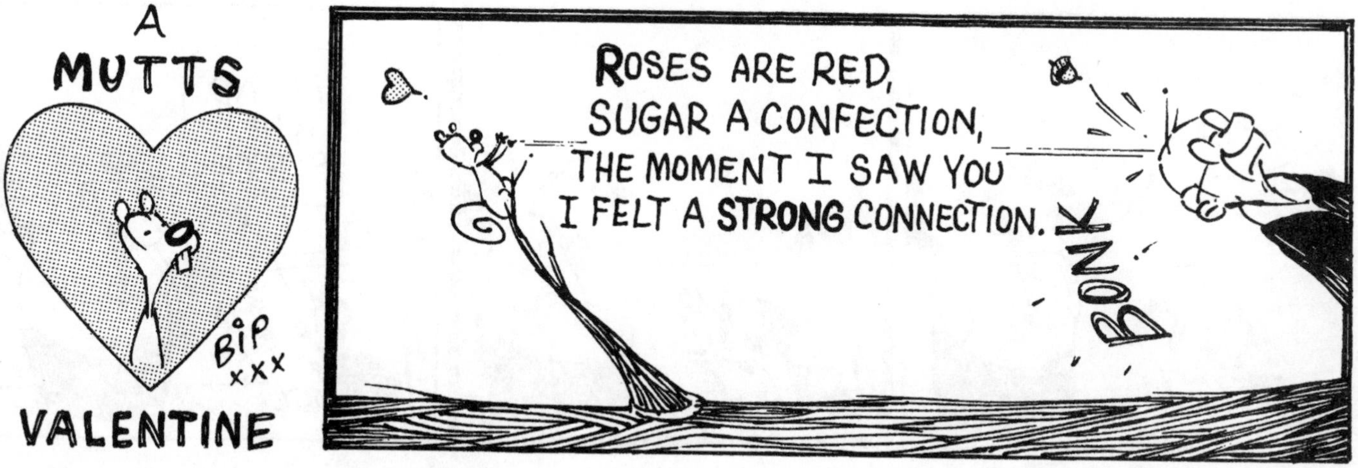
A MUTTS VALENTINE
BIP XXX
ROSES ARE RED,
SUGAR A CONFECTION,
THE MOMENT I SAW YOU
I FELT A STRONG CONNECTION.
BONK

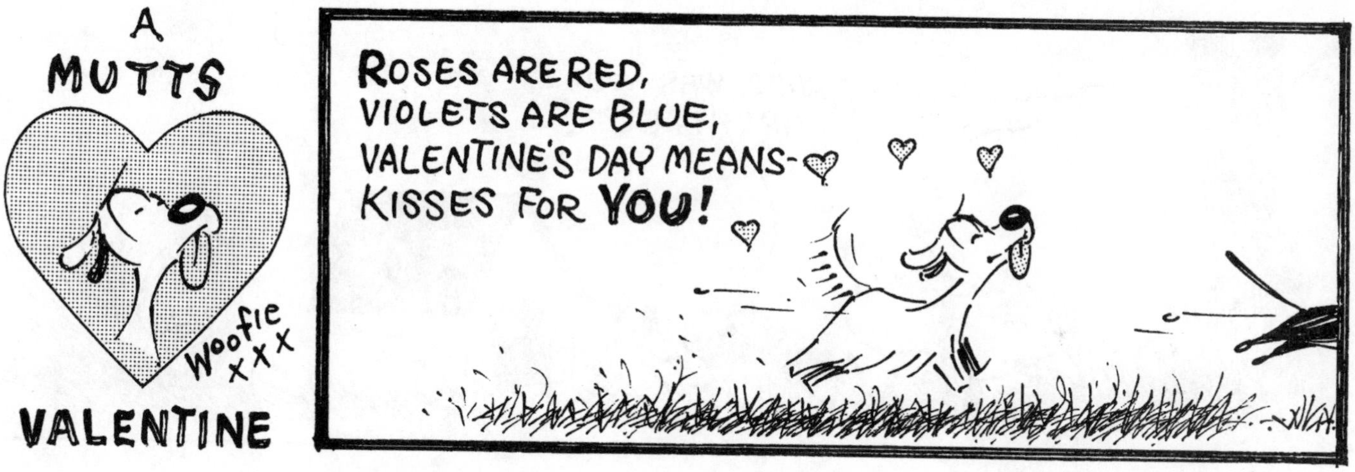
A MUTTS VALENTINE
Woofie XXX
ROSES ARE RED,
VIOLETS ARE BLUE,
VALENTINE'S DAY MEANS-
KISSES FOR YOU!

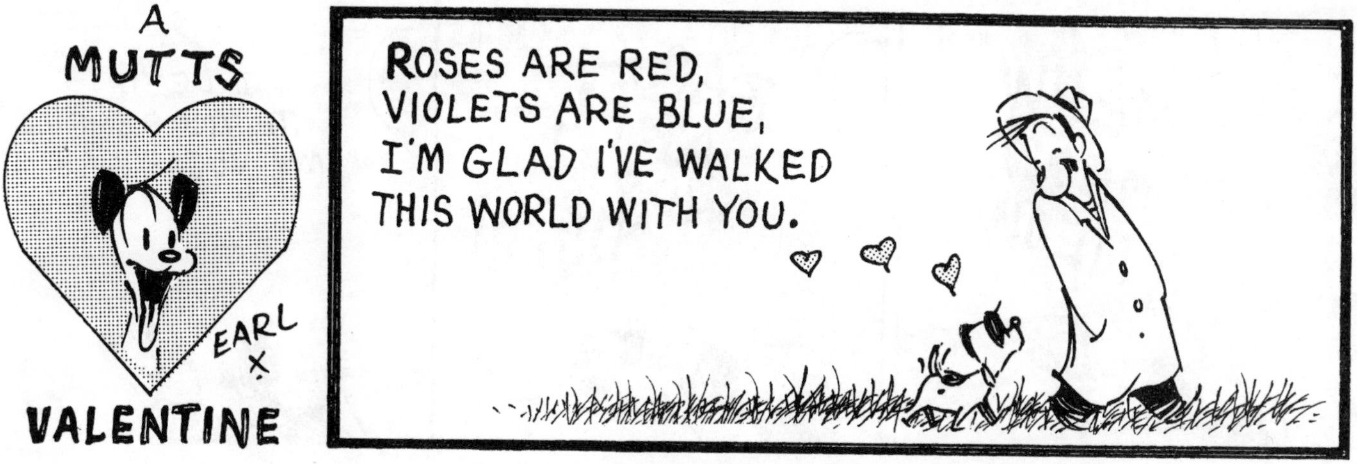
A MUTTS VALENTINE
EARL X
ROSES ARE RED,
VIOLETS ARE BLUE,
I'M GLAD I'VE WALKED
THIS WORLD WITH YOU.

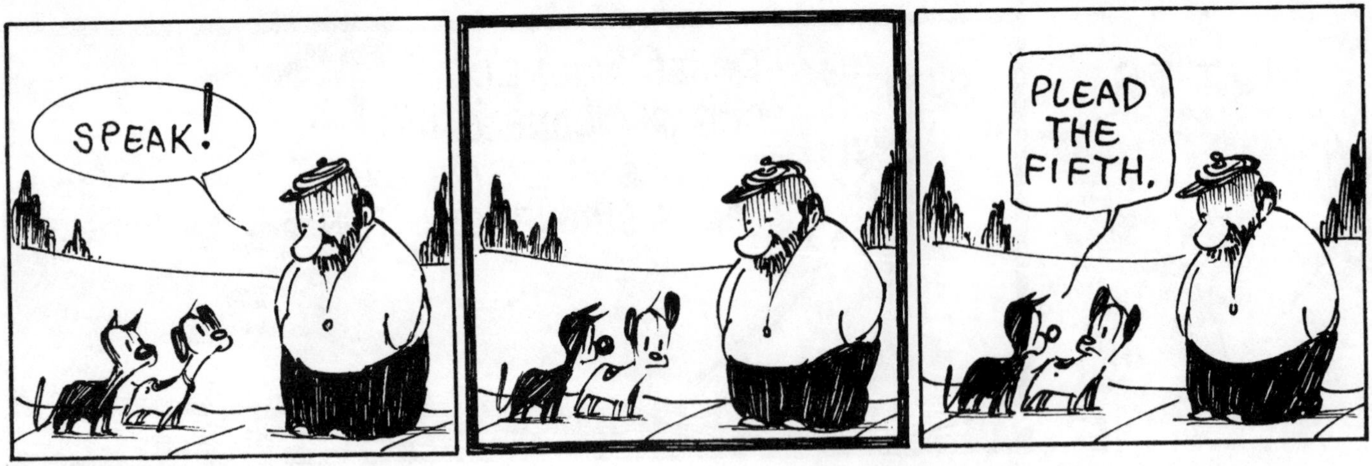
SPEAK!
PLEAD THE FIFTH.

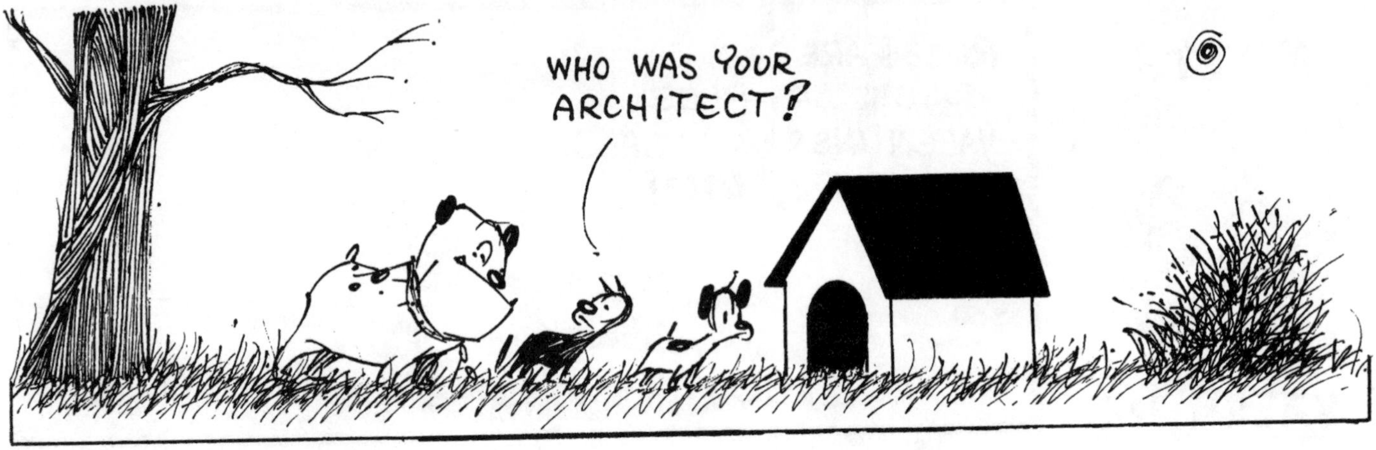
WHO WAS YOUR ARCHITECT?

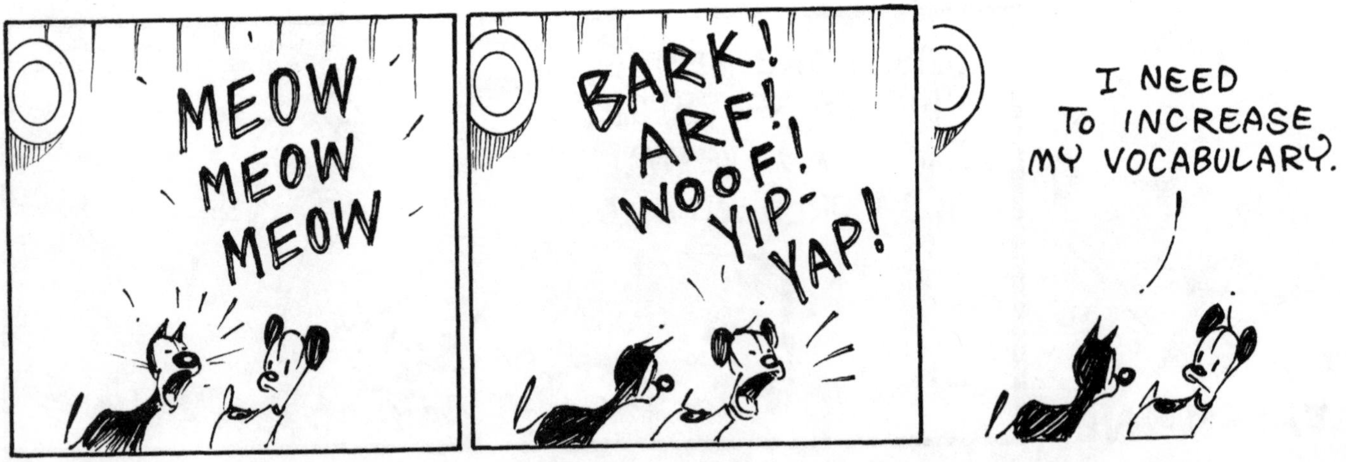
MEOW MEOW MEOW
BARK! ARF! WOOF! YIP-YAP!
I NEED TO INCREASE MY VOCABULARY.

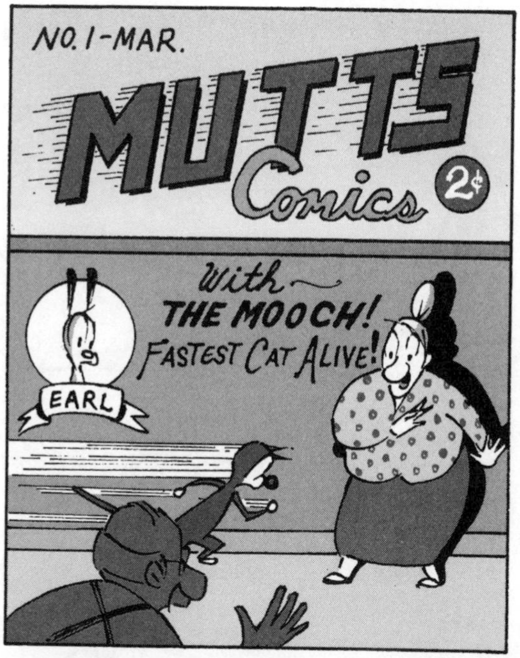
NO. 1-MAR.
MUTTS
Comics
2¢
with
THE MOOCH!
FASTEST CAT ALIVE!
EARL

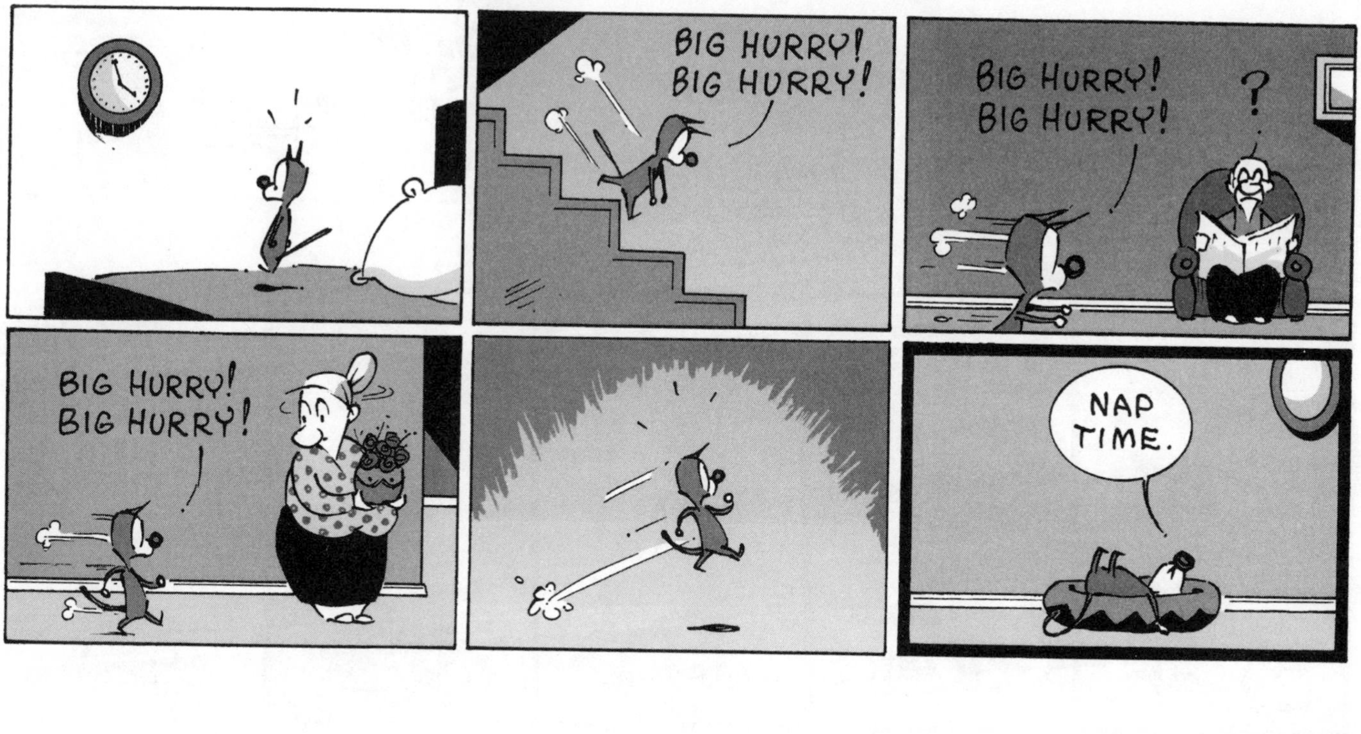
BIG HURRY!
BIG HURRY!
BIG HURRY!
BIG HURRY!
BIG HURRY!
BIG HURRY!
?
NAP TIME.

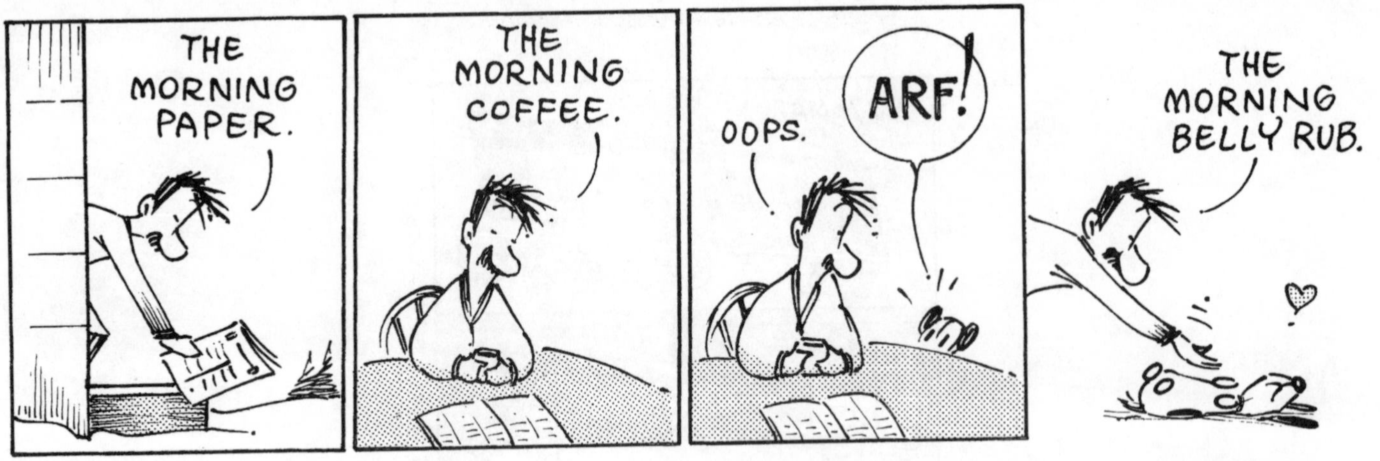
THE MORNING PAPER.
THE MORNING COFFEE.
OOPS.
ARF!
THE MORNING BELLY RUB.

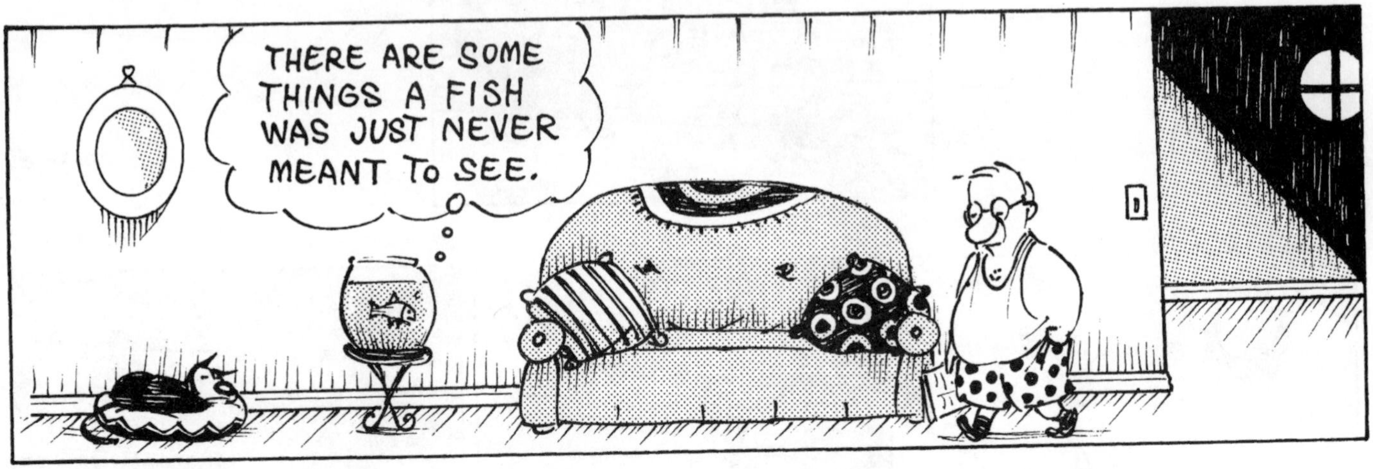
THERE ARE SOME THINGS A FISH WAS JUST NEVER MEANT TO SEE.

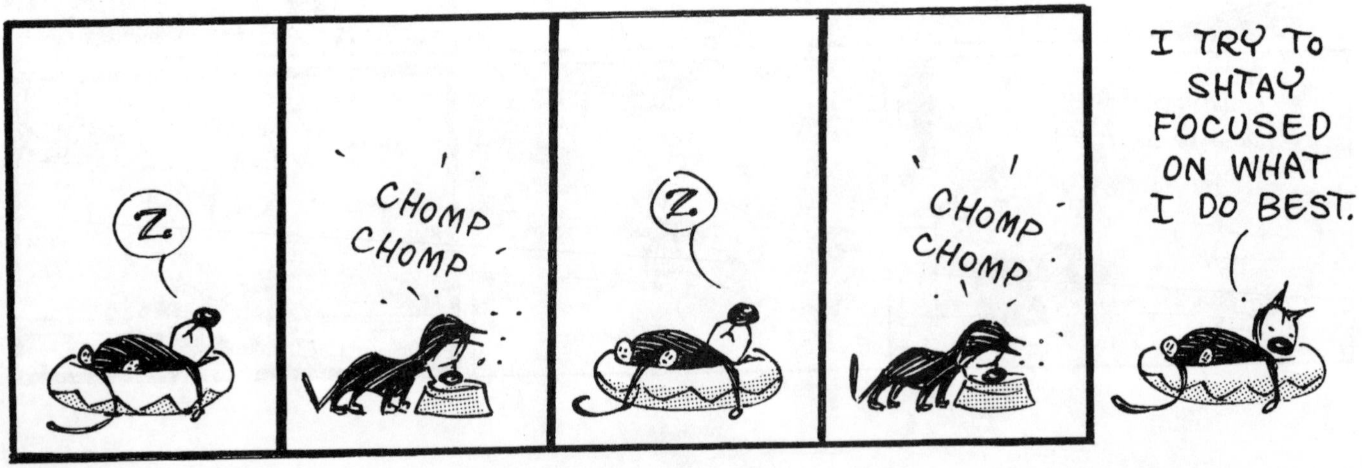
Z
CHOMP CHOMP
Z
CHOMP CHOMP
I TRY TO SHTAY FOCUSED ON WHAT I DO BEST.

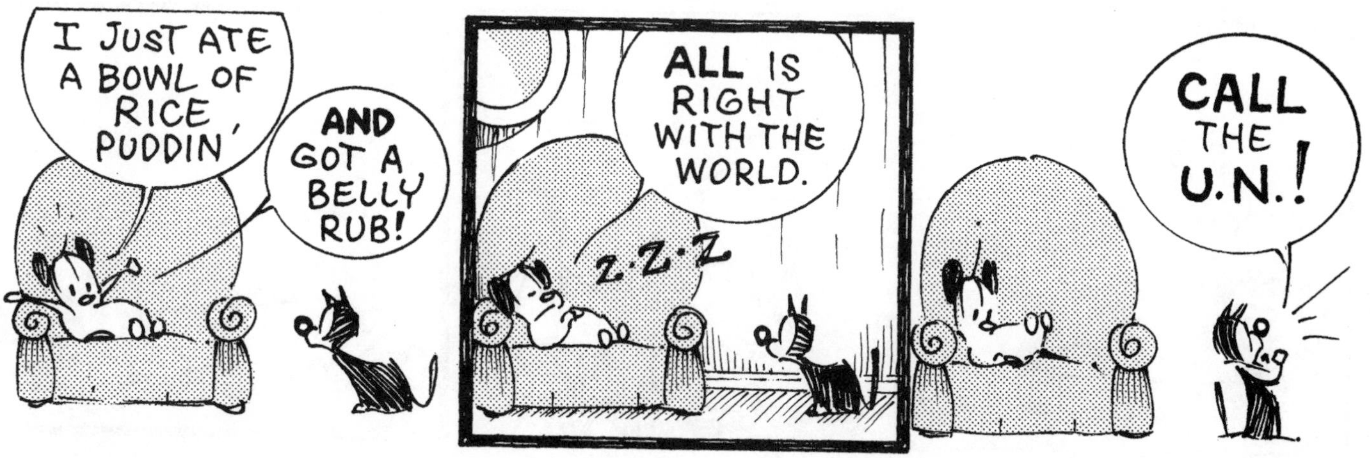
I JUST ATE A BOWL OF RICE PUDDIN'
AND GOT A BELLY RUB!
ALL IS RIGHT WITH THE WORLD.
Z·Z·Z
CALL THE U.N.!

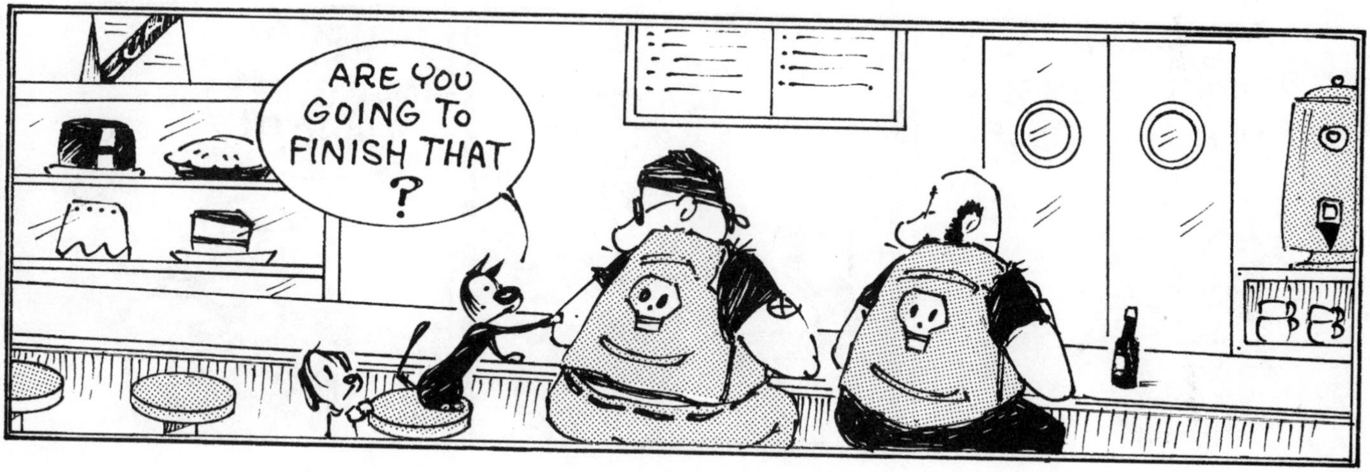
ARE YOU GOING TO FINISH THAT?

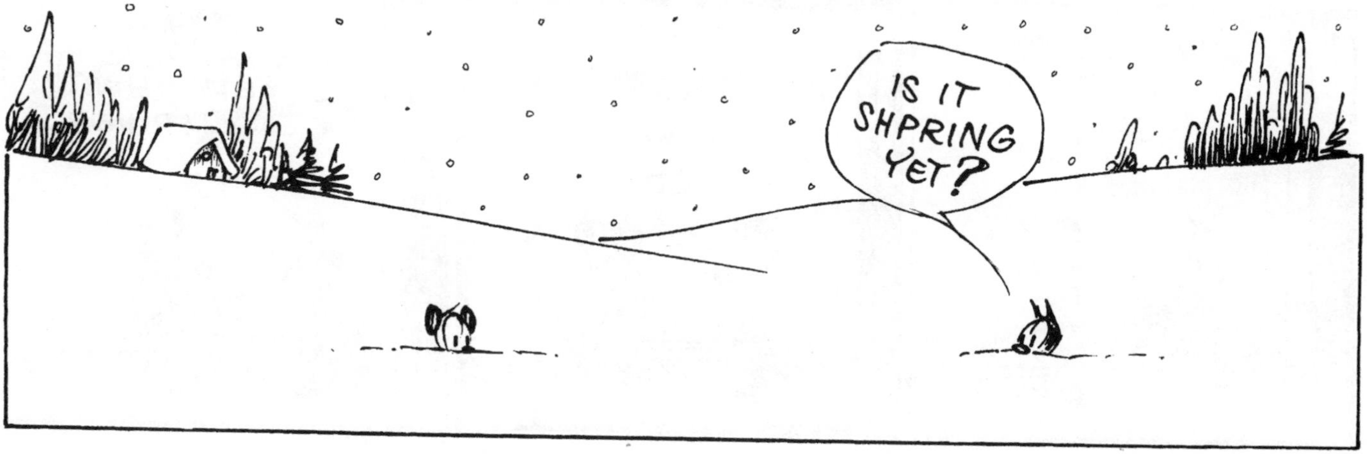
IS IT SHPRING YET?

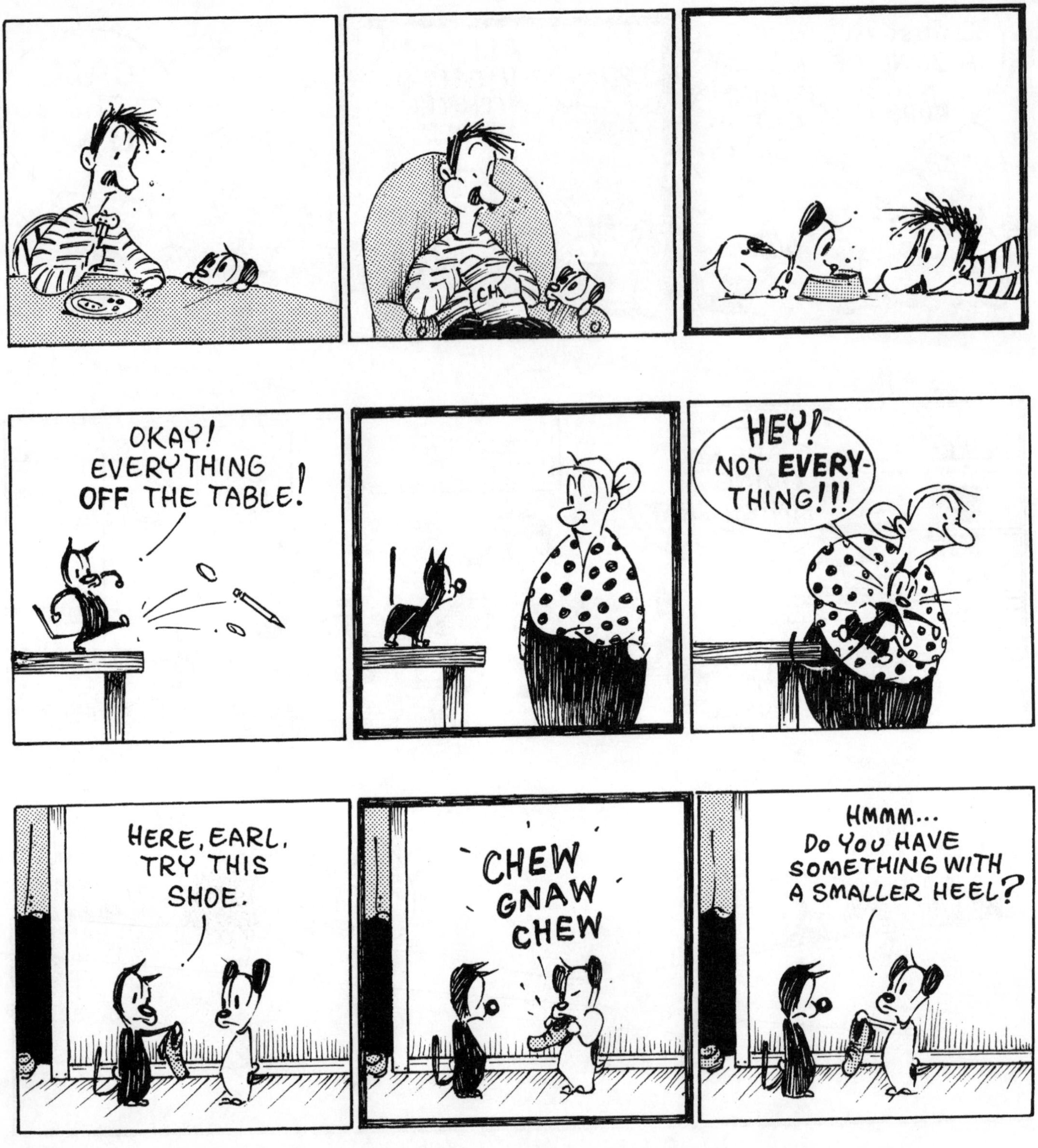
OKAY! EVERYTHING OFF THE TABLE!
HEY! NOT EVERY-THING!!!
HERE, EARL. TRY THIS SHOE.
CHEW GNAW CHEW
HMMM... DO YOU HAVE SOMETHING WITH A SMALLER HEEL?

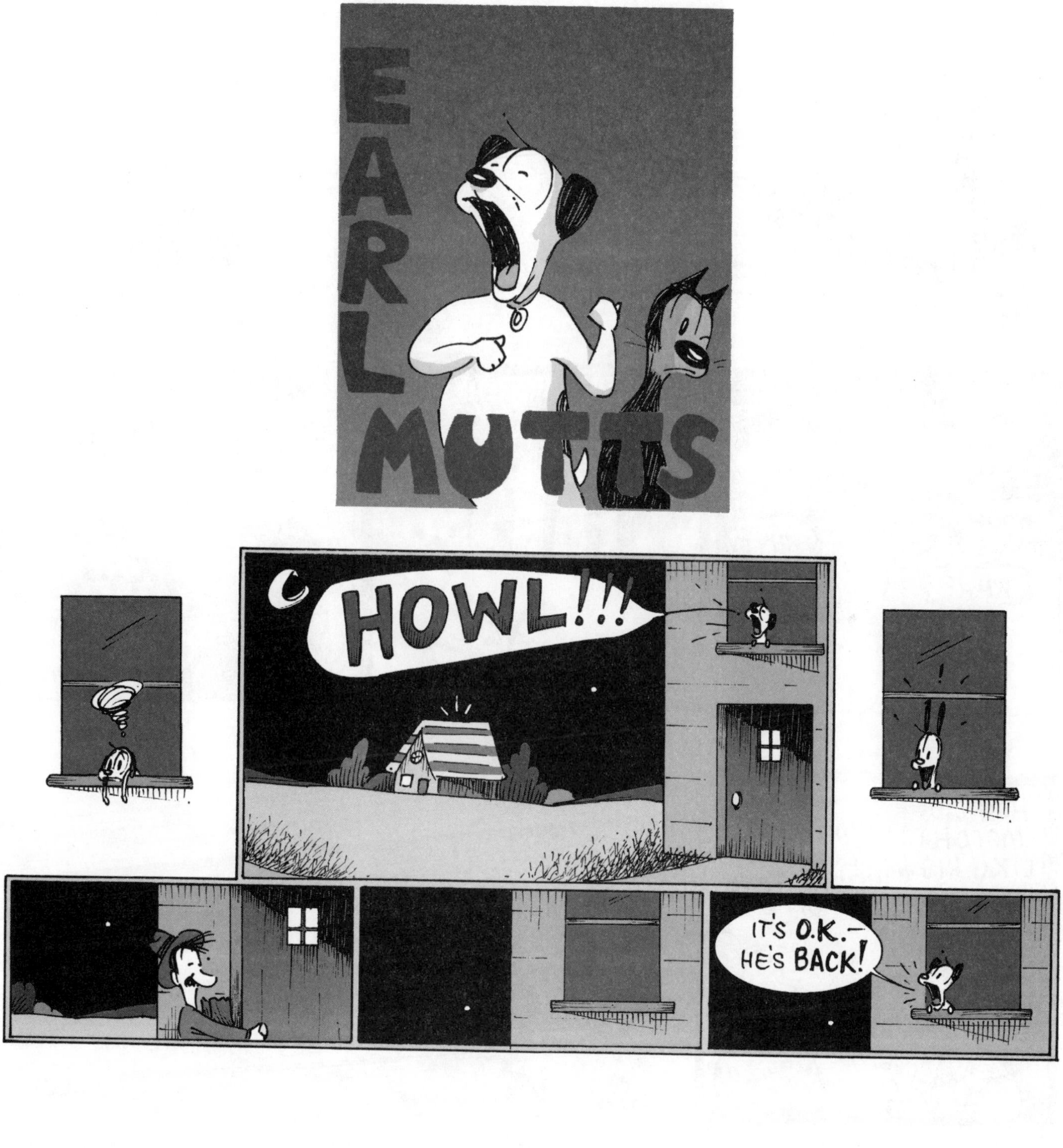
EARL
MUTTS
HOWL!!!
IT'S O.K.– HE'S BACK!

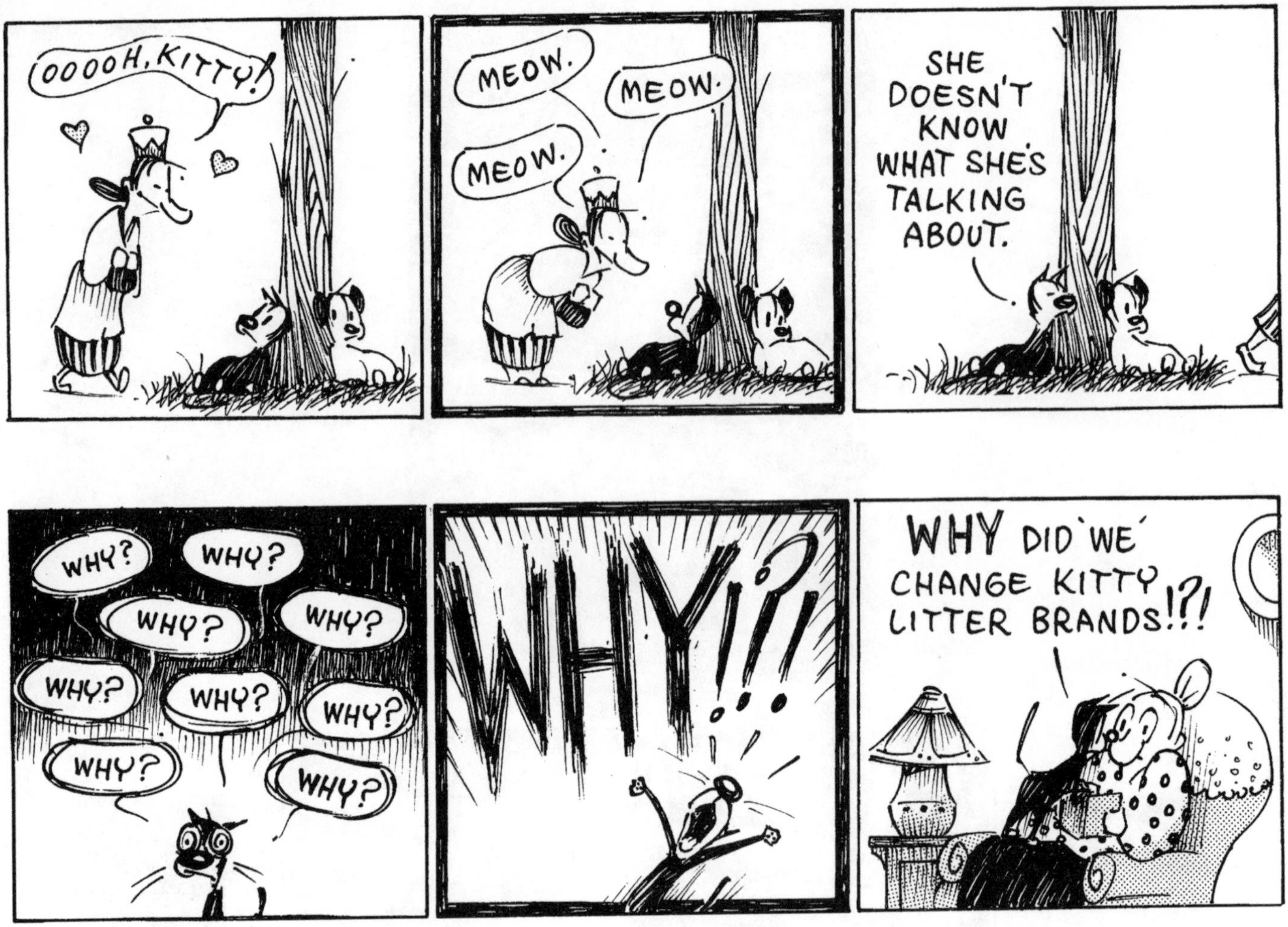
OOOOH, KITTY!
MEOW.
MEOW.
MEOW.
SHE DOESN'T KNOW WHAT SHE'S TALKING ABOUT.
WHY?
WHY?
WHY?
WHY?
WHY?
WHY?
WHY?
WHY?
WHY?
WHY!!!
WHY DID WE CHANGE KITTY LITTER BRANDS!?!

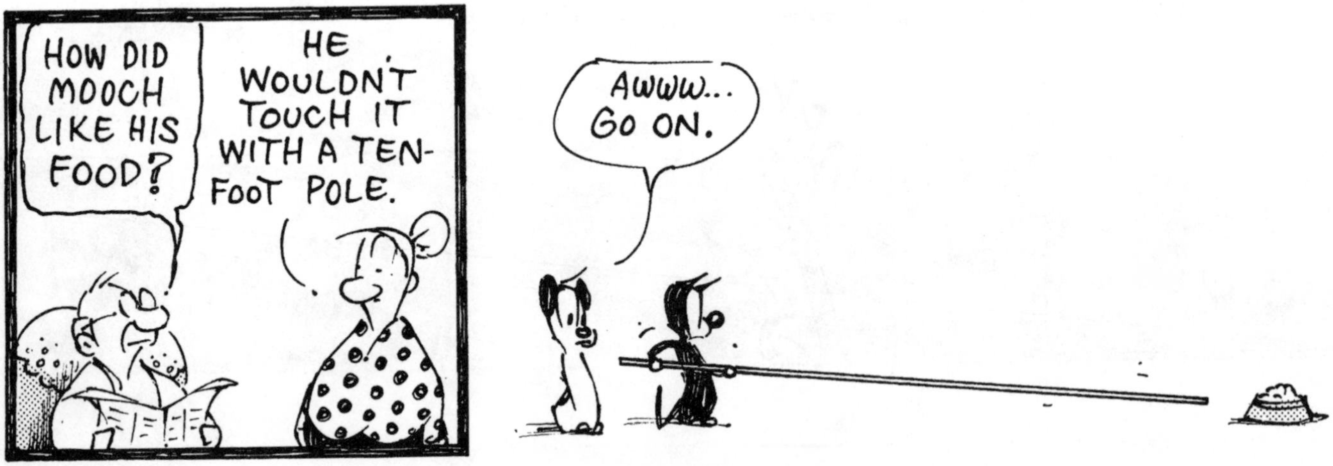
HOW DID MOOCH LIKE HIS FOOD?
HE WOULDN'T TOUCH IT WITH A TEN-FOOT POLE.
AWWW... GO ON.

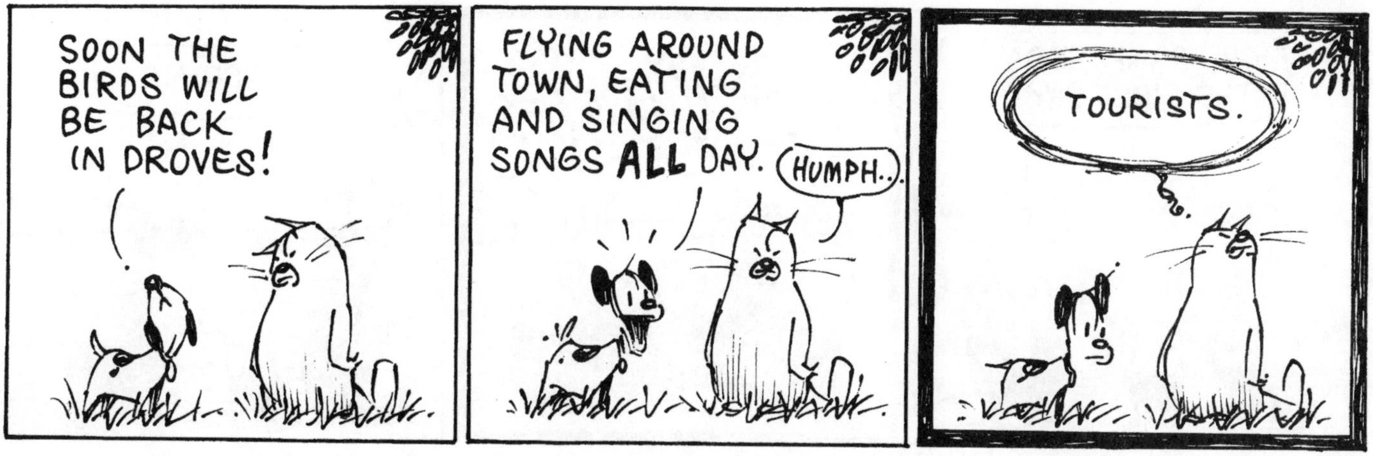
SOON THE BIRDS WILL BE BACK IN DROVES!
FLYING AROUND TOWN, EATING AND SINGING SONGS ALL DAY.
HUMPH..
TOURISTS.

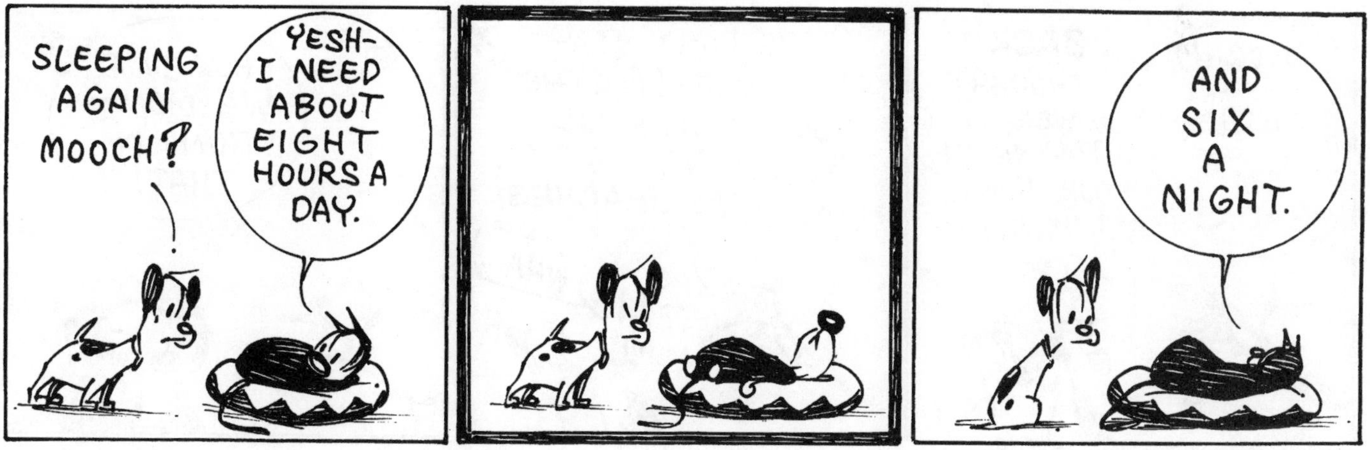
SLEEPING AGAIN MOOCH?
YESH- I NEED ABOUT EIGHT HOURS A DAY.
AND SIX A NIGHT.

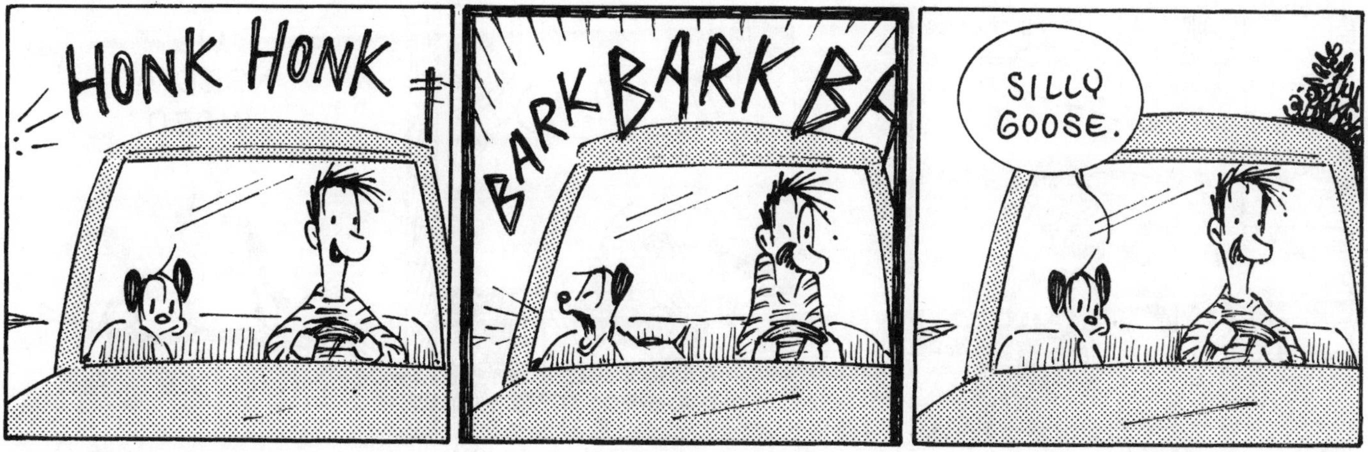
HONK HONK
BARK BARK BA
SILLY GOOSE.

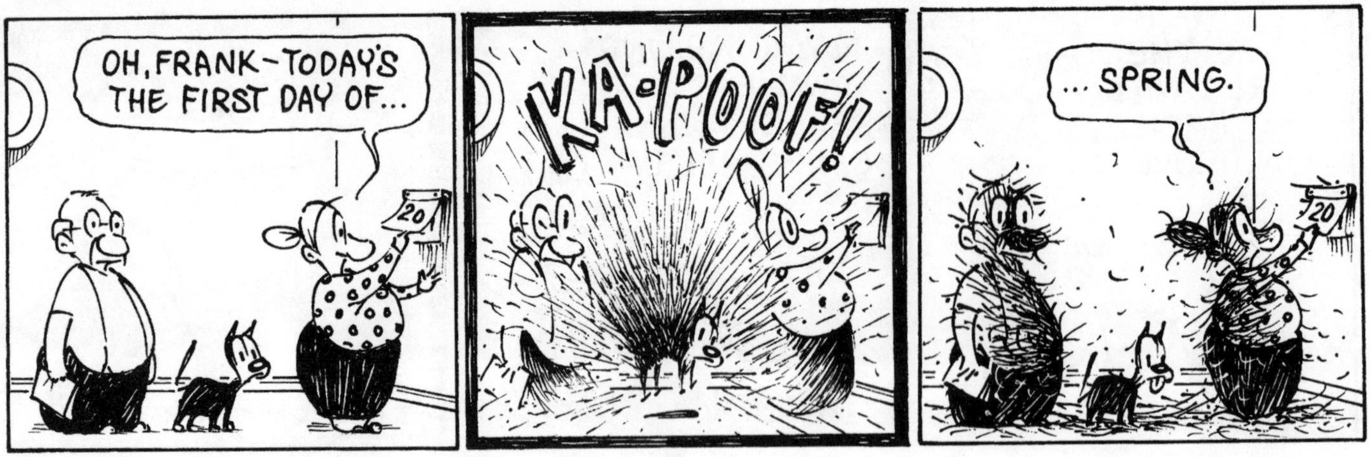
OH, FRANK–TODAY'S THE FIRST DAY OF...
KA-POOF!
... SPRING.

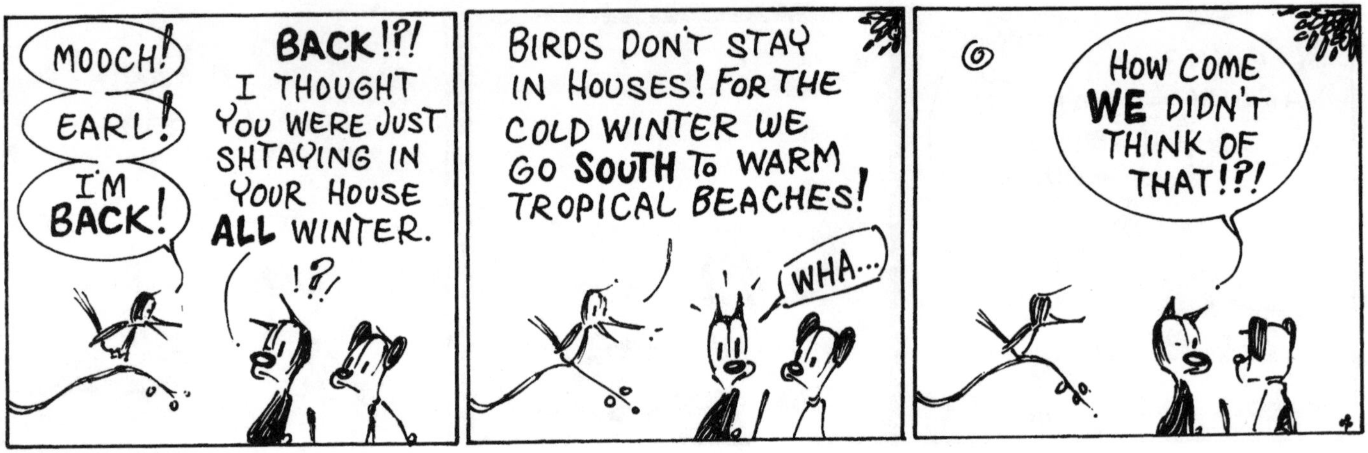
MOOCH!
EARL!
I'M BACK!
BACK!?! I THOUGHT YOU WERE JUST SHTAYING IN YOUR HOUSE ALL WINTER.
!?!
BIRDS DON'T STAY IN HOUSES! FOR THE COLD WINTER WE GO SOUTH TO WARM TROPICAL BEACHES!
WHA...
HOW COME WE DIDN'T THINK OF THAT!?!

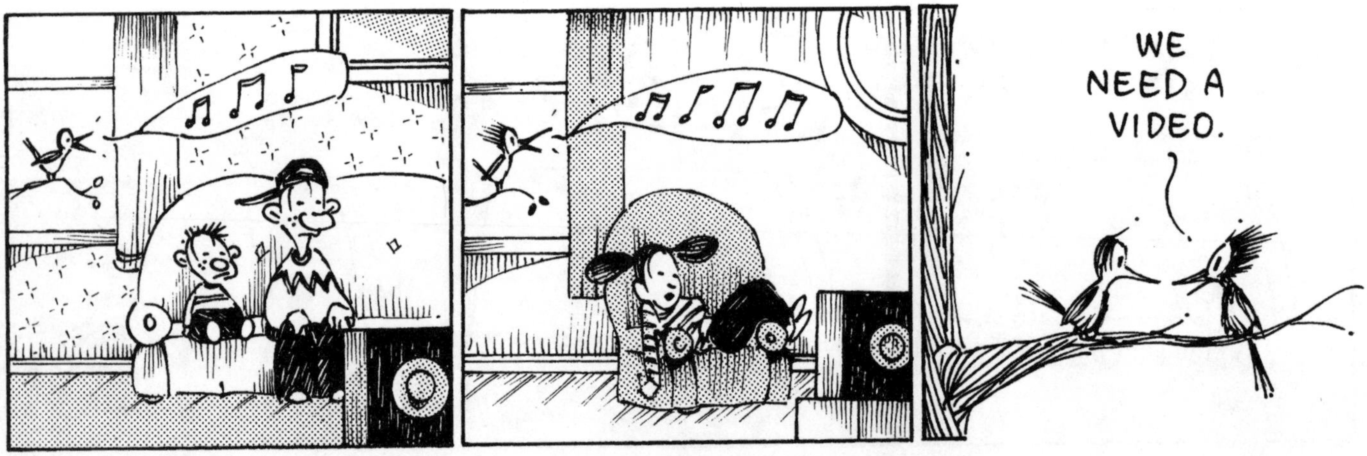
WE NEED A VIDEO.

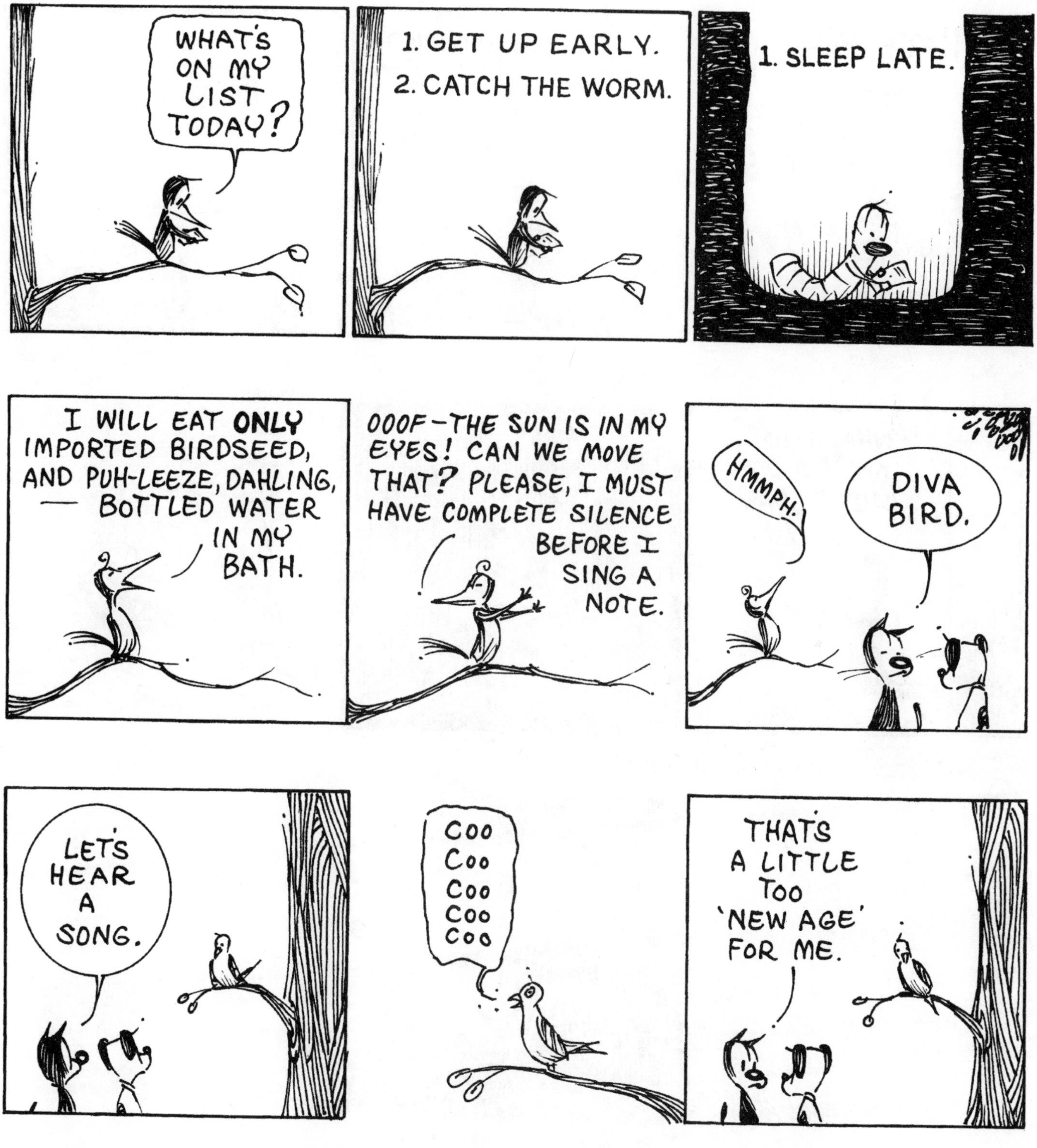
WHAT'S ON MY LIST TODAY?
1. GET UP EARLY.
2. CATCH THE WORM.
1. SLEEP LATE.
I WILL EAT ONLY IMPORTED BIRDSEED, AND PUH-LEEZE, DAHLING, — BOTTLED WATER IN MY BATH.
OOOF—THE SUN IS IN MY EYES! CAN WE MOVE THAT? PLEASE, I MUST HAVE COMPLETE SILENCE BEFORE I SING A NOTE.
HMMPH.
DIVA BIRD.
LET'S HEAR A SONG.
COO COO COO COO COO
THAT'S A LITTLE TOO 'NEW AGE' FOR ME.

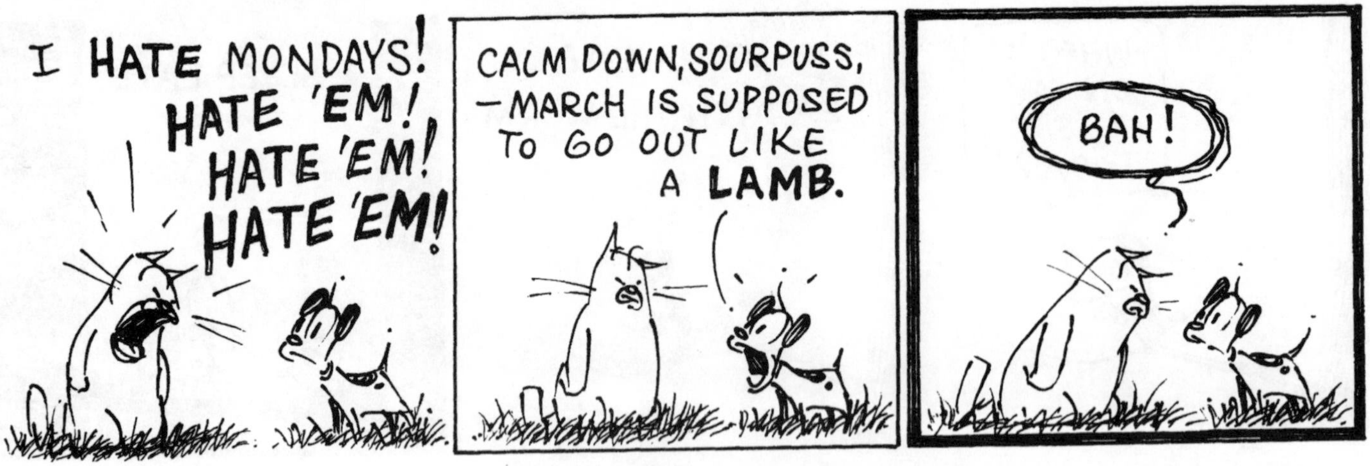
I HATE MONDAYS! HATE 'EM! HATE 'EM! HATE 'EM!
CALM DOWN, SOURPUSS, —MARCH IS SUPPOSED TO GO OUT LIKE A LAMB.
BAH!

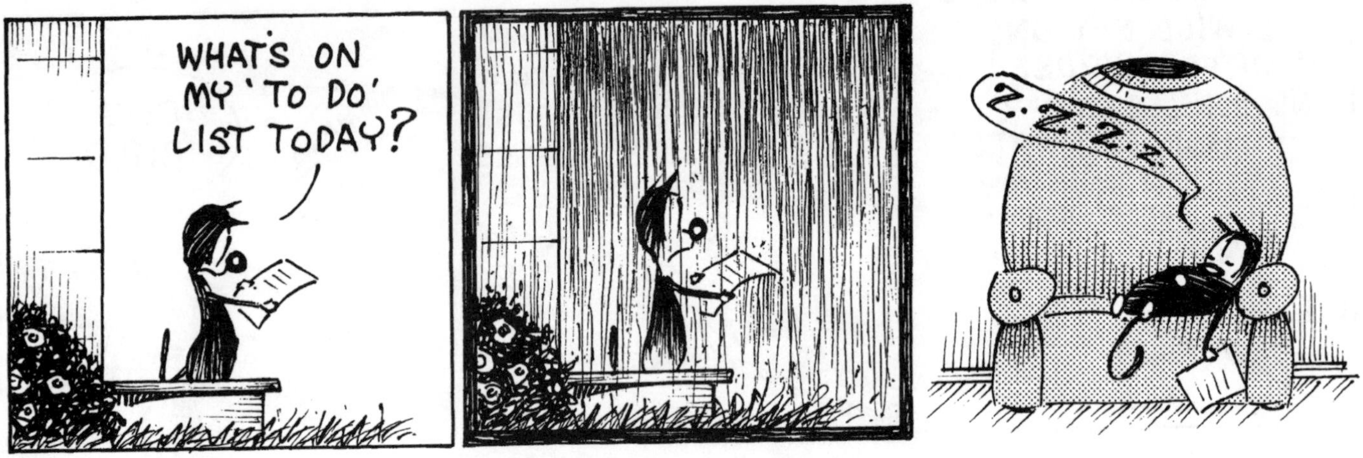
WHAT'S ON MY 'TO DO' LIST TODAY?
Z.Z.Z.Z

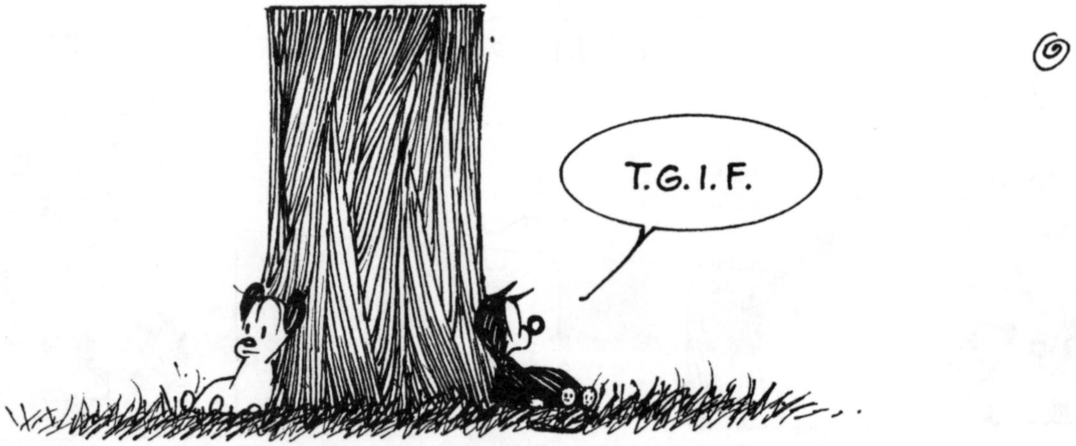
T.G.I.F.

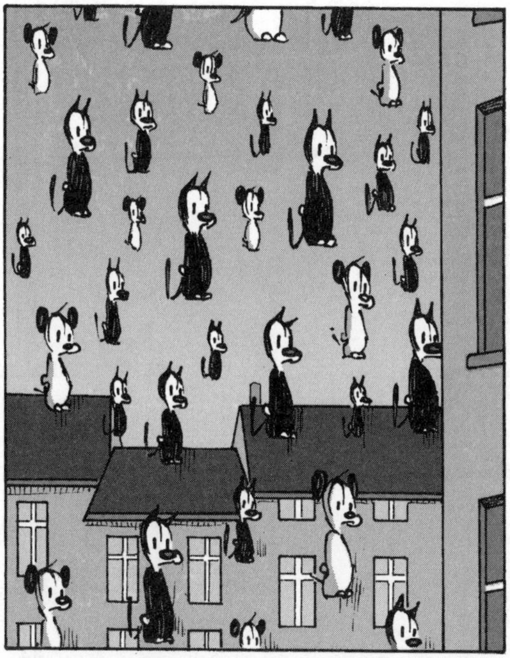

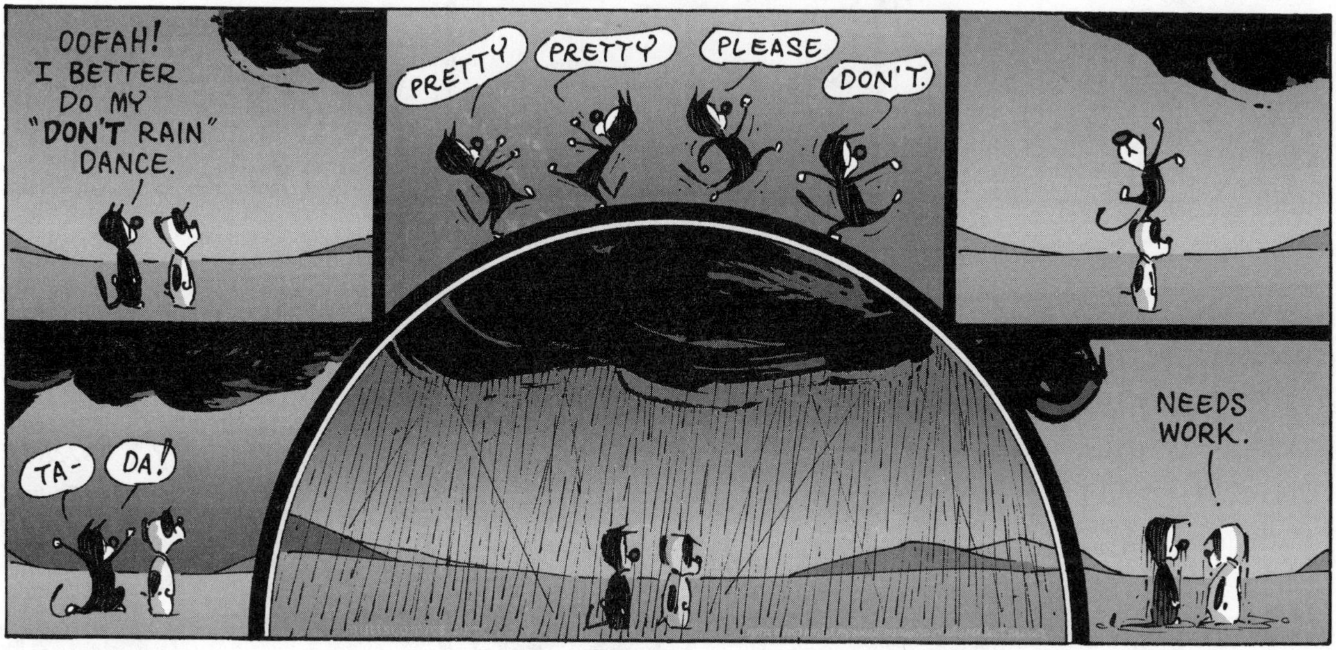
OOFAH! I BETTER DO MY "DON'T RAIN" DANCE.
PRETTY
PRETTY
PLEASE
DON'T.
TA-
DA!
NEEDS WORK.

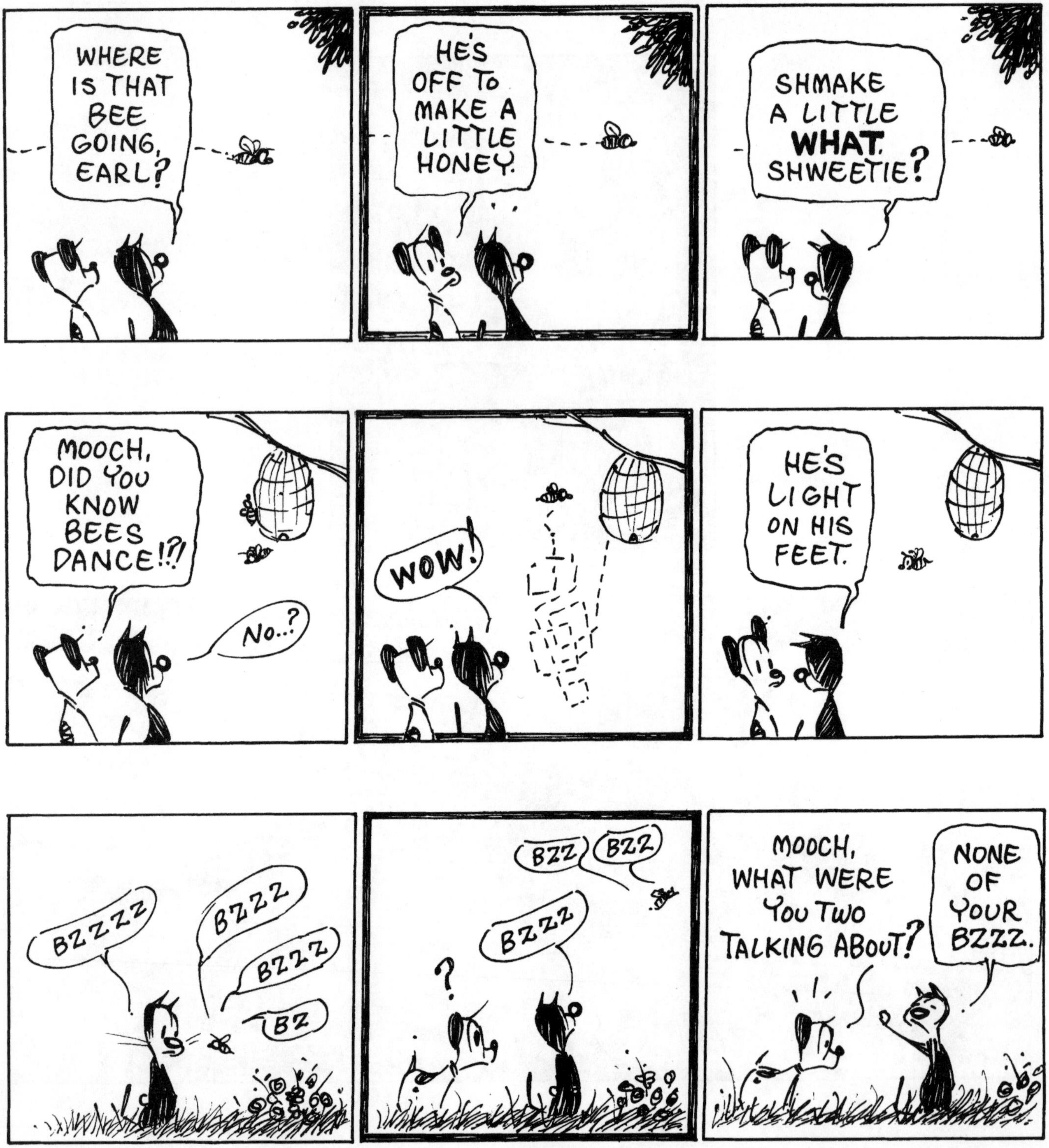

WHERE IS THAT BEE GOING, EARL?
HE'S OFF TO MAKE A LITTLE HONEY.
SHMAKE A LITTLE **WHAT**, SHWEETIE?
MOOCH, DID YOU KNOW BEES DANCE!?!
No..?
WOW!
HE'S LIGHT ON HIS FEET.
BZZZZ
BZZZ
BZZZ
BZ
BZZ
BZZ
BZZZ
?
MOOCH, WHAT WERE YOU TWO TALKING ABOUT?
NONE OF YOUR BZZZ.

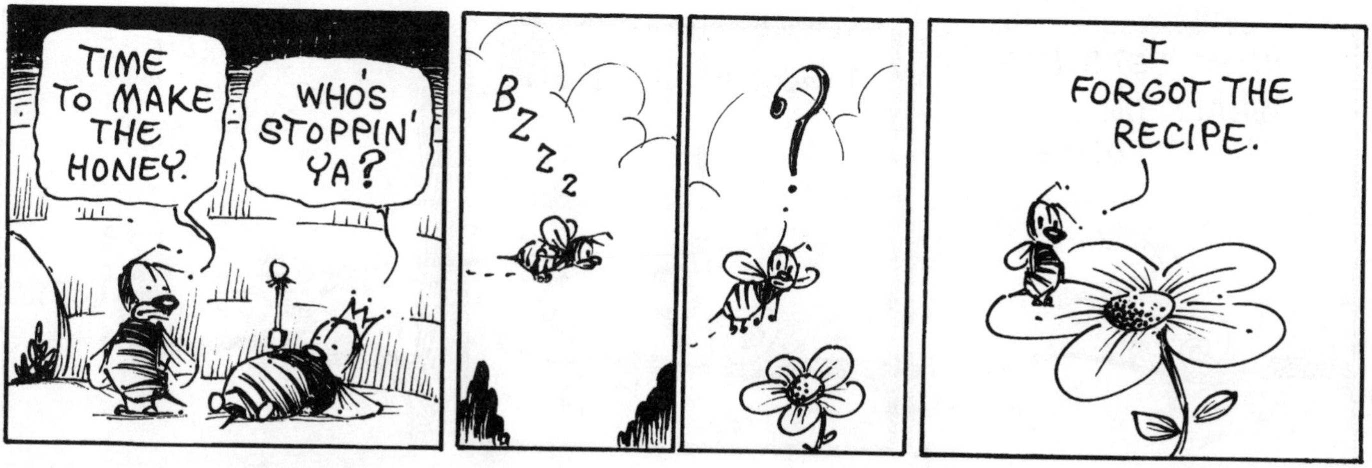
TIME TO MAKE THE HONEY.
WHO'S STOPPIN' YA?
BZZZ
?
I FORGOT THE RECIPE.

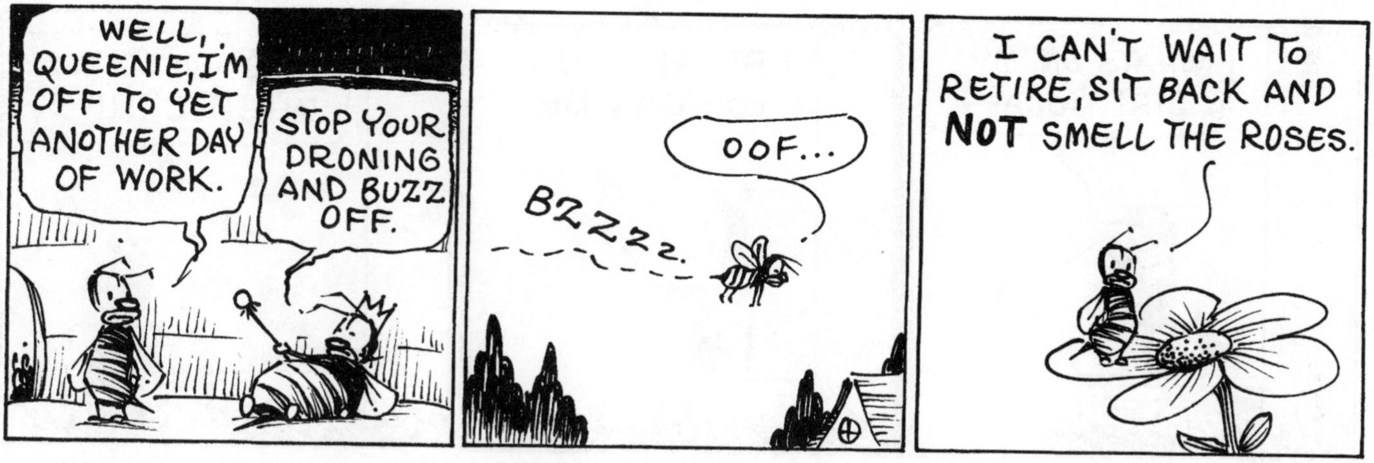
WELL, QUEENIE, I'M OFF TO YET ANOTHER DAY OF WORK.
STOP YOUR DRONING AND BUZZ OFF.
BZZZZZ.
OOF...
I CAN'T WAIT TO RETIRE, SIT BACK AND **NOT** SMELL THE ROSES.

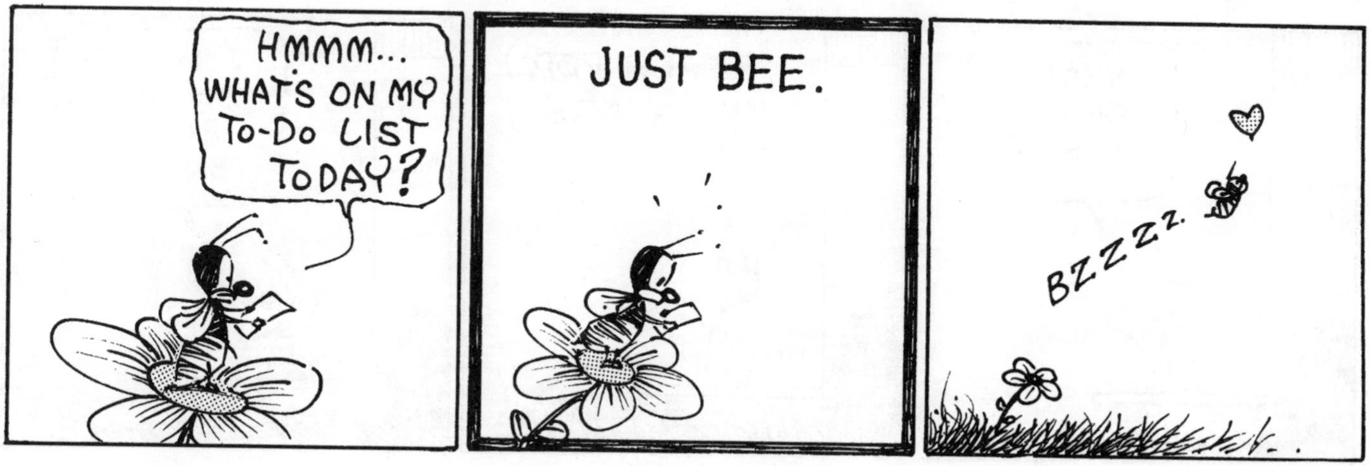
HMMM... WHAT'S ON MY TO-DO LIST TODAY?
JUST BEE.
BZZZZ.

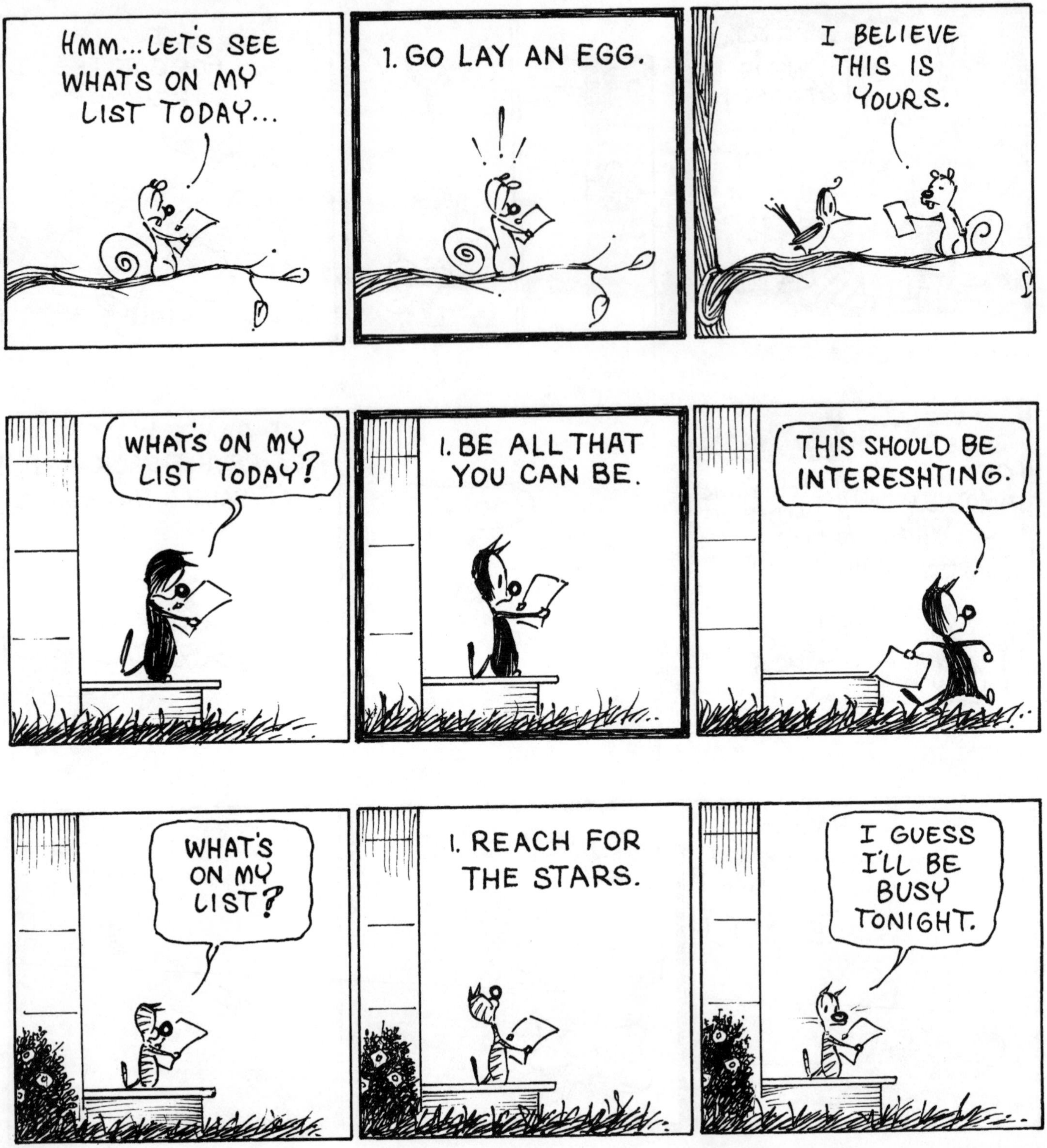
HMM...LET'S SEE WHAT'S ON MY LIST TODAY...
1. GO LAY AN EGG.
!
I BELIEVE THIS IS YOURS.
WHAT'S ON MY LIST TODAY?
1. BE ALL THAT YOU CAN BE.
THIS SHOULD BE INTERESHTING.
WHAT'S ON MY LIST?
1. REACH FOR THE STARS.
I GUESS I'LL BE BUSY TONIGHT.

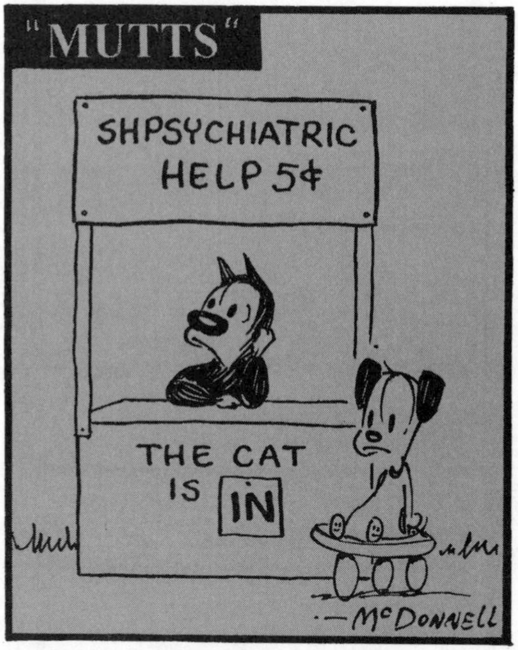
"MUTTS"
SHPSYCHIATRIC HELP 5¢
THE CAT IS IN
McDONNELL

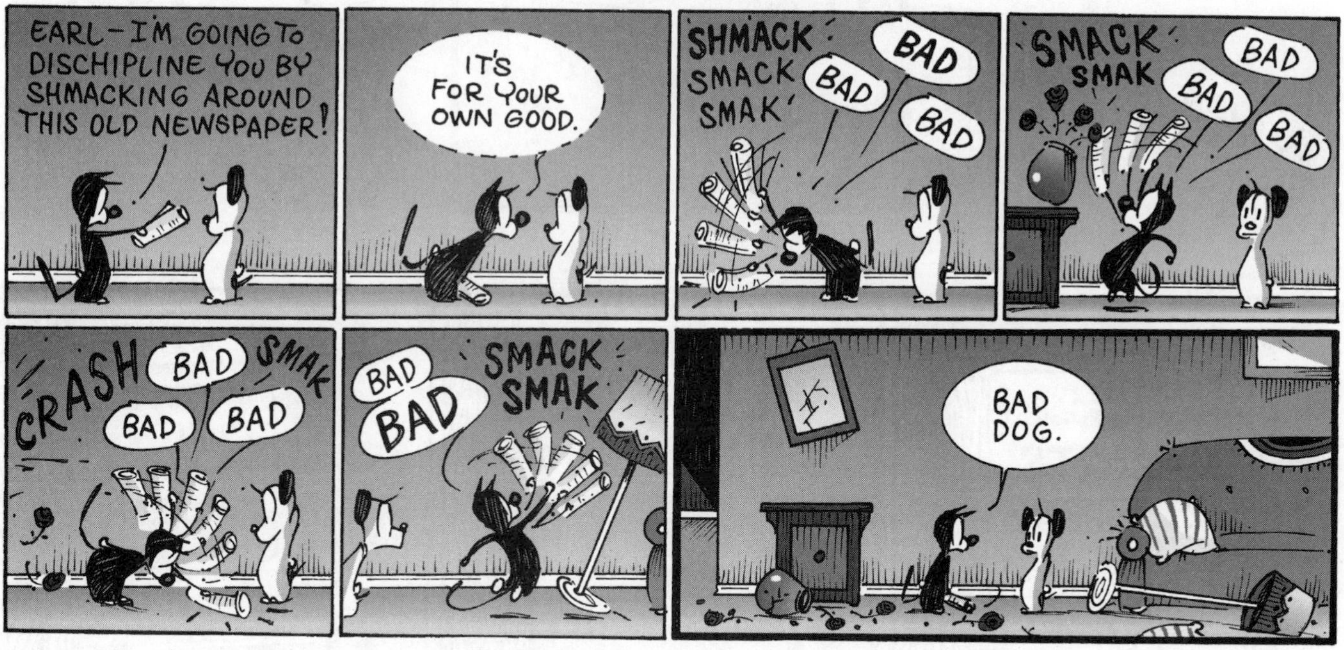
EARL—I'M GOING TO DISCHIPLINE YOU BY SHMACKING AROUND THIS OLD NEWSPAPER!
IT'S FOR YOUR OWN GOOD.
SHMACK SMACK SMAK
BAD
BAD
BAD
SMACK SMAK
BAD
BAD
BAD
CRASH
BAD
SMAK
BAD
BAD
BAD
BAD
SMACK SMAK
BAD DOG.

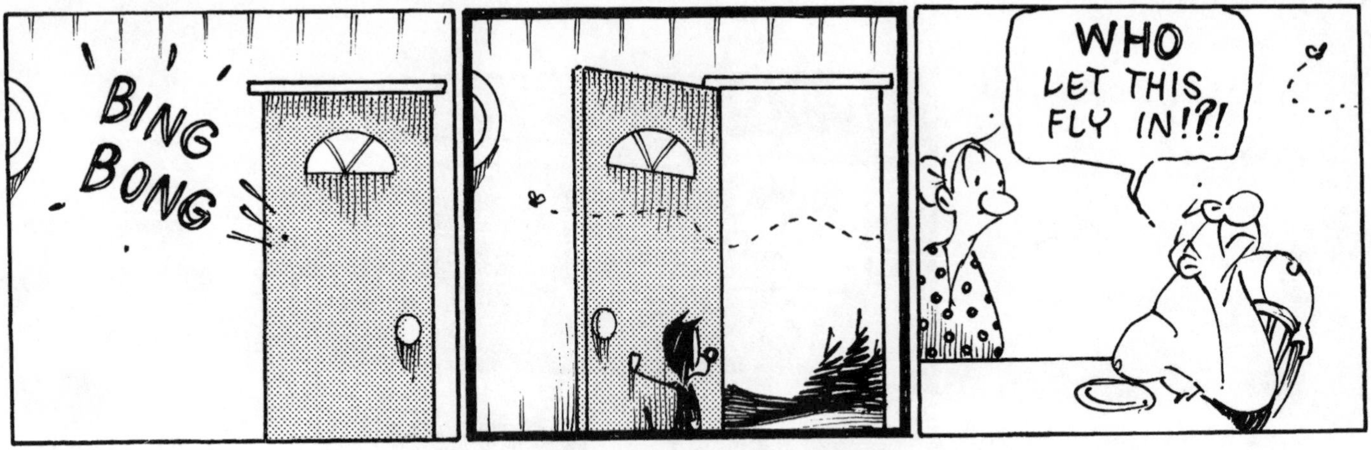
BING BONG
WHO LET THIS FLY IN!?!

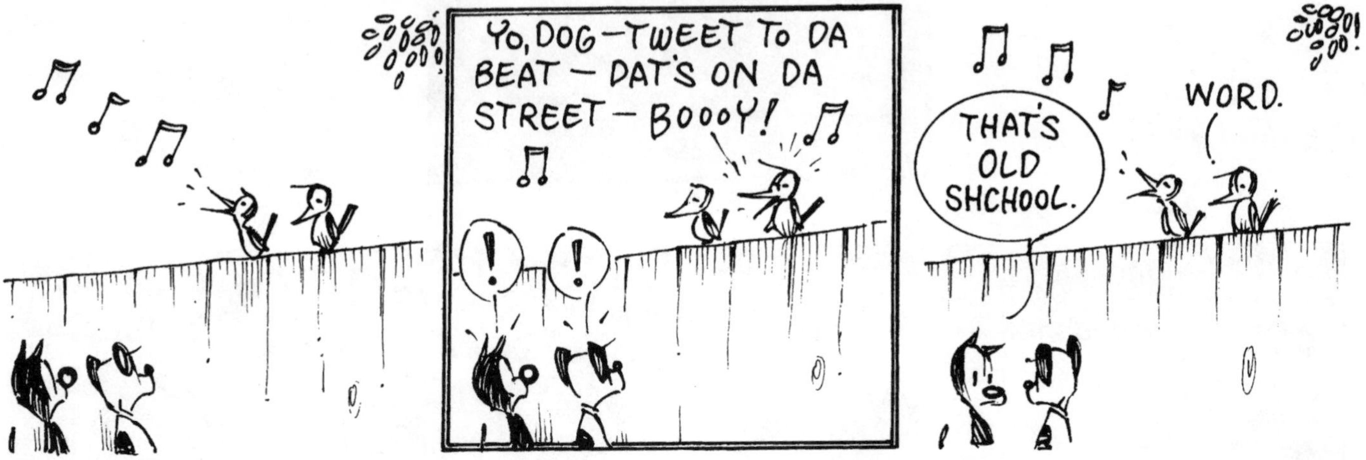
YO, DOG—TWEET TO DA BEAT—DAT'S ON DA STREET—BOOOY!
!
!
THAT'S OLD SHCHOOL.
WORD.

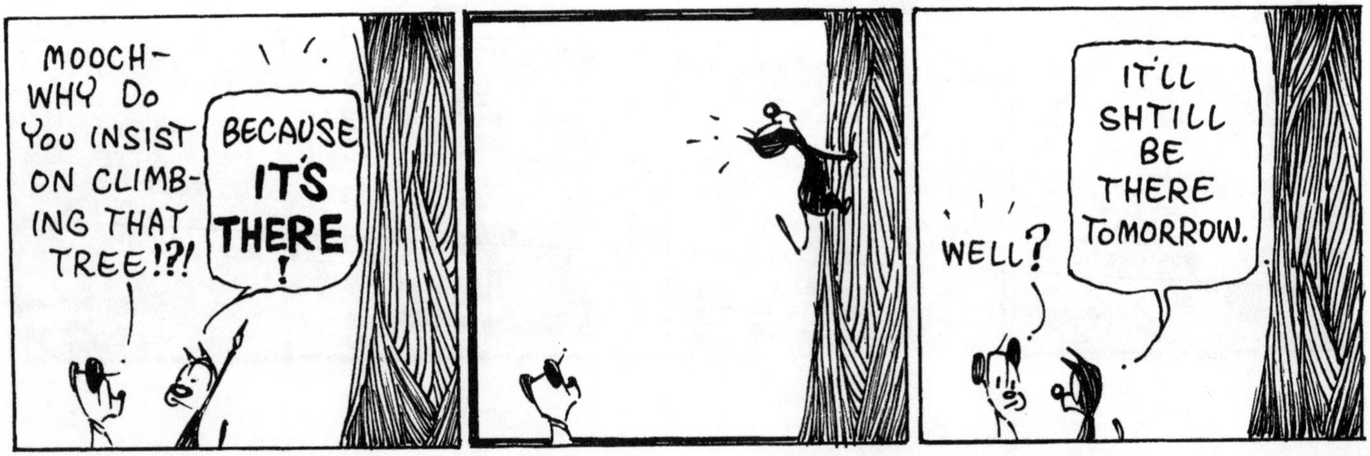
MOOCH—WHY DO YOU INSIST ON CLIMBING THAT TREE!?!
BECAUSE IT'S THERE!
WELL?
IT'LL SHTILL BE THERE TOMORROW.

Mutts
by P. L. McDonnell

WHO ELSE WOULD GENTLY WASH YOUR DIRTY WITTLE FACE?
WHO ELSE WOULD KEEP YOUR WITTLE FOOTSIES WARM ALL NIGHT?
WHO ELSE WOULD UNCONDITIONALLY LOVE AND PROTECT YOUR WITTLE SELF?
WHO ELSE WOULD REGURGITATE A BUGGY SNACK INTO YOUR HUNGRY WITTLE MOUTH?
SIGH...
MOM

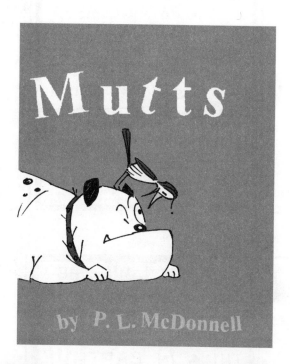

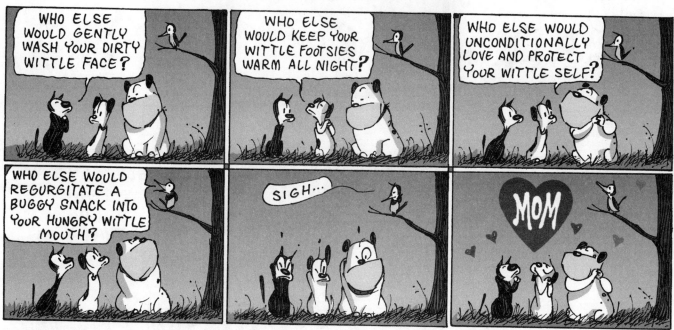

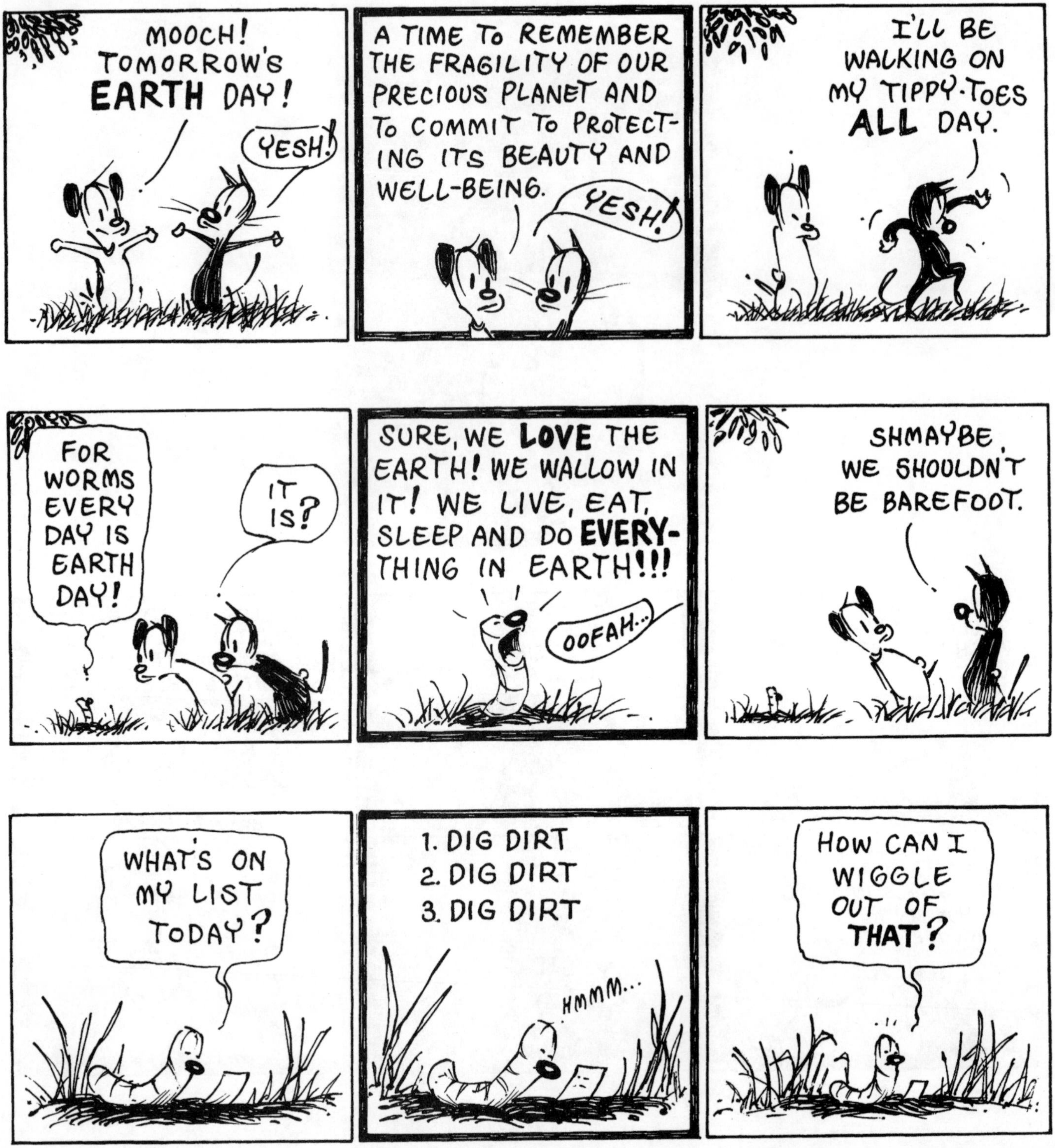
MOOCH! TOMORROW'S EARTH DAY!
YESH!
A TIME TO REMEMBER THE FRAGILITY OF OUR PRECIOUS PLANET AND TO COMMIT TO PROTECTING ITS BEAUTY AND WELL-BEING.
YESH!
I'LL BE WALKING ON MY TIPPY-TOES ALL DAY.
FOR WORMS EVERY DAY IS EARTH DAY!
IT IS?
SURE, WE LOVE THE EARTH! WE WALLOW IN IT! WE LIVE, EAT, SLEEP AND DO EVERYTHING IN EARTH!!!
OOFAH...
SHMAYBE, WE SHOULDN'T BE BAREFOOT.
WHAT'S ON MY LIST TODAY?
1. DIG DIRT
2. DIG DIRT
3. DIG DIRT
HMMM...
HOW CAN I WIGGLE OUT OF THAT?

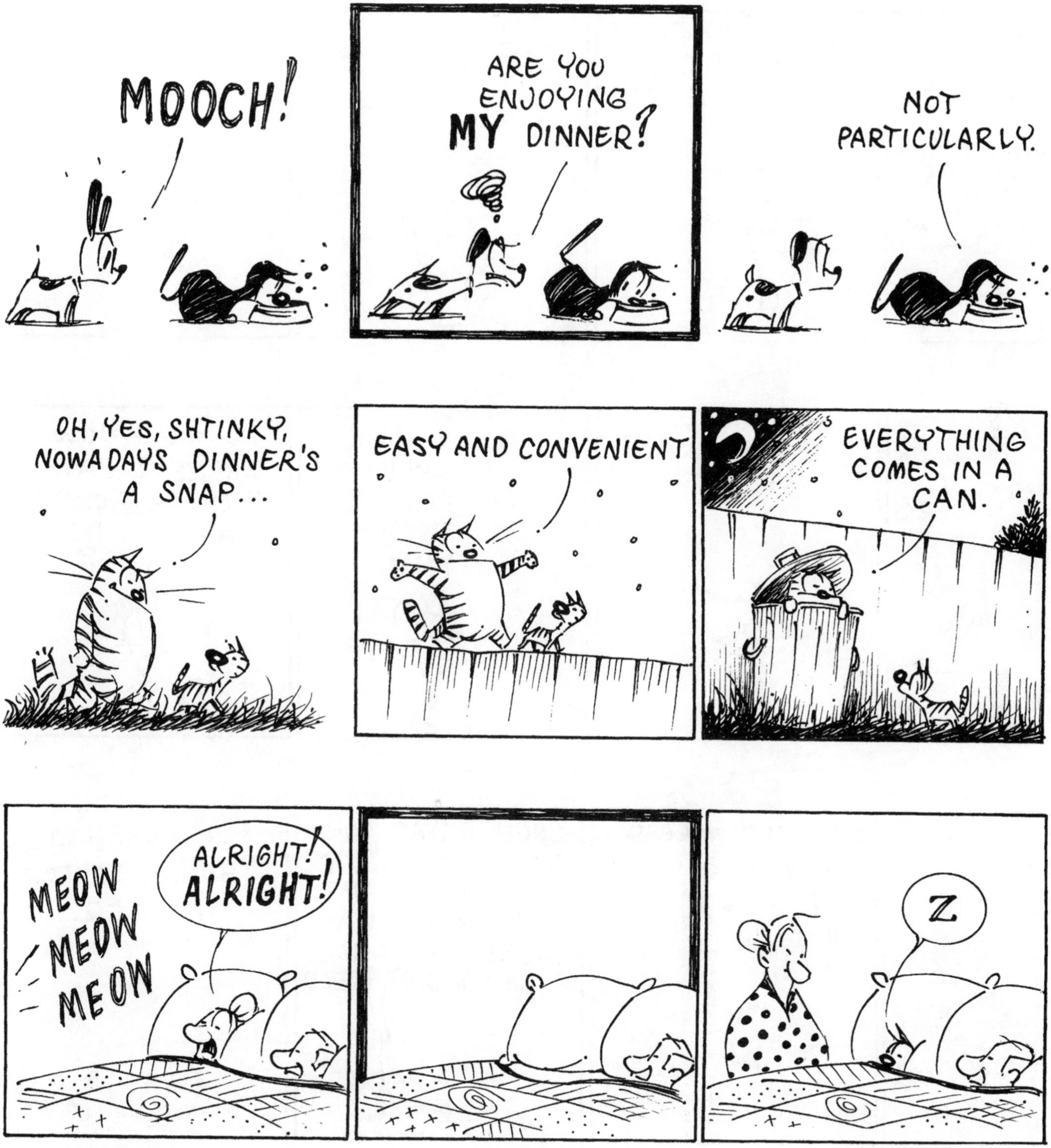
MOOCH!
ARE YOU ENJOYING MY DINNER?
NOT PARTICULARLY.
OH, YES, SHTINKY, NOWADAYS DINNER'S A SNAP...
EASY AND CONVENIENT
EVERYTHING COMES IN A CAN.
MEOW MEOW MEOW
ALRIGHT! ALRIGHT!
Z

Strip 1

Shelter Stories — "SAMMY"

OKAY—SO MY FIRST OWNERS DIDN'T APPRECIATE ME ...SIGH...

IT'S THEIR LOSS.

AND YOUR GAIN?

Strip 2

Shelter Stories — "BRANDO"

I'M NEW AROUND HERE.

DO YOU KNOW WHERE I CAN FIND A GOOD LAP IN THIS TOWN?

Strip 3

Shelter Stories — "PETER"

THE KIDS WERE SO HAPPY TO GET ME THAT SUNDAY MORNING. BUT...

SOON I WAS FORGOTTEN IN A CAGE IN THE BACKYARD—AND THEN I WAS TOSSED OUT ONTO A SMALL DIRT FIELD.

THE CHOCOLATE BUNNY LASTED LONGER.

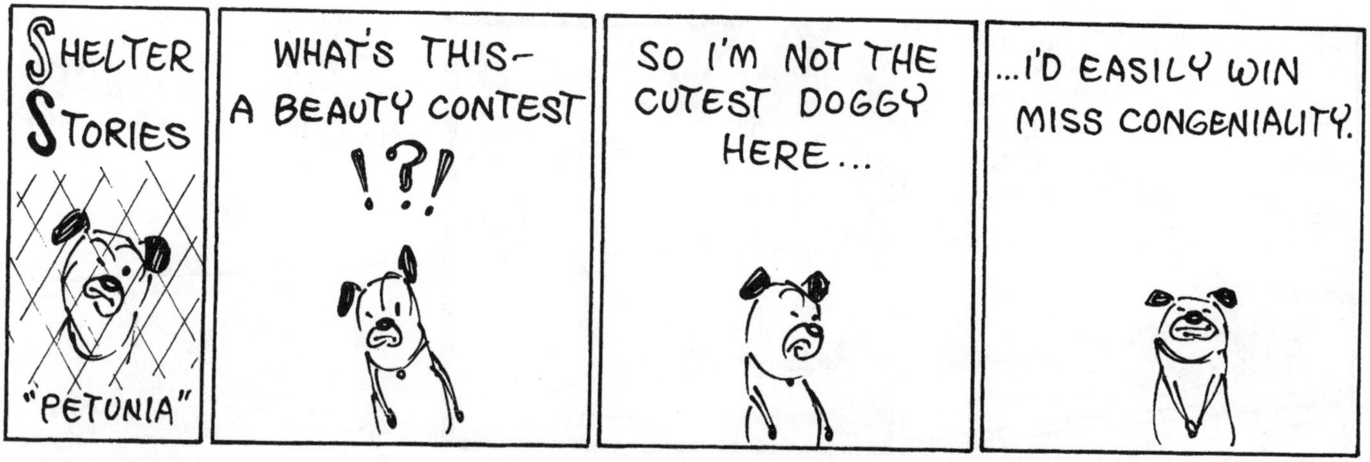
SHELTER STORIES
"PETUNIA"
WHAT'S THIS- A BEAUTY CONTEST
!?!
SO I'M NOT THE CUTEST DOGGY HERE...
...I'D EASILY WIN MISS CONGENIALITY.

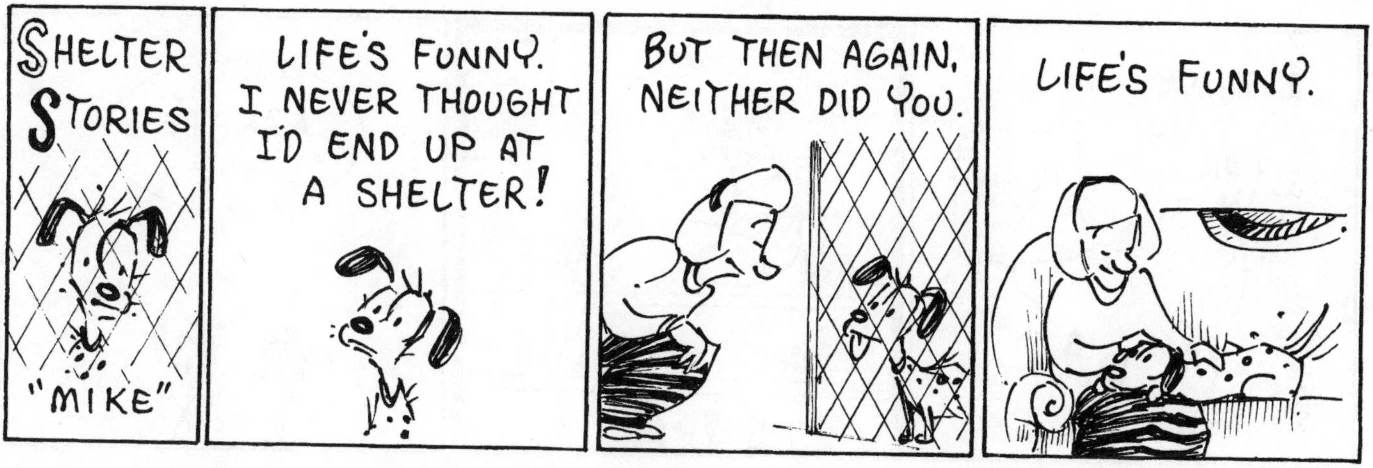
SHELTER STORIES
"MIKE"
LIFE'S FUNNY. I NEVER THOUGHT I'D END UP AT A SHELTER!
BUT THEN AGAIN, NEITHER DID YOU.
LIFE'S FUNNY.

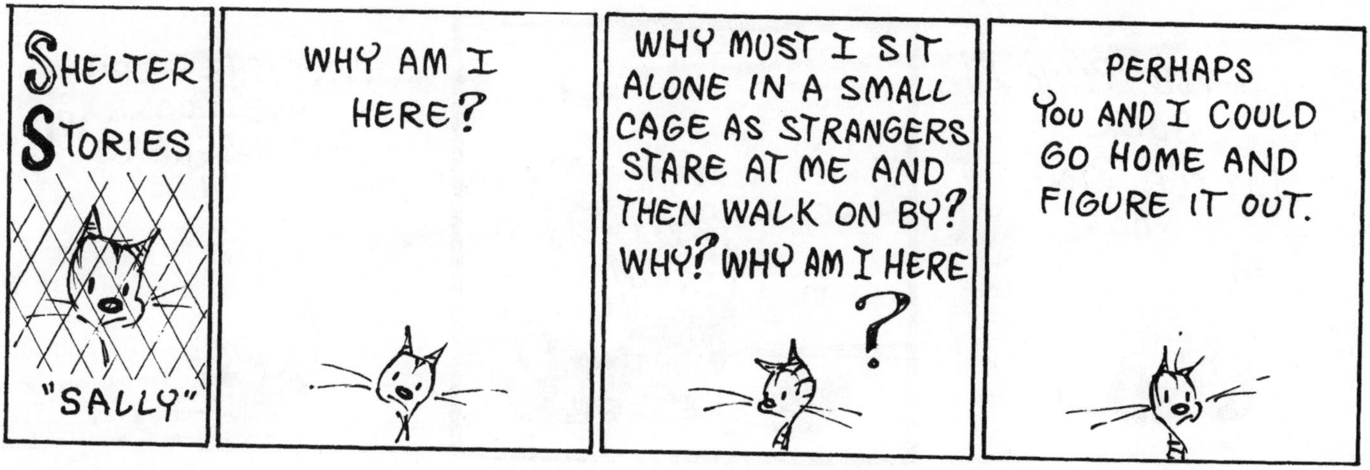
SHELTER STORIES
"SALLY"
WHY AM I HERE?
WHY MUST I SIT ALONE IN A SMALL CAGE AS STRANGERS STARE AT ME AND THEN WALK ON BY? WHY? WHY AM I HERE
?
PERHAPS YOU AND I COULD GO HOME AND FIGURE IT OUT.

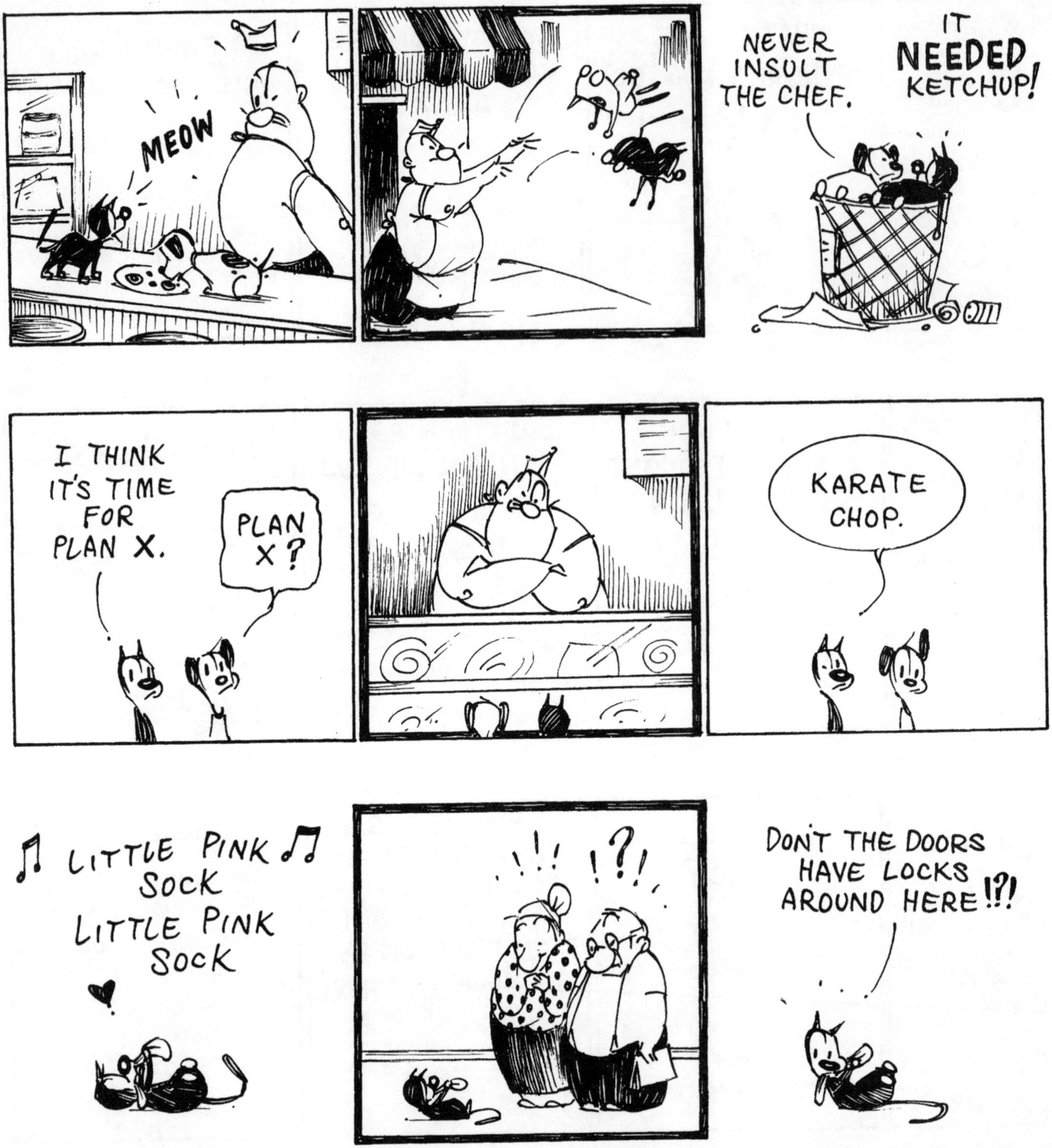
MEOW
NEVER INSULT THE CHEF.
IT NEEDED KETCHUP!
I THINK IT'S TIME FOR PLAN X.
PLAN X?
KARATE CHOP.
♫ LITTLE PINK ♫ SOCK LITTLE PINK SOCK
!!!
!?!
DON'T THE DOORS HAVE LOCKS AROUND HERE!?!

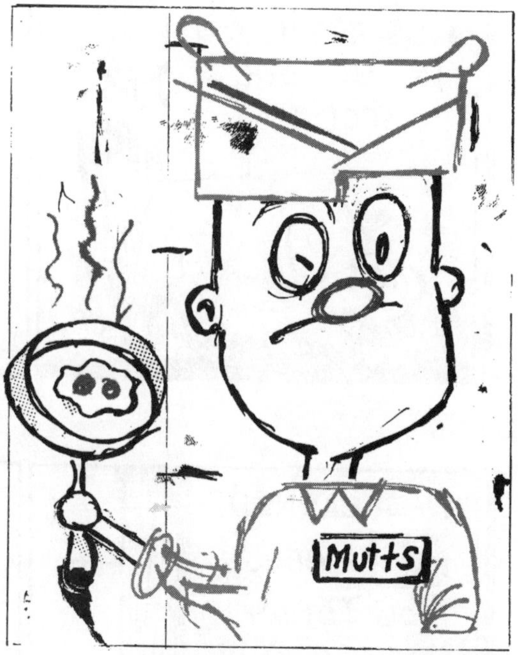
Mutts

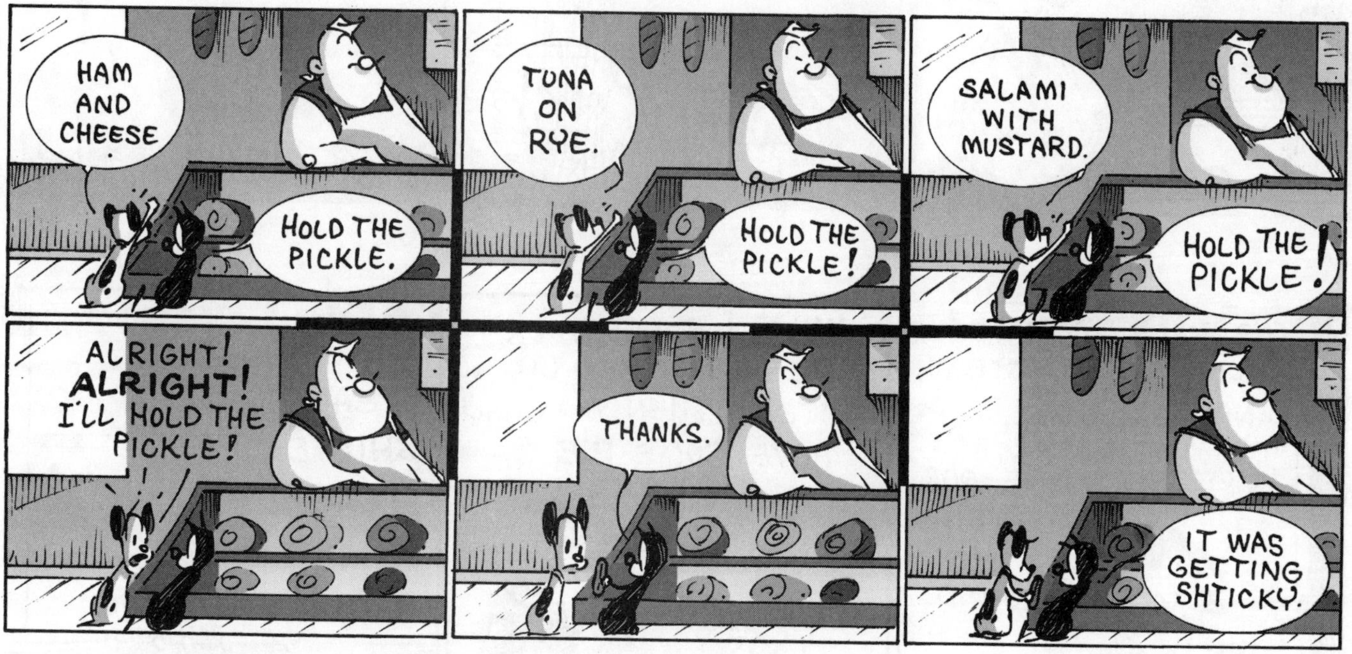
HAM AND CHEESE
HOLD THE PICKLE.
TUNA ON RYE.
HOLD THE PICKLE!
SALAMI WITH MUSTARD.
HOLD THE PICKLE!
ALRIGHT! ALRIGHT! I'LL HOLD THE PICKLE!
THANKS.
IT WAS GETTING SHTICKY.

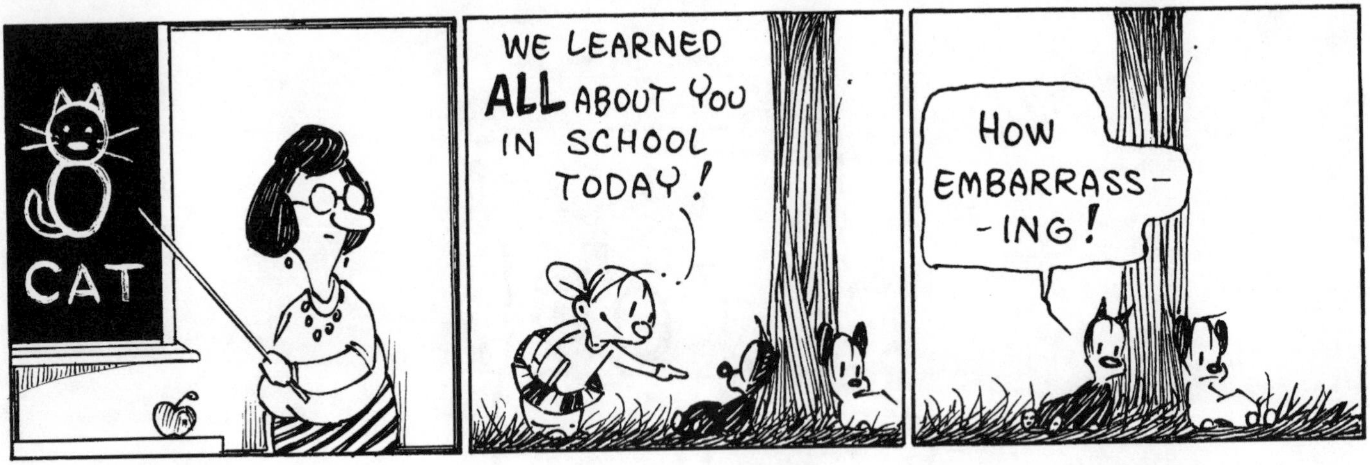
CAT
WE LEARNED ALL ABOUT YOU IN SCHOOL TODAY!
HOW EMBARRASS- -ING!

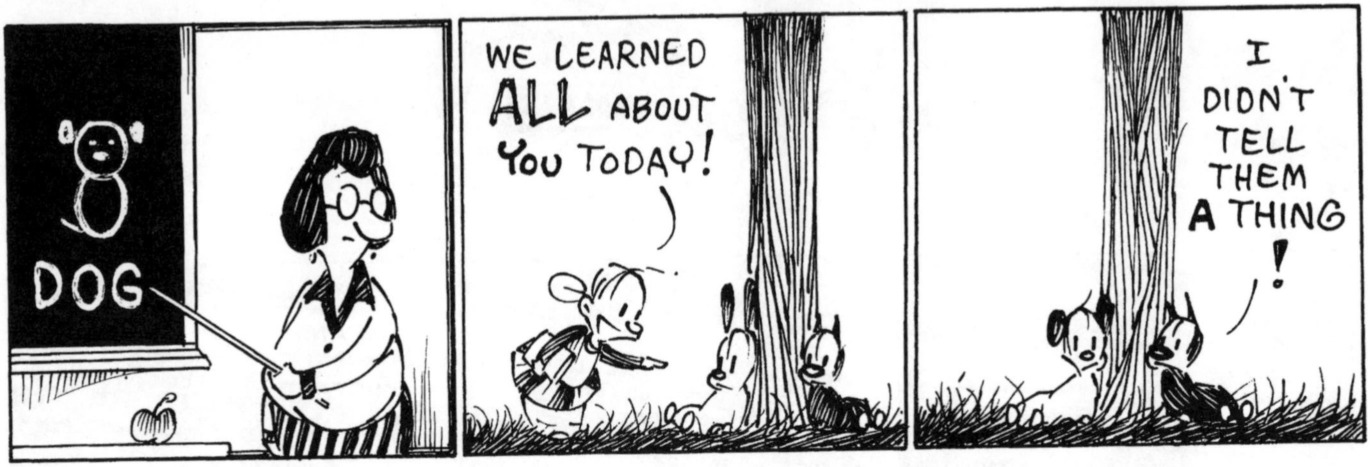
DOG
WE LEARNED ALL ABOUT YOU TODAY!
I DIDN'T TELL THEM A THING!

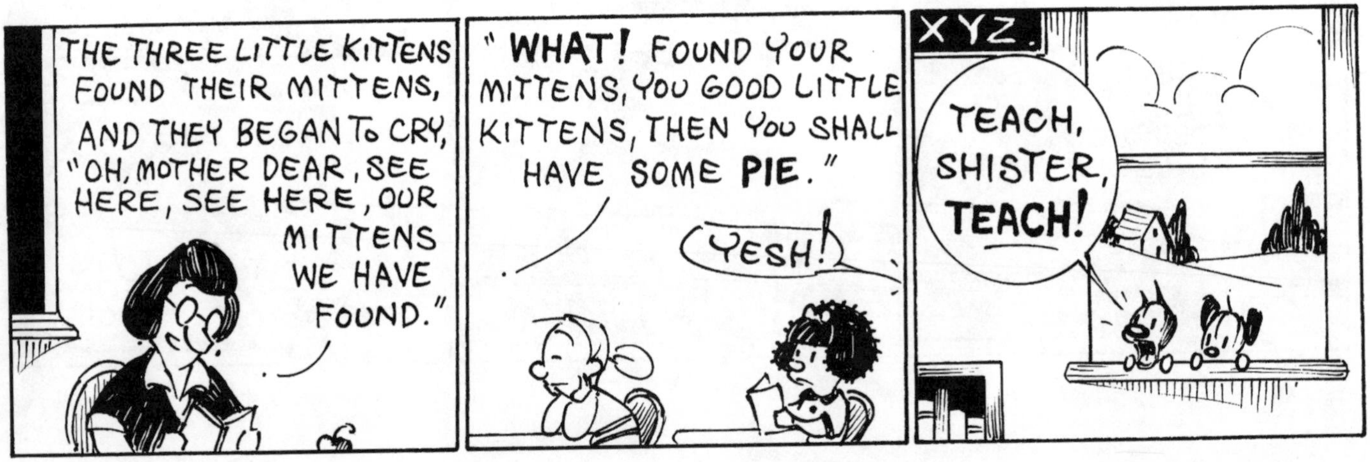
THE THREE LITTLE KITTENS FOUND THEIR MITTENS, AND THEY BEGAN TO CRY, "OH, MOTHER DEAR, SEE HERE, SEE HERE, OUR MITTENS WE HAVE FOUND."
"WHAT! FOUND YOUR MITTENS, YOU GOOD LITTLE KITTENS, THEN YOU SHALL HAVE SOME PIE."
YESH!
XYZ.
TEACH, SHISTER, TEACH!

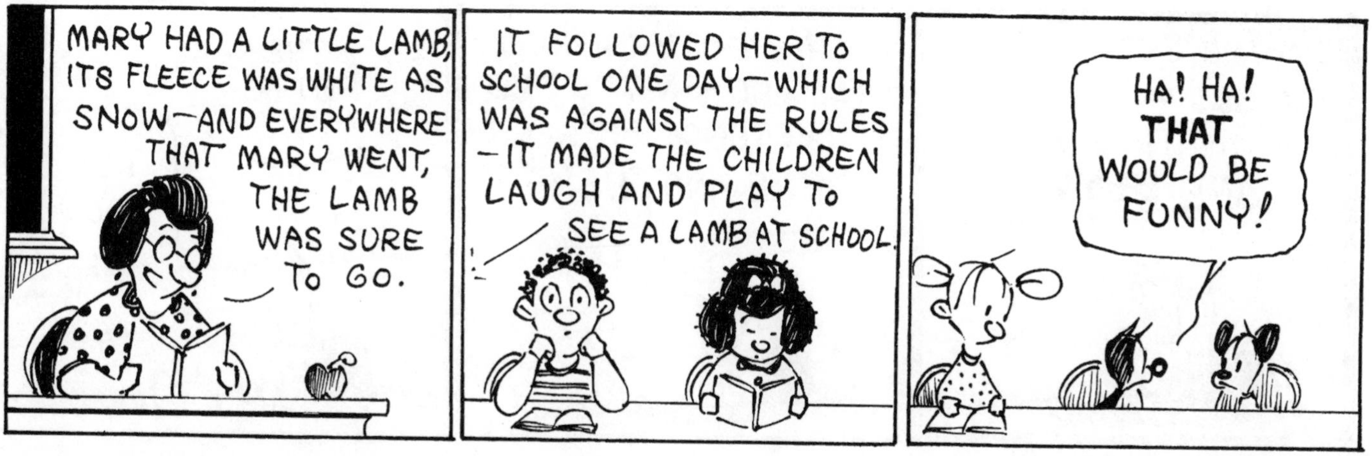
MARY HAD A LITTLE LAMB, ITS FLEECE WAS WHITE AS SNOW—AND EVERYWHERE THAT MARY WENT, THE LAMB WAS SURE TO GO.
IT FOLLOWED HER TO SCHOOL ONE DAY—WHICH WAS AGAINST THE RULES—IT MADE THE CHILDREN LAUGH AND PLAY TO SEE A LAMB AT SCHOOL.
HA! HA! **THAT** WOULD BE FUNNY!

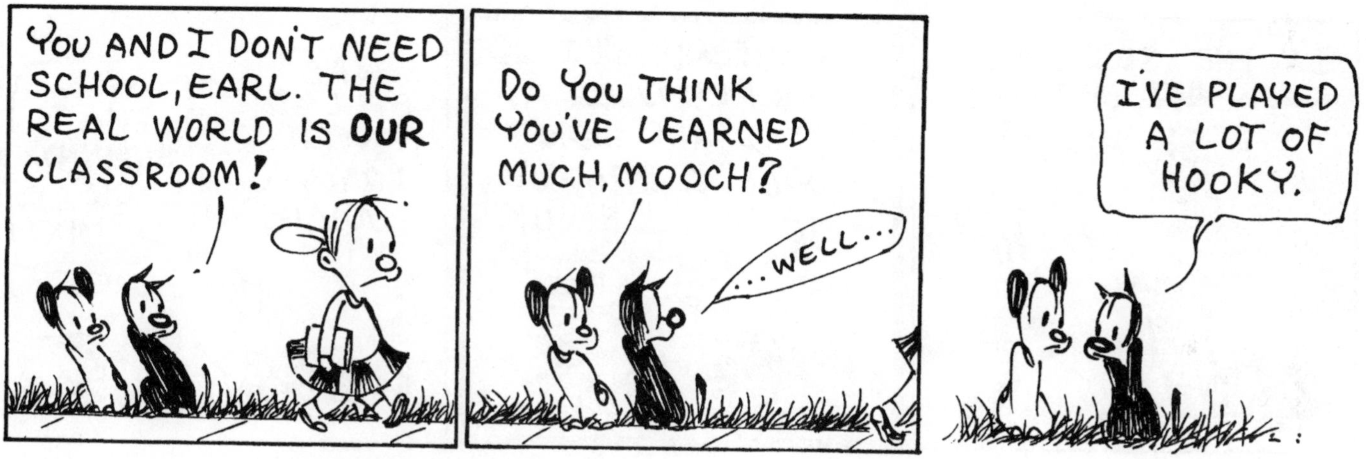
YOU AND I DON'T NEED SCHOOL, EARL. THE REAL WORLD IS **OUR** CLASSROOM!
DO YOU THINK YOU'VE LEARNED MUCH, MOOCH?
...WELL...
I'VE PLAYED A LOT OF HOOKY.

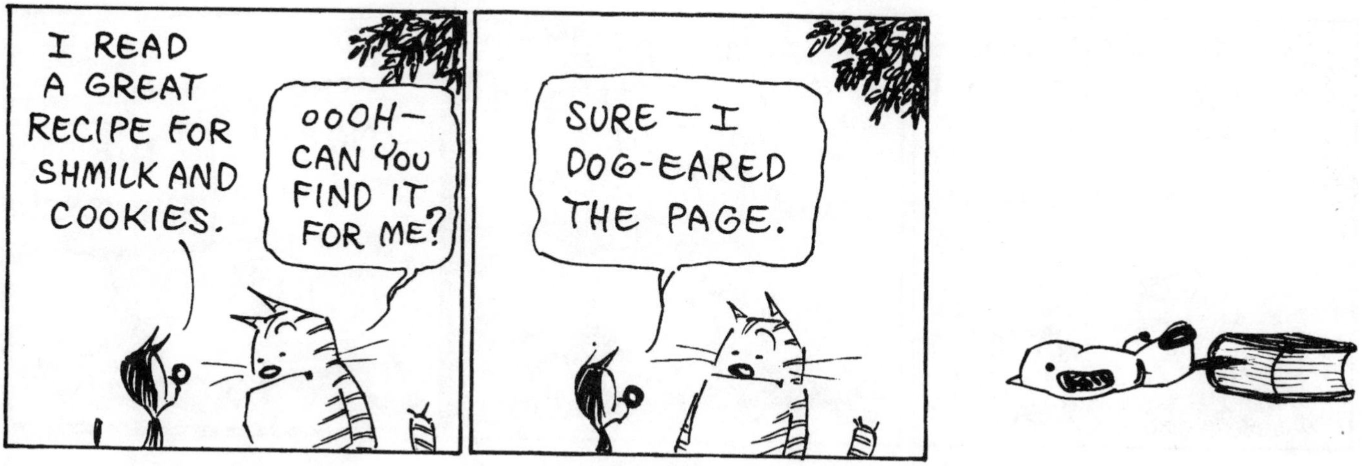
I READ A GREAT RECIPE FOR SHMILK AND COOKIES.
OOOH—CAN YOU FIND IT FOR ME?
SURE—I DOG-EARED THE PAGE.

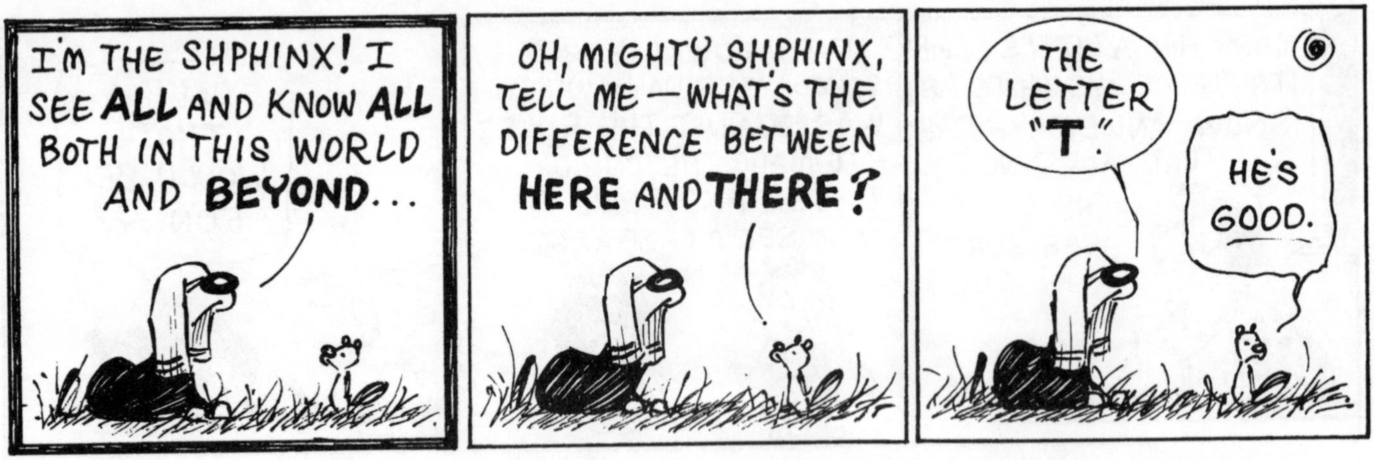
I'M THE SHPHINX! I SEE ALL AND KNOW ALL BOTH IN THIS WORLD AND BEYOND...
OH, MIGHTY SHPHINX, TELL ME — WHAT'S THE DIFFERENCE BETWEEN HERE AND THERE?
THE LETTER "T".
HE'S GOOD.

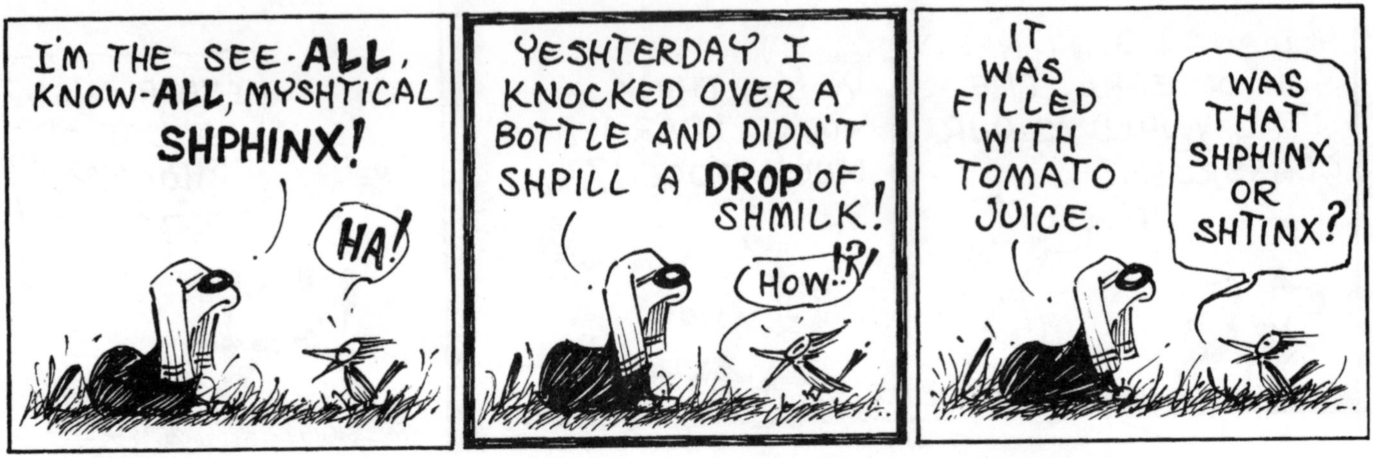
I'M THE SEE-ALL, KNOW-ALL, MYSHTICAL SHPHINX!
HA!
YESHTERDAY I KNOCKED OVER A BOTTLE AND DIDN'T SHPILL A DROP OF SHMILK!
HOW!?
IT WAS FILLED WITH TOMATO JUICE.
WAS THAT SHPHINX OR SHTINX?

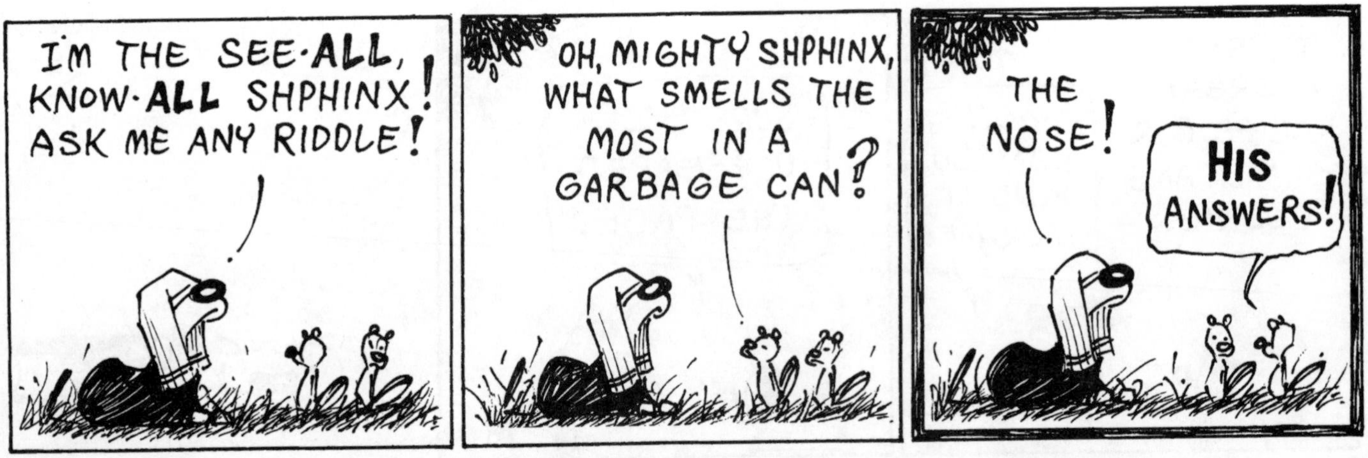
I'M THE SEE-ALL, KNOW-ALL SHPHINX! ASK ME ANY RIDDLE!
OH, MIGHTY SHPHINX, WHAT SMELLS THE MOST IN A GARBAGE CAN?
THE NOSE!
HIS ANSWERS!

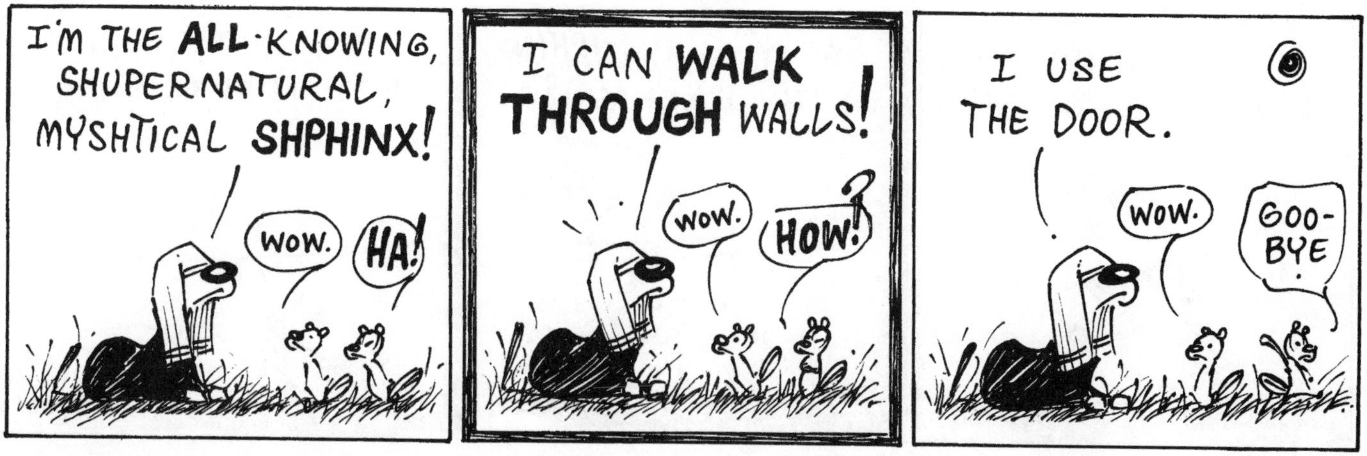
I'M THE ALL-KNOWING, SHUPERNATURAL, MYSHTICAL SHPHINX!
WOW.
HA!
I CAN WALK THROUGH WALLS!
WOW.
HOW?
I USE THE DOOR.
WOW.
GOO-BYE

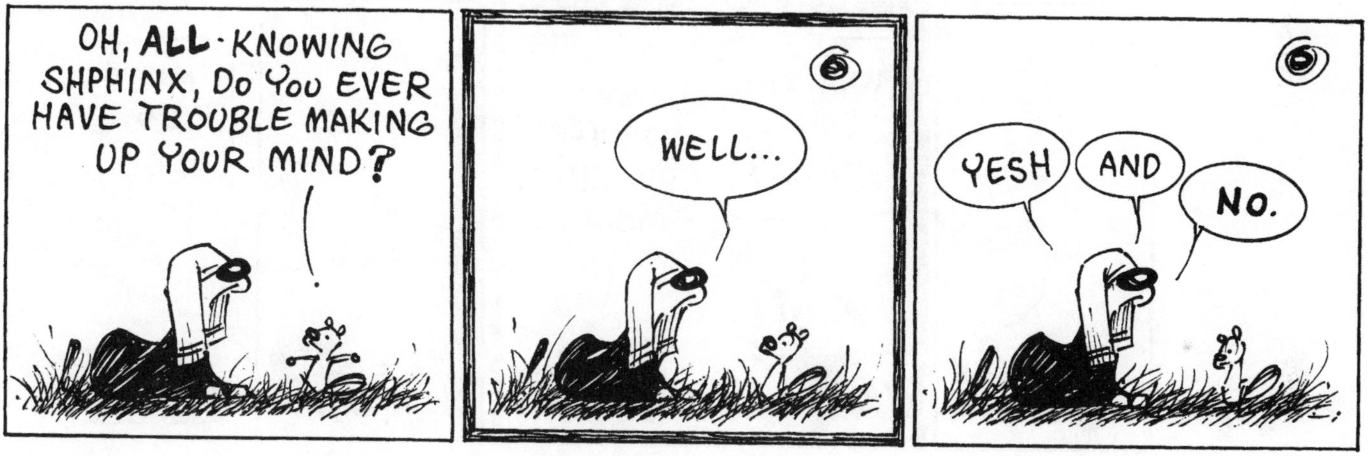
OH, ALL-KNOWING SHPHINX, DO YOU EVER HAVE TROUBLE MAKING UP YOUR MIND?
WELL...
YESH
AND
NO.

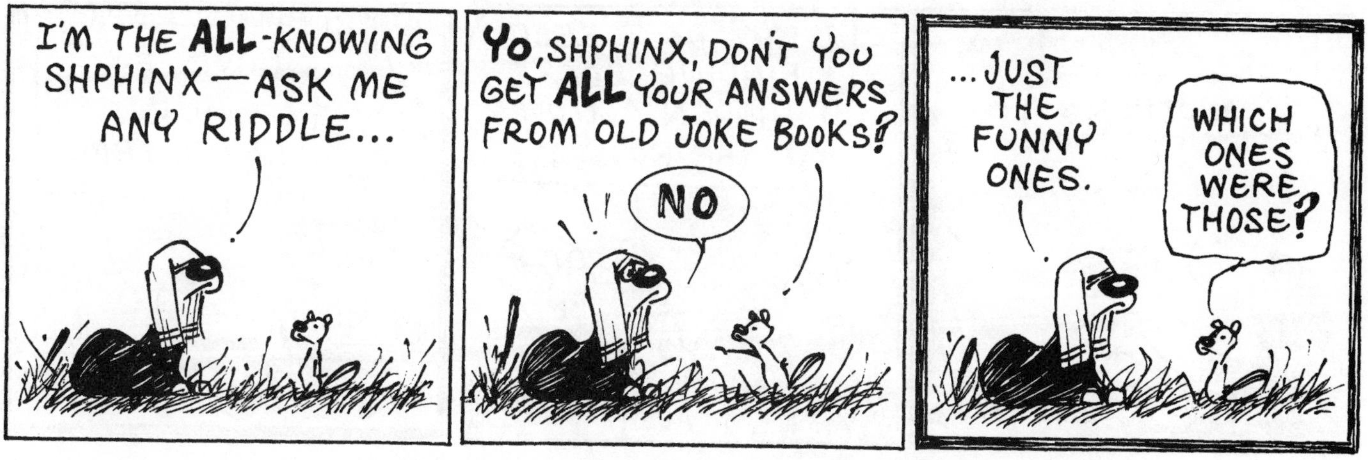
I'M THE ALL-KNOWING SHPHINX—ASK ME ANY RIDDLE...
YO, SHPHINX, DON'T YOU GET ALL YOUR ANSWERS FROM OLD JOKE BOOKS?
NO
...JUST THE FUNNY ONES.
WHICH ONES WERE THOSE?

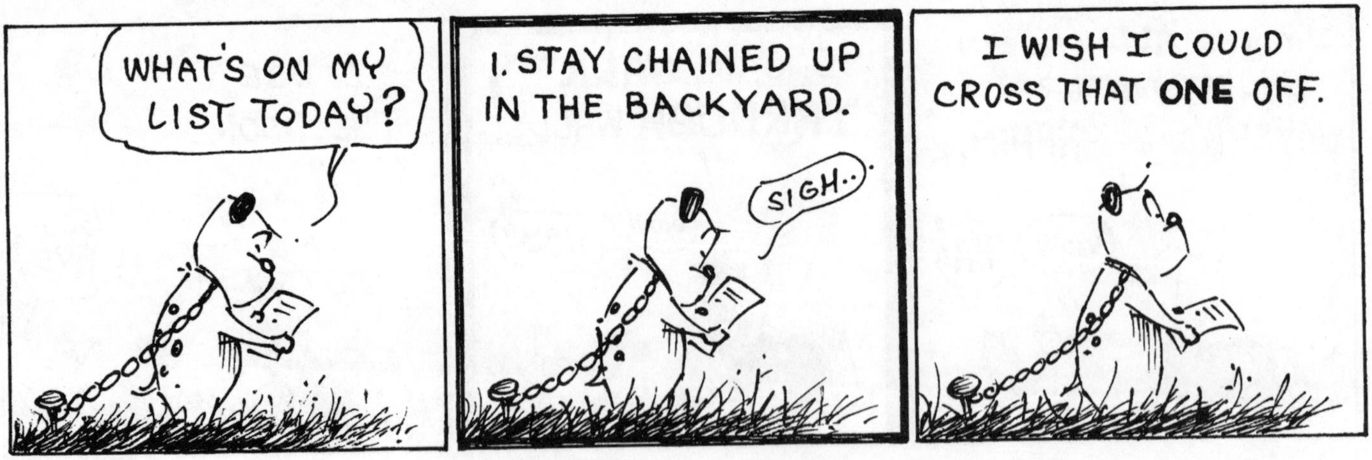
WHAT'S ON MY LIST TODAY?
I. STAY CHAINED UP IN THE BACKYARD.
SIGH..
I WISH I COULD CROSS THAT **ONE** OFF.

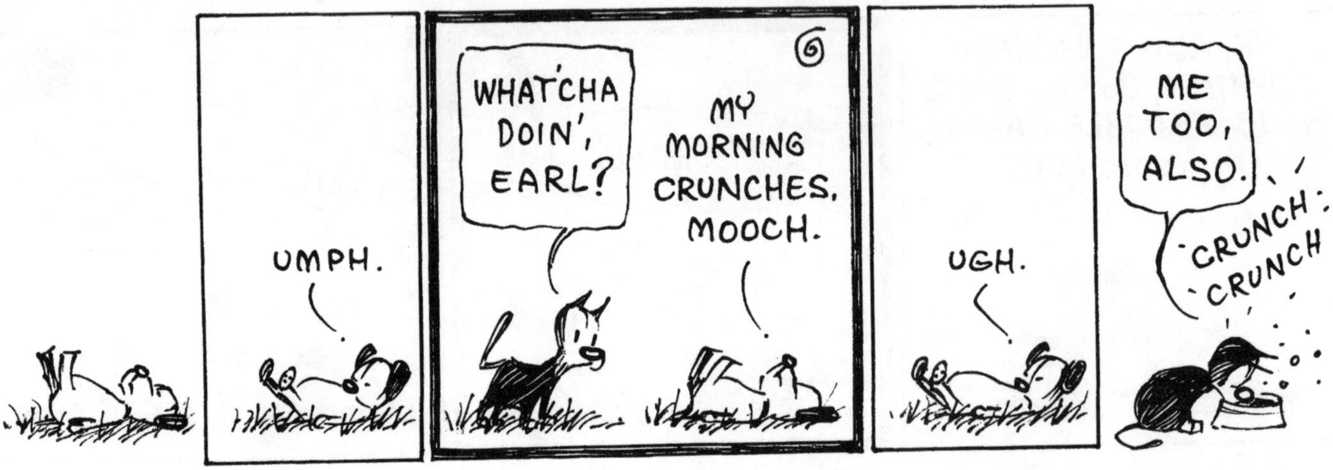
UMPH.
WHAT'CHA DOIN', EARL?
MY MORNING CRUNCHES, MOOCH.
UGH.
ME TOO, ALSO.
CRUNCH CRUNCH

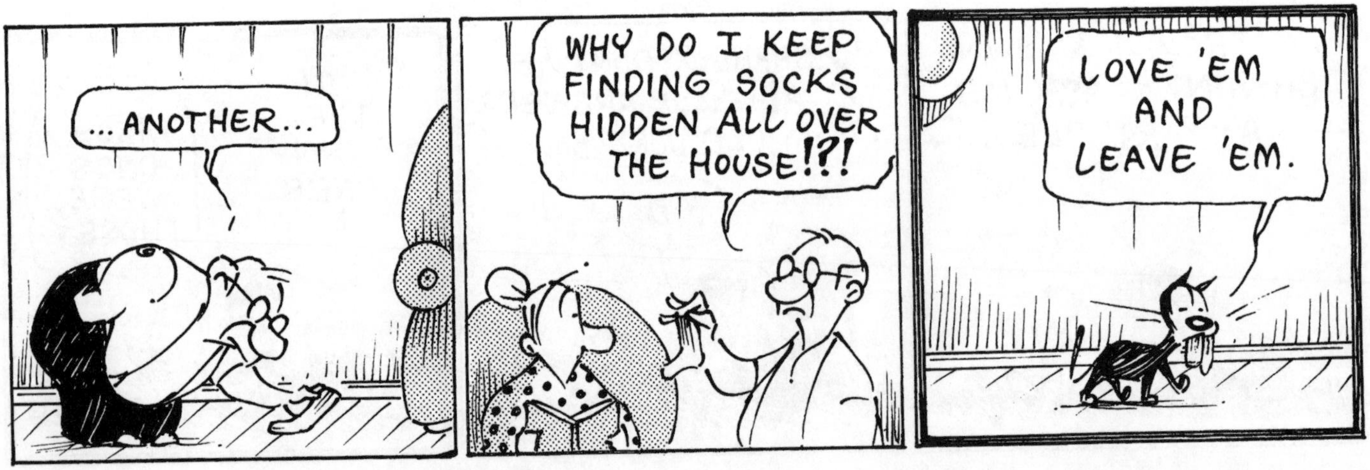
... ANOTHER ...
WHY DO I KEEP FINDING SOCKS HIDDEN ALL OVER THE HOUSE!?!
LOVE 'EM AND LEAVE 'EM.

MUTTS
PATRICK McDONNELL

RRRRRRRRRRRR
FOO.
EVERY NIGHT IT'S THE SAME DANCE WITH YOU TWO.

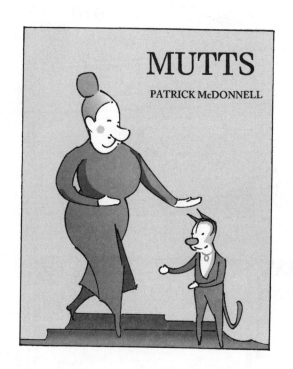

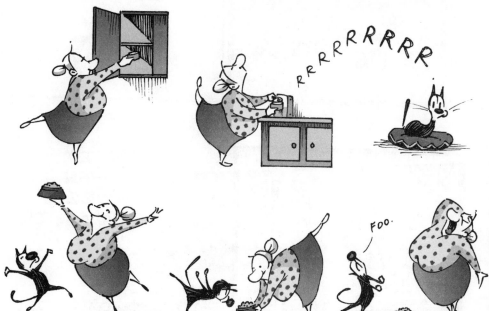

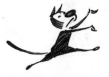

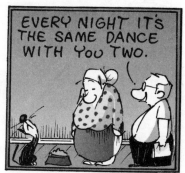

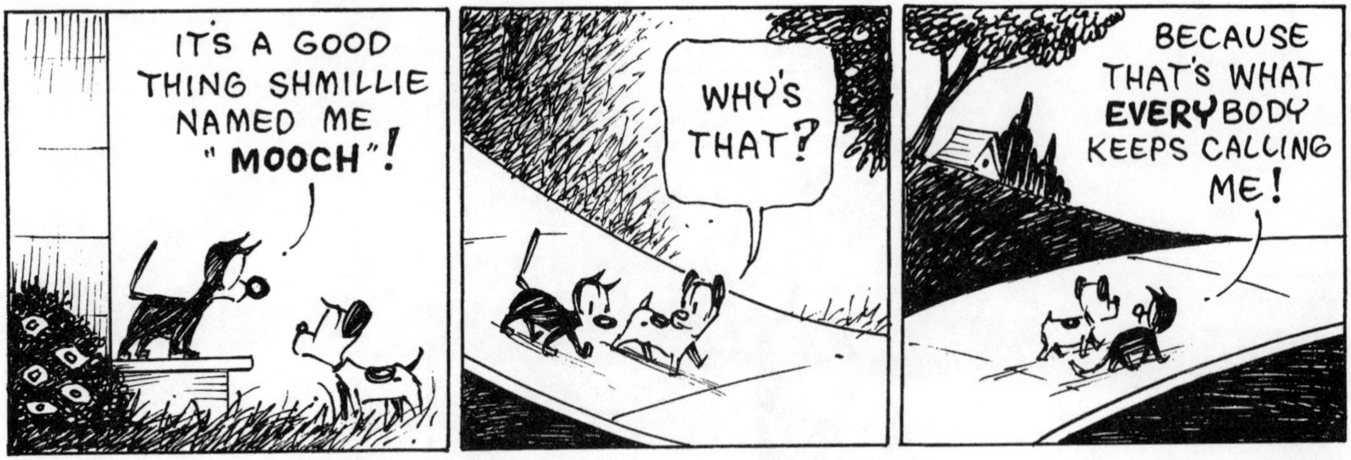
IT'S A GOOD THING SHMILLIE NAMED ME "MOOCH"!
WHY'S THAT?
BECAUSE THAT'S WHAT EVERYBODY KEEPS CALLING ME!

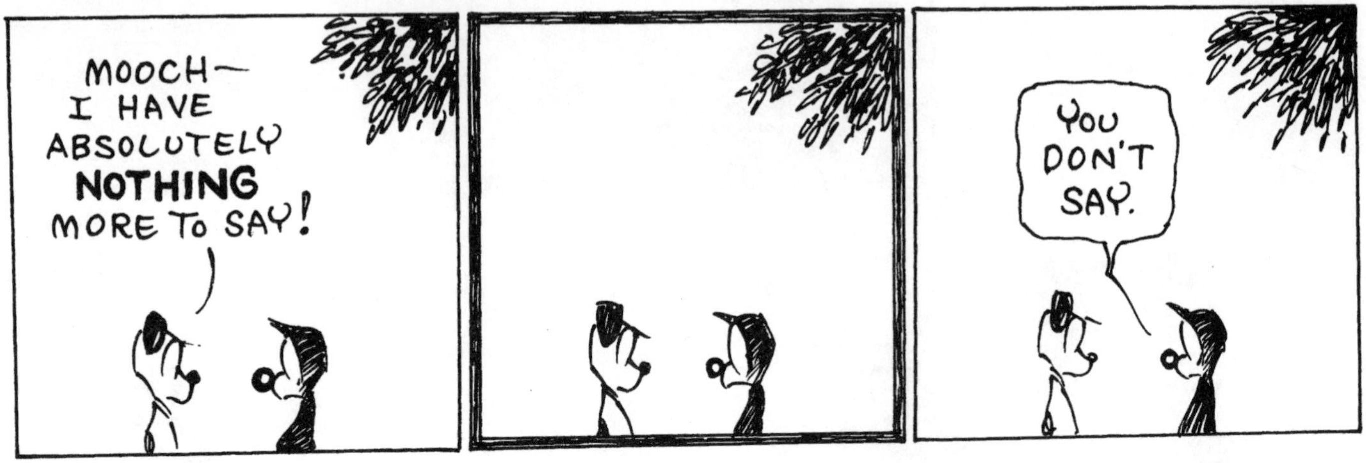
MOOCH— I HAVE ABSOLUTELY NOTHING MORE TO SAY!
YOU DON'T SAY.

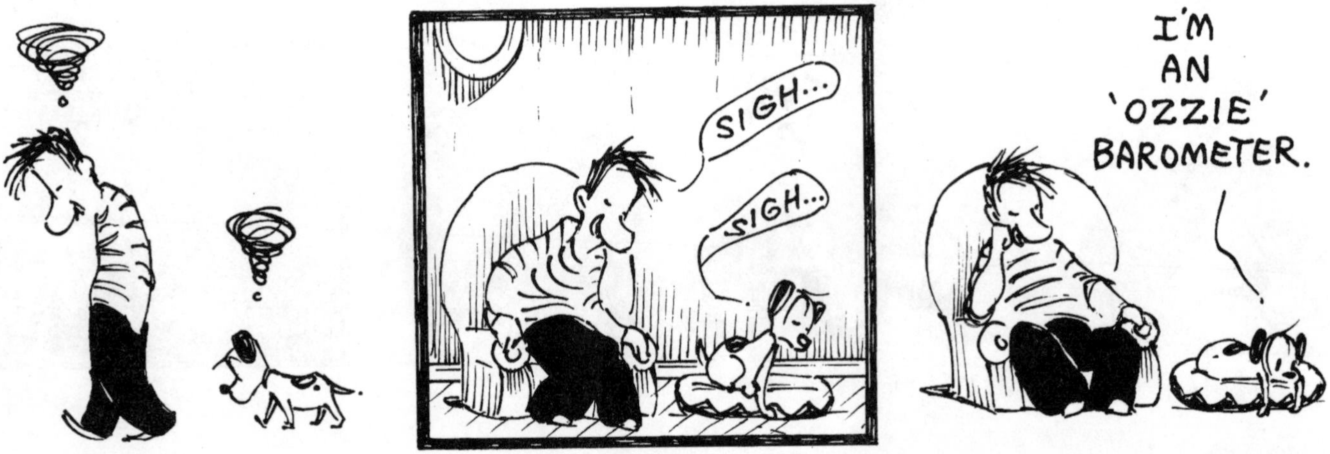
SIGH...
SIGH...
I'M AN 'OZZIE' BAROMETER.

Mutts

PATRICK McDONNELL

MY HUSBAND WILL BE RIGHT WITH YOU.
HELLO, KITTY.
POOM POOM POOM
YOU'RE IN HIS CHAIR.

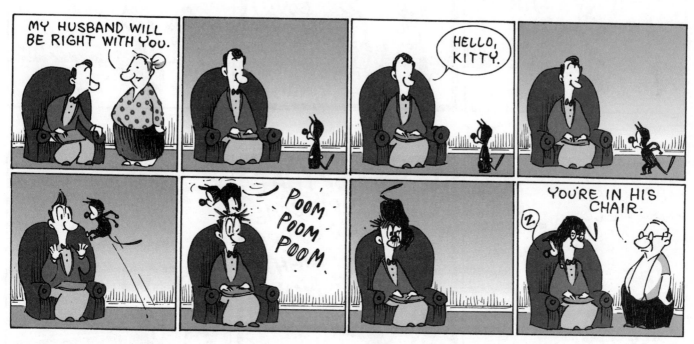

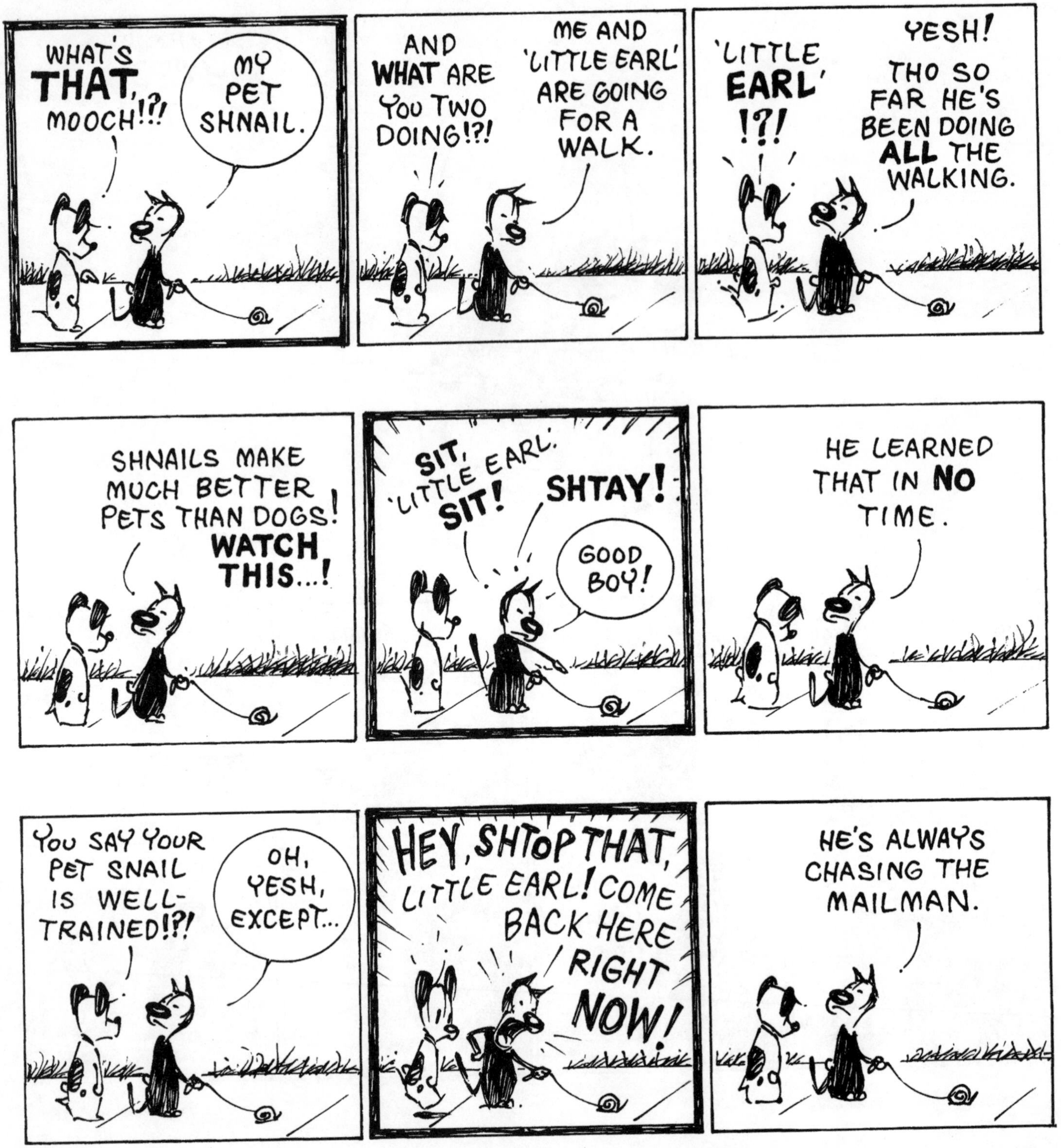
WHAT'S THAT, MOOCH!?!
MY PET SHNAIL.
AND WHAT ARE YOU TWO DOING!?!
ME AND 'LITTLE EARL' ARE GOING FOR A WALK.
'LITTLE EARL' !?!
YESH! THO SO FAR HE'S BEEN DOING ALL THE WALKING.
SHNAILS MAKE MUCH BETTER PETS THAN DOGS! WATCH THIS...!
SIT, 'LITTLE EARL.' SIT!
SHTAY!
GOOD BOY!
HE LEARNED THAT IN NO TIME.
YOU SAY YOUR PET SNAIL IS WELL-TRAINED!?!
OH, YESH, EXCEPT...
HEY, SHTOP THAT, LITTLE EARL! COME BACK HERE RIGHT NOW!
HE'S ALWAYS CHASING THE MAILMAN.

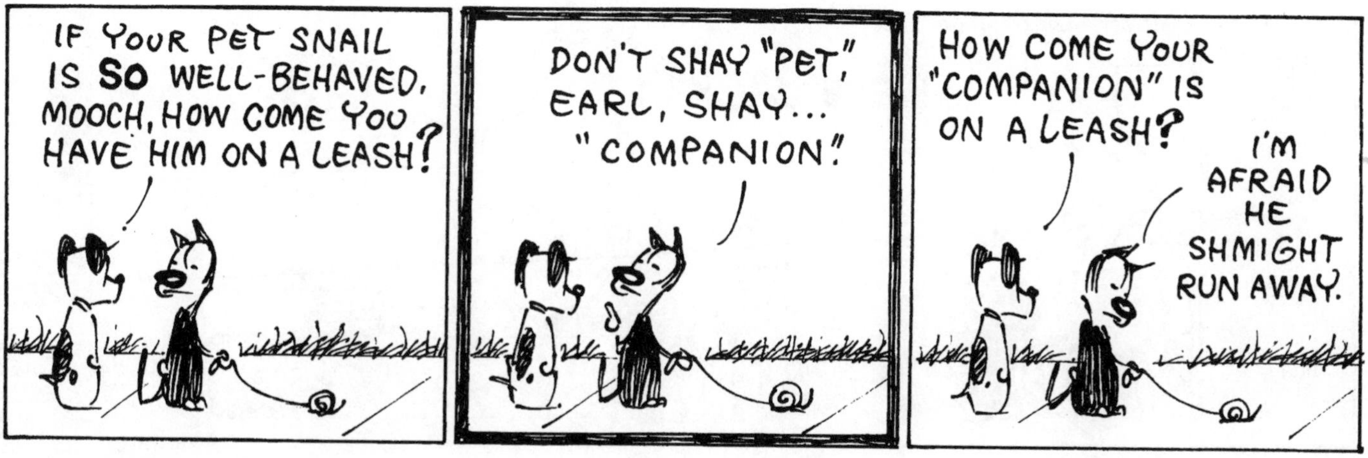
IF YOUR PET SNAIL IS SO WELL-BEHAVED, MOOCH, HOW COME YOU HAVE HIM ON A LEASH?
DON'T SHAY "PET," EARL, SHAY... "COMPANION."
HOW COME YOUR "COMPANION" IS ON A LEASH?
I'M AFRAID HE SHMIGHT RUN AWAY.

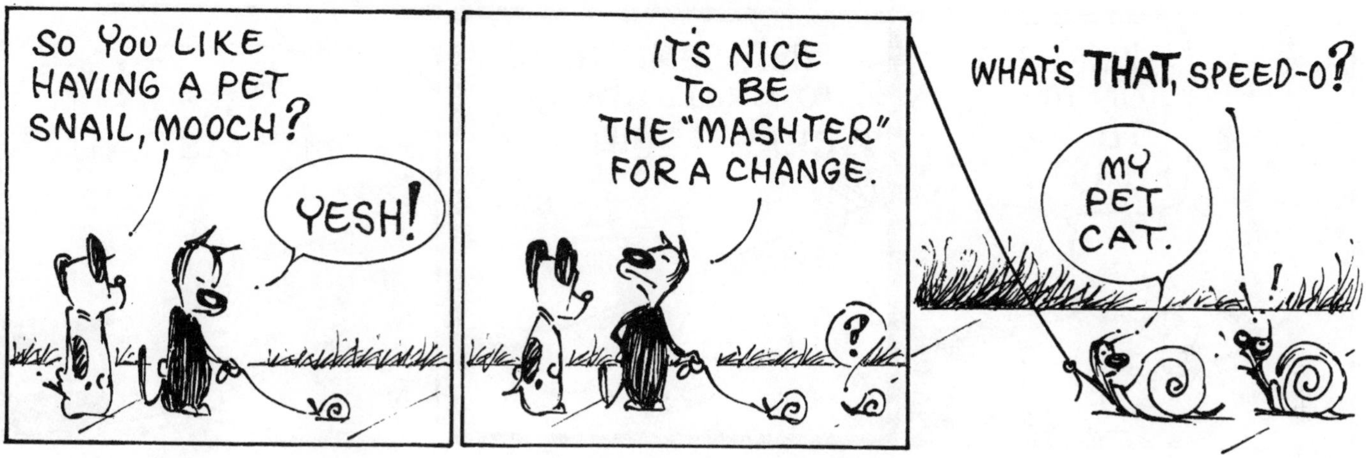
SO YOU LIKE HAVING A PET SNAIL, MOOCH?
YESH!
IT'S NICE TO BE THE "MASHTER" FOR A CHANGE.
?
WHAT'S THAT, SPEED-O?
MY PET CAT.
!

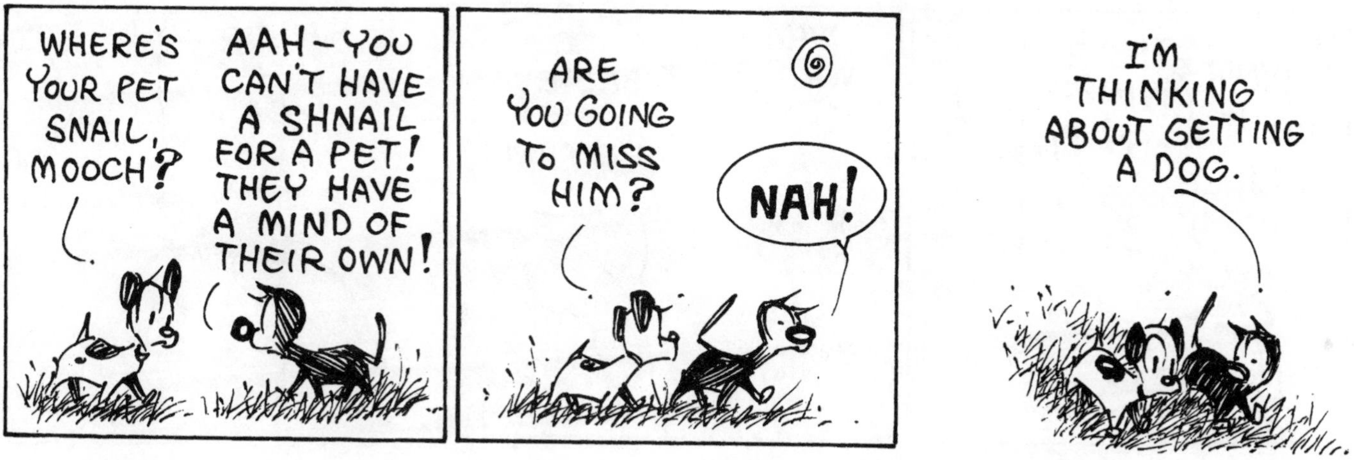
WHERE'S YOUR PET SNAIL, MOOCH?
AAH–YOU CAN'T HAVE A SHNAIL FOR A PET! THEY HAVE A MIND OF THEIR OWN!
ARE YOU GOING TO MISS HIM?
NAH!
I'M THINKING ABOUT GETTING A DOG.

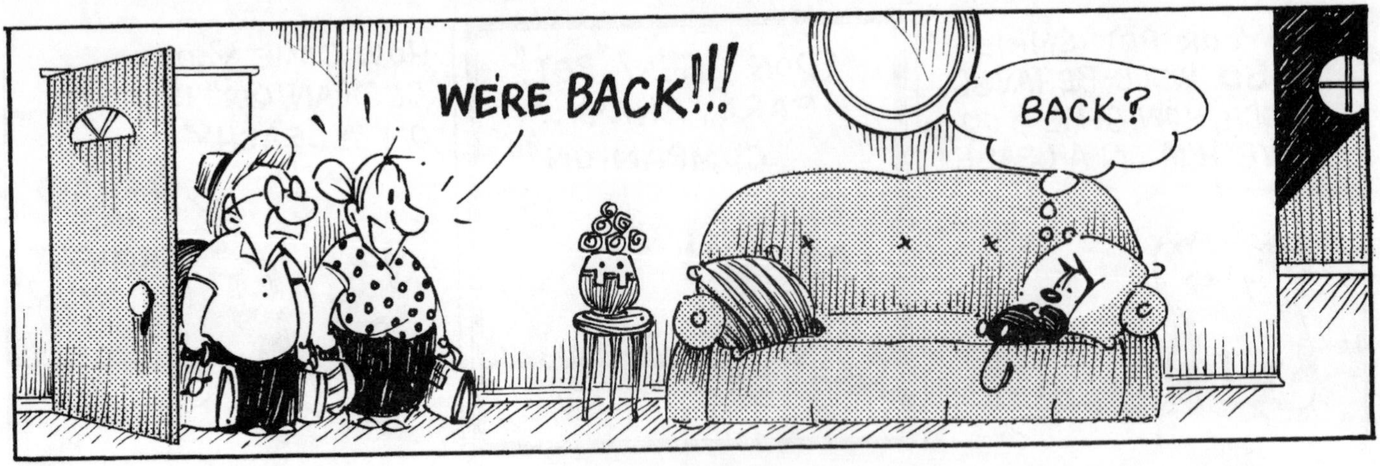
WE'RE BACK!!!
BACK?

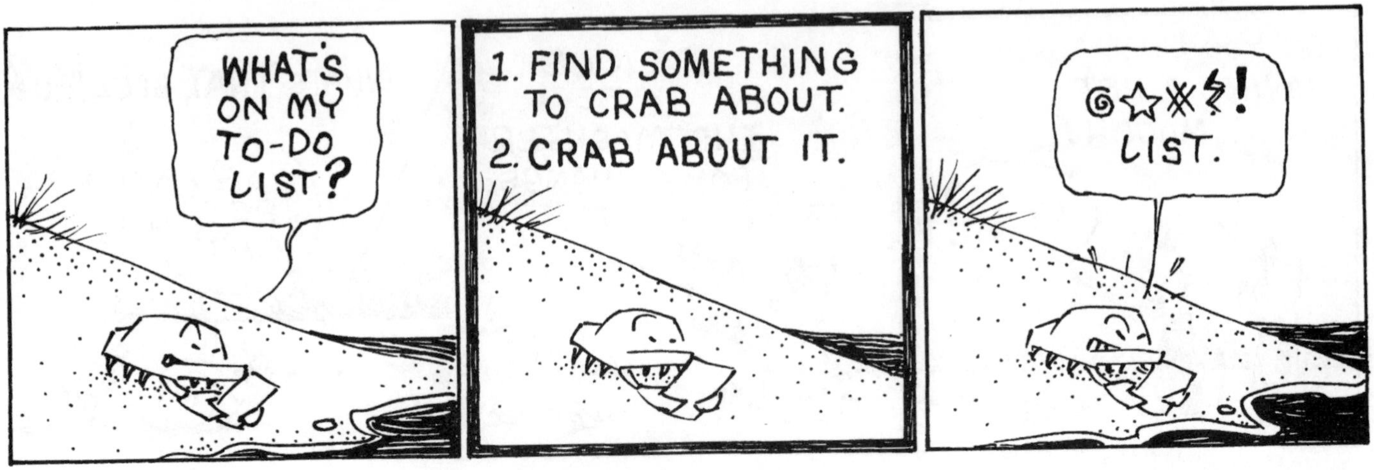
WHAT'S ON MY TO-DO LIST?
1. FIND SOMETHING TO CRAB ABOUT.
2. CRAB ABOUT IT.
LIST.

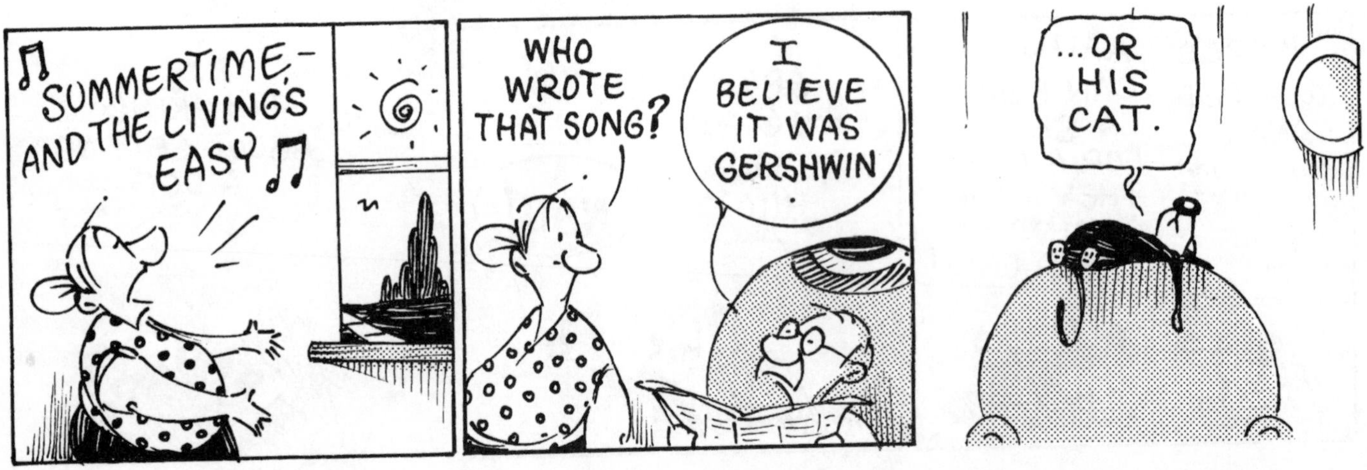
SUMMERTIME, AND THE LIVING'S EASY
WHO WROTE THAT SONG?
I BELIEVE IT WAS GERSHWIN.
...OR HIS CAT.

The adventures of...
MUTTS
by PATRICK McDONNELL

MUTTS
WHO'S BEEN EATING MY DIN-DIN?
CRIMESHTOPPERS
WATCH YOUR PLATE.
WHO WOULD COMMIT SUCH A DELECTABLE CRIME? WHO? WHO? WHO? I SHMELL DOG!
WHICH CAGEY CANINE CULPRIT COULD IT BE?
SHQUEAKEE TOYEE
POUCH POOCH
LITTLE FACE FIDO
DOG BREATH MAHONEY
AUGH! I MUST SHOLVE THIS CHOWHOUND 'WHO-DID-IT'!
I WILL GET TO THE BOTTOM OF THIS!
CHOMP CHOMP
MOOCH! WHAT ARE YOU DOING IN MY HOUSE EATING MY DINNER?
HMMM...
... ANOTHER MYSHTERY.

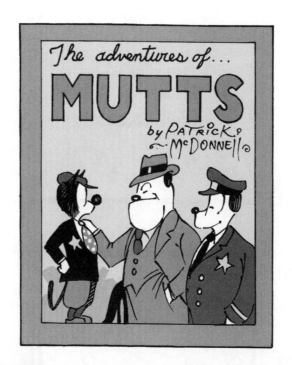

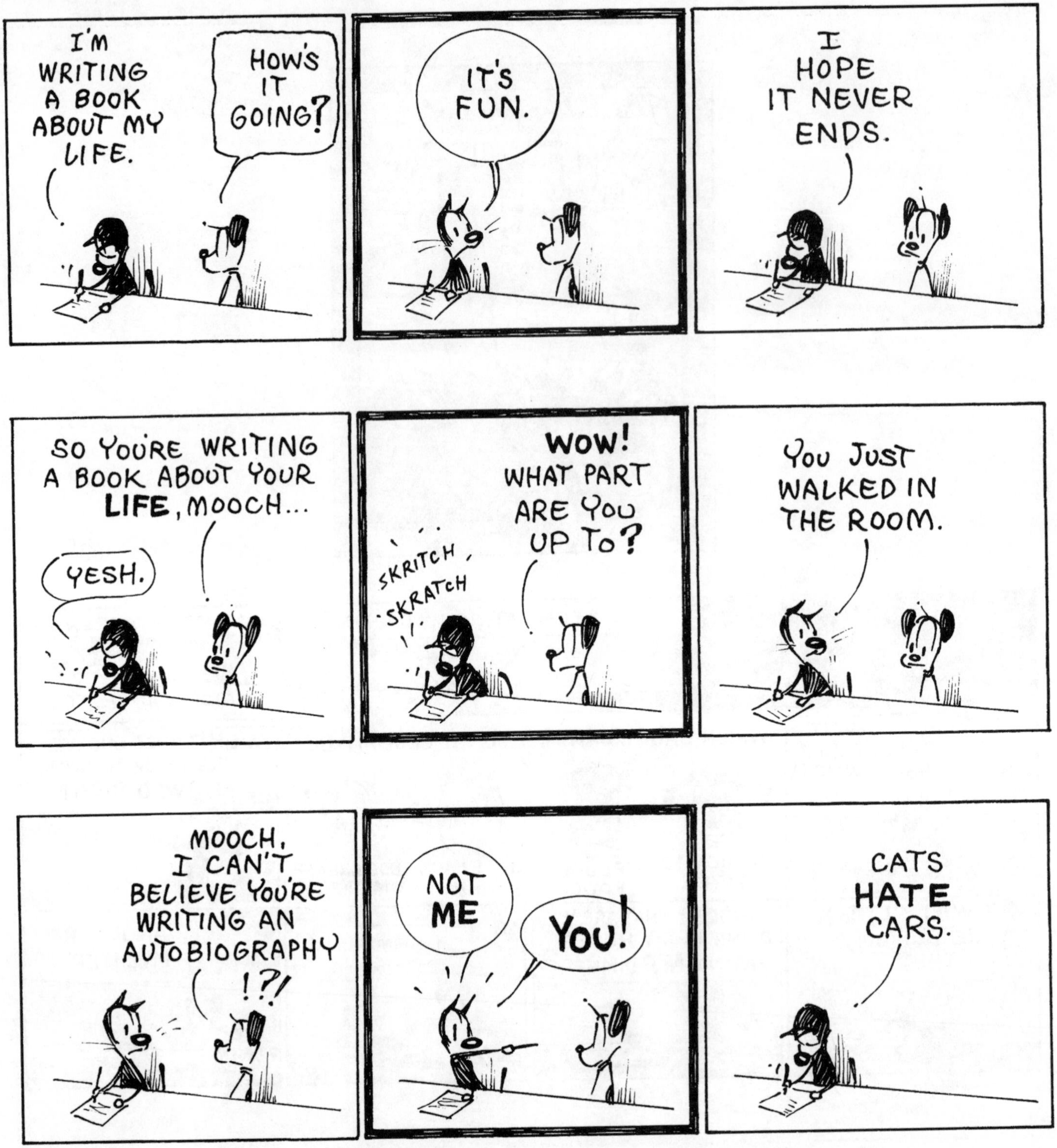
I'M WRITING A BOOK ABOUT MY LIFE.
HOW'S IT GOING?
IT'S FUN.
I HOPE IT NEVER ENDS.
SO YOU'RE WRITING A BOOK ABOUT YOUR **LIFE**, MOOCH...
YESH.
SKRITCH SKRATCH
WOW! WHAT PART ARE YOU UP TO?
YOU JUST WALKED IN THE ROOM.
MOOCH, I CAN'T BELIEVE YOU'RE WRITING AN AUTOBIOGRAPHY !?!
NOT **ME**
YOU!
CATS **HATE** CARS.

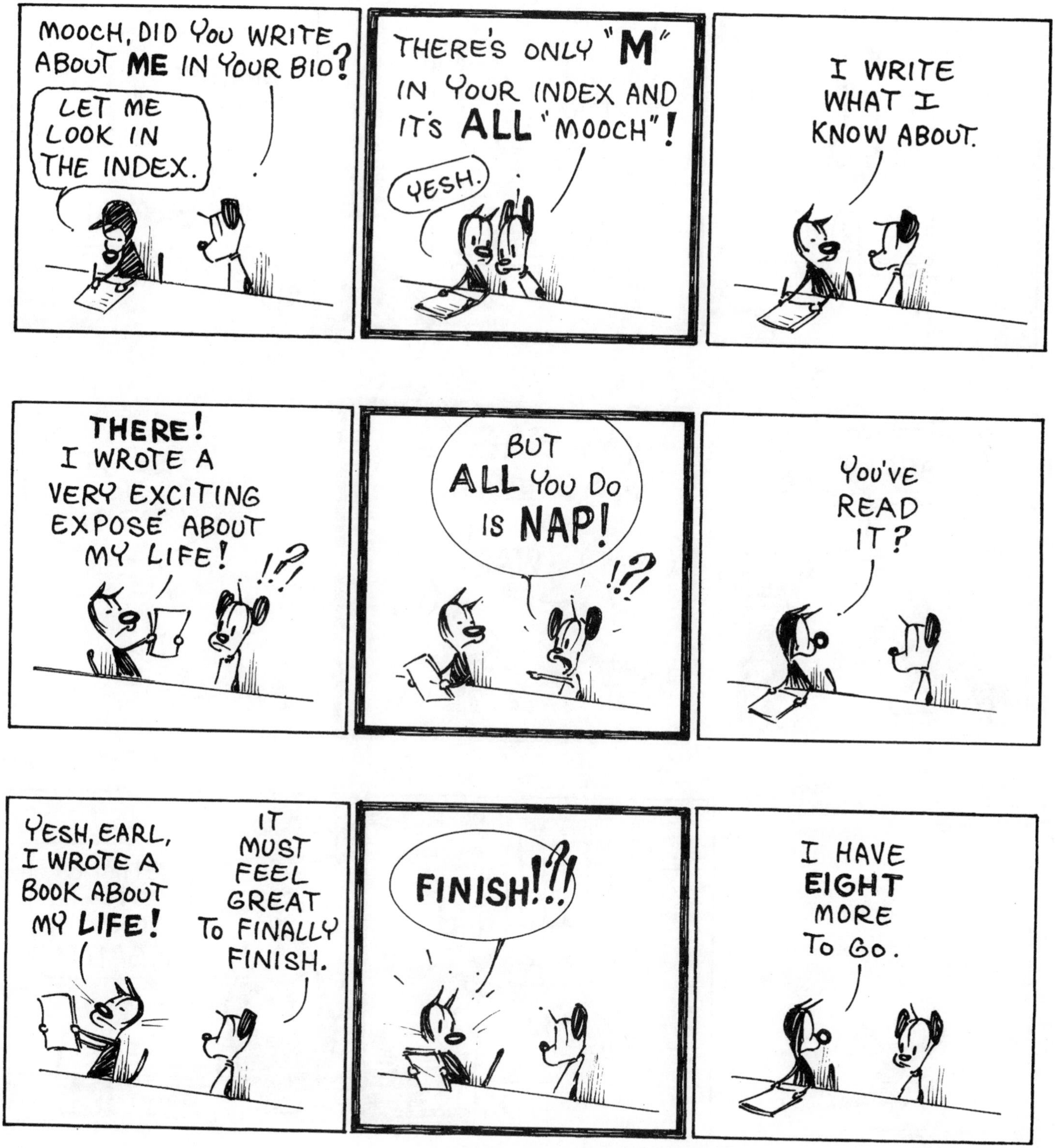
MOOCH, DID YOU WRITE ABOUT ME IN YOUR BIO?
LET ME LOOK IN THE INDEX.
THERE'S ONLY "M" IN YOUR INDEX AND IT'S ALL "MOOCH"!
YESH.
I WRITE WHAT I KNOW ABOUT.
THERE! I WROTE A VERY EXCITING EXPOSÉ ABOUT MY LIFE!
!?
BUT ALL YOU DO IS NAP!
!?
YOU'VE READ IT?
YESH, EARL, I WROTE A BOOK ABOUT MY LIFE!
IT MUST FEEL GREAT TO FINALLY FINISH.
FINISH!?!
I HAVE EIGHT MORE TO GO.

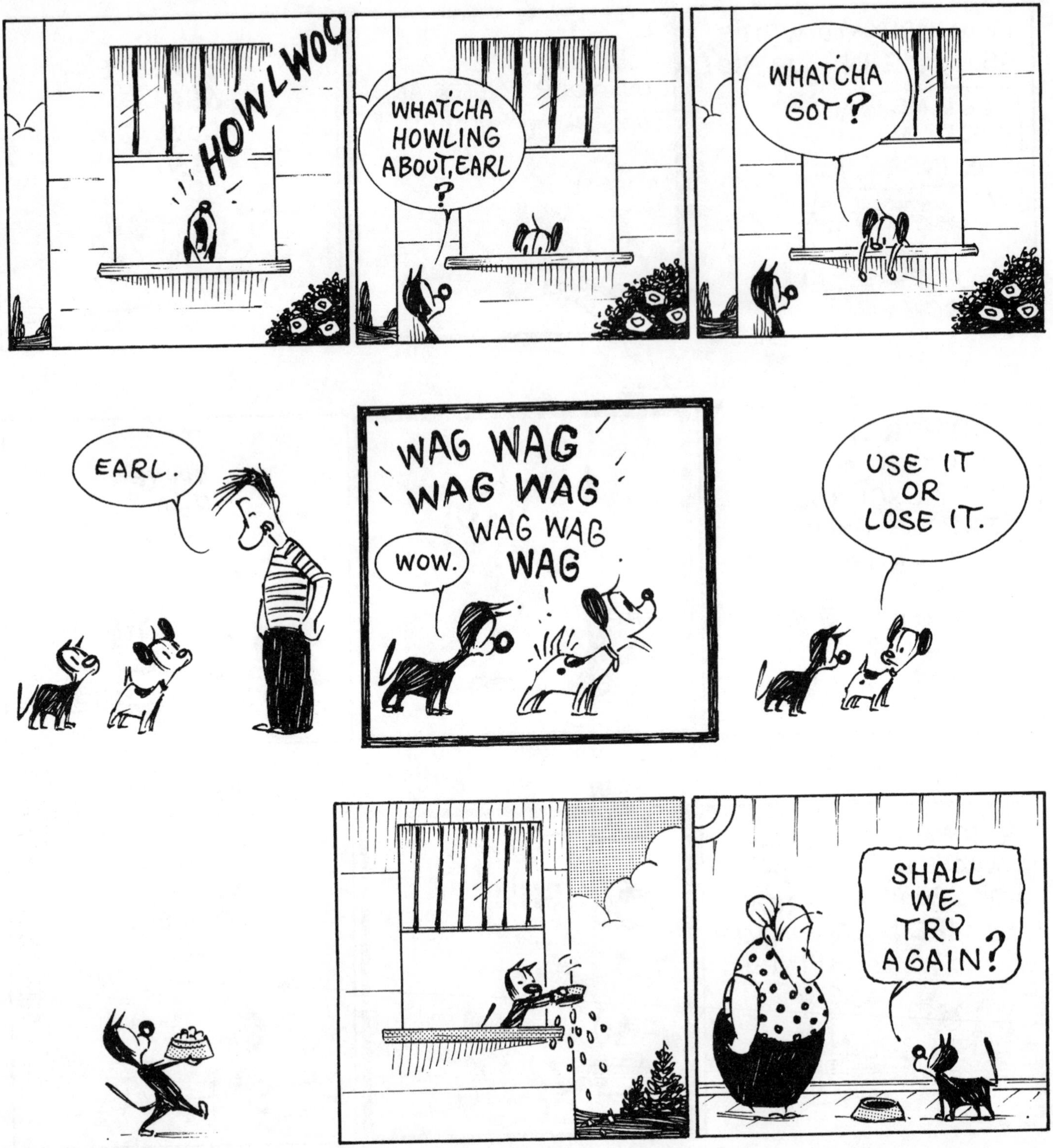
HOWLWOO
WHATCHA HOWLING ABOUT, EARL?
WHATCHA GOT?
EARL.
WAG WAG WAG WAG WAG WAG WAG
WOW.
USE IT OR LOSE IT.
SHALL WE TRY AGAIN?

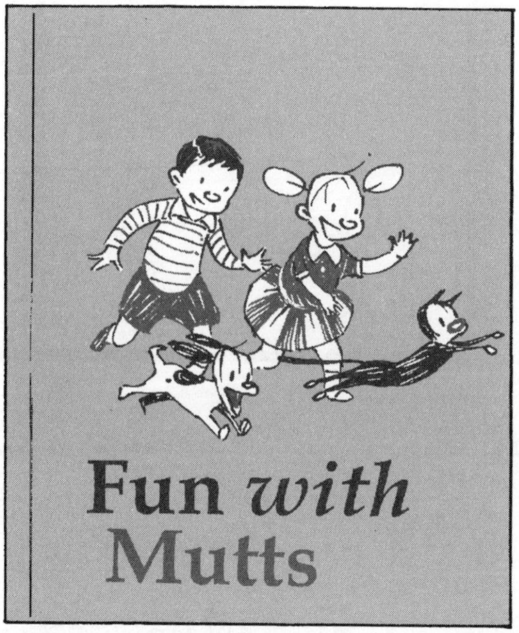
Fun *with*
Mutts

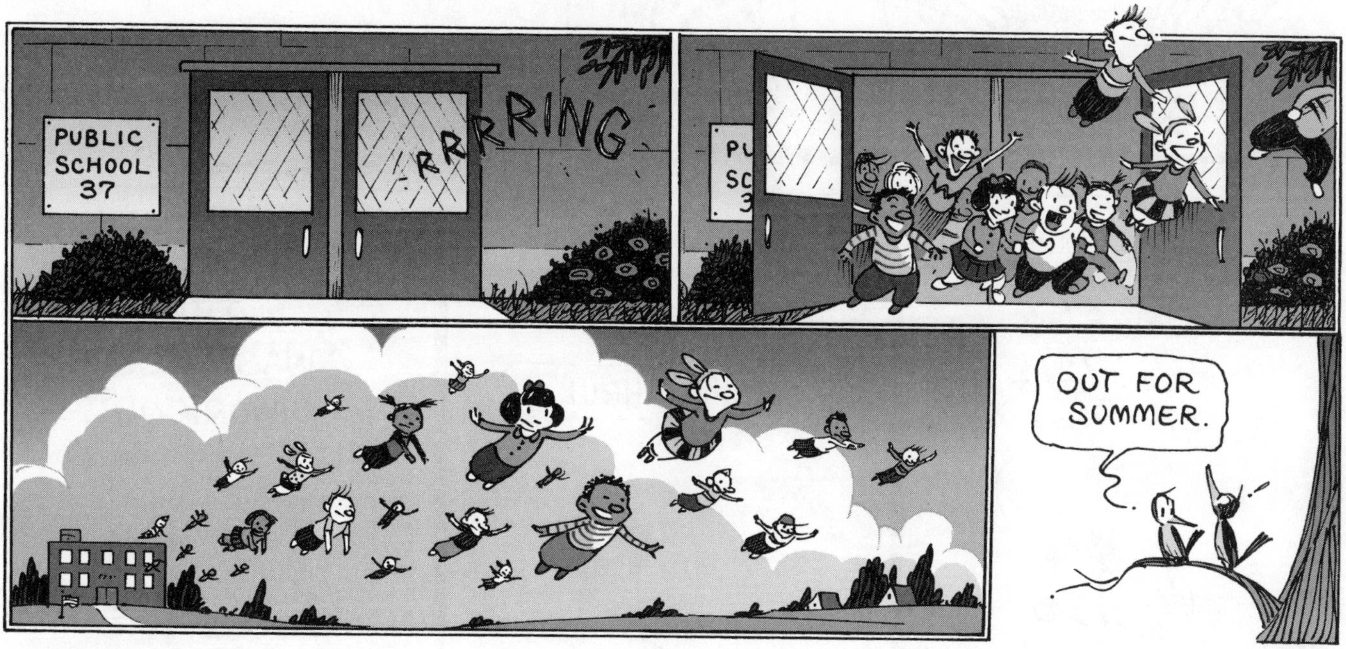
PUBLIC SCHOOL 37
RRRRING
OUT FOR SUMMER.

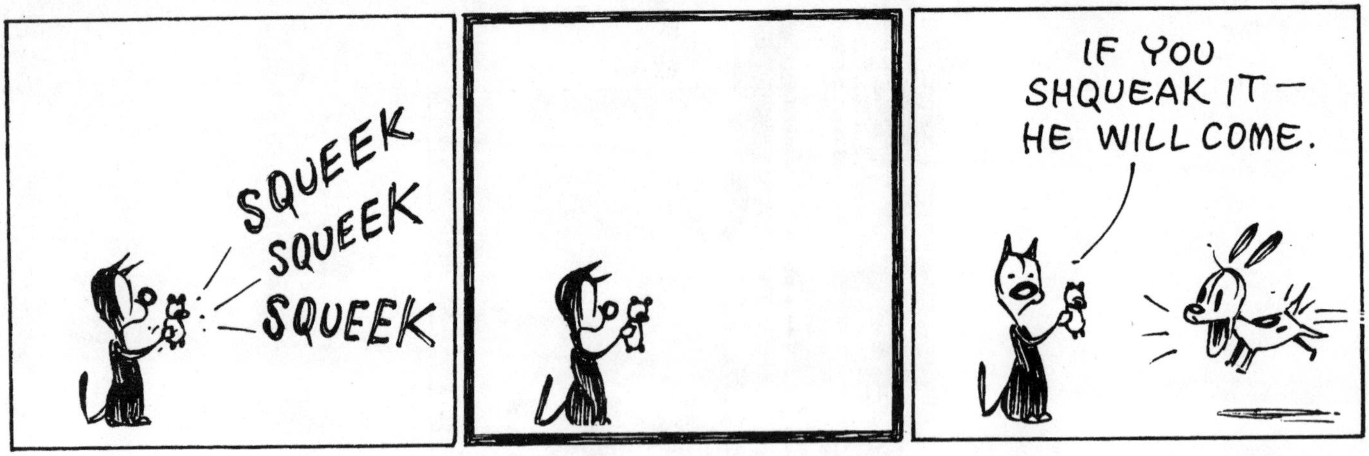
SQUEEK
SQUEEK
SQUEEK
IF YOU SHQUEAK IT — HE WILL COME.

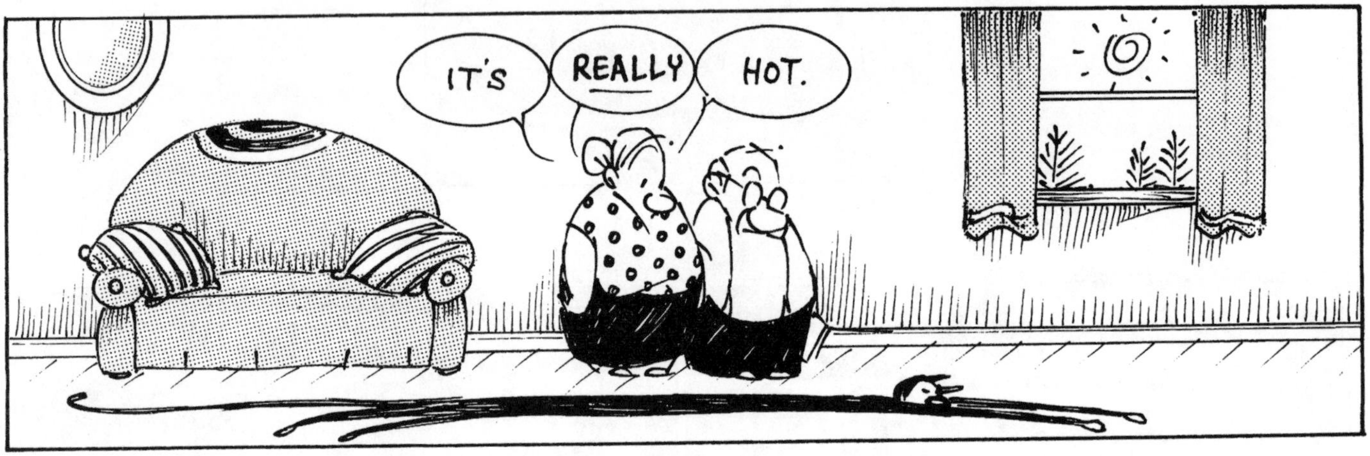
IT'S
REALLY
HOT.

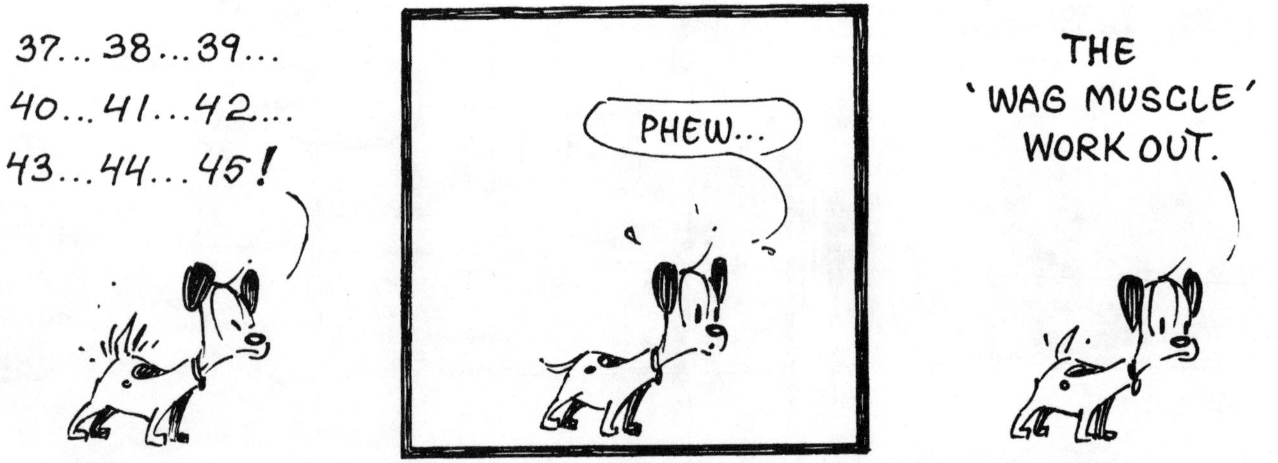
37... 38... 39... 40... 41... 42... 43... 44... 45!
PHEW...
THE 'WAG MUSCLE' WORK OUT.

MUTTS

I'M TRYING TO ORGANIZE A NATIONAL 'PURR IN' FOR WORLD PEACE.
A "PURR IN" !?!
YESH! IF EVERYONE EVERYWHERE DID EVERYTHING THEY CAN TO SHMAKE THEIR CATS PURR ALL AT THE SHAME DESIGNATED TIME
THAT HUMONGOUS PURR WOULD VIBRATE AND RESHONATE THROUGHOUT THE COSHMOS!!!
AND HOW DOES THAT HELP WORLD PEACE?
THE KITTIES WILL BE HAPPY.
...AND THAT'S A SHTART!

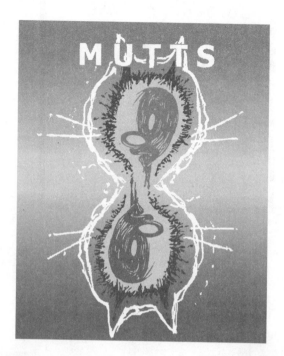

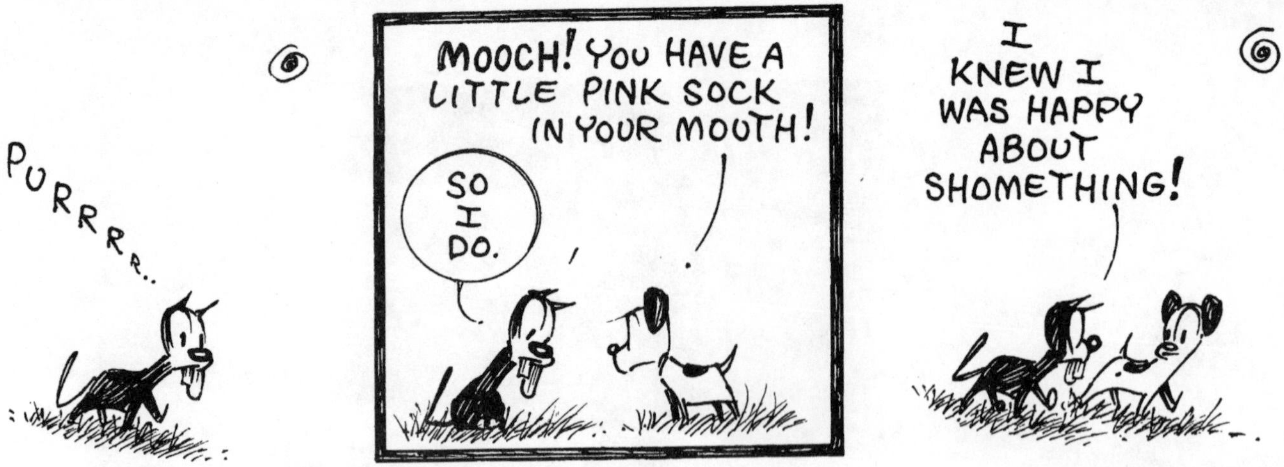
PURRRR...
MOOCH! YOU HAVE A LITTLE PINK SOCK IN YOUR MOUTH!
SO I DO.
I KNEW I WAS HAPPY ABOUT SHOMETHING!

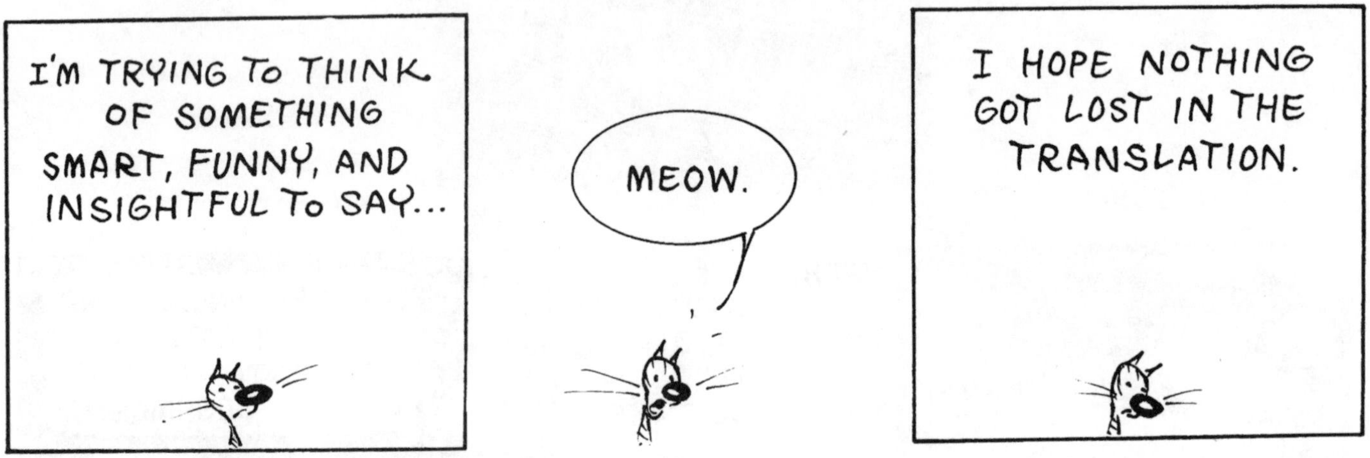
I'M TRYING TO THINK OF SOMETHING SMART, FUNNY, AND INSIGHTFUL TO SAY...
MEOW.
I HOPE NOTHING GOT LOST IN THE TRANSLATION.

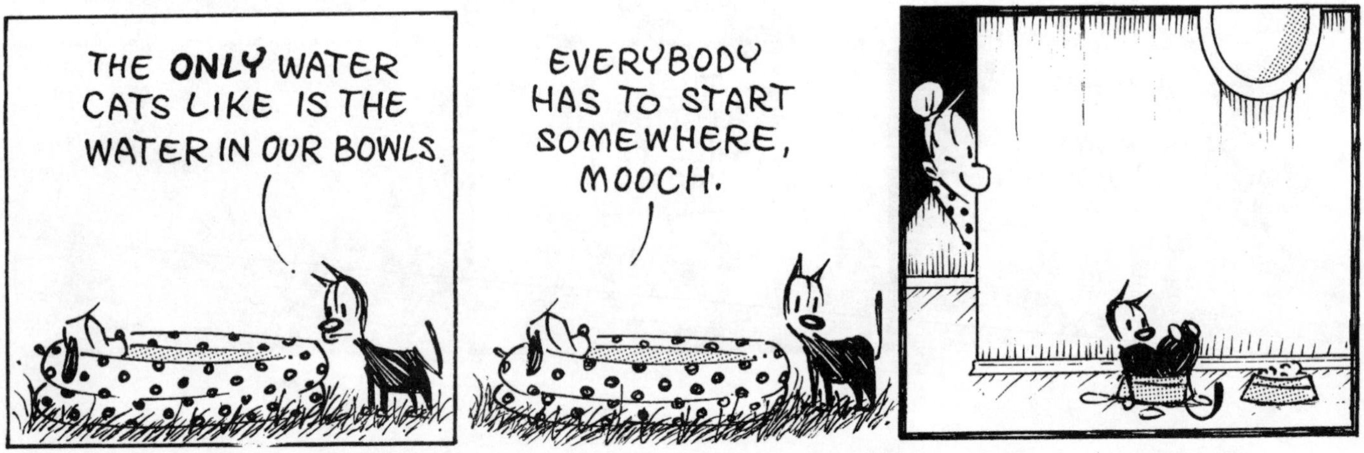
THE **ONLY** WATER CATS LIKE IS THE WATER IN OUR BOWLS.
EVERYBODY HAS TO START SOMEWHERE, MOOCH.

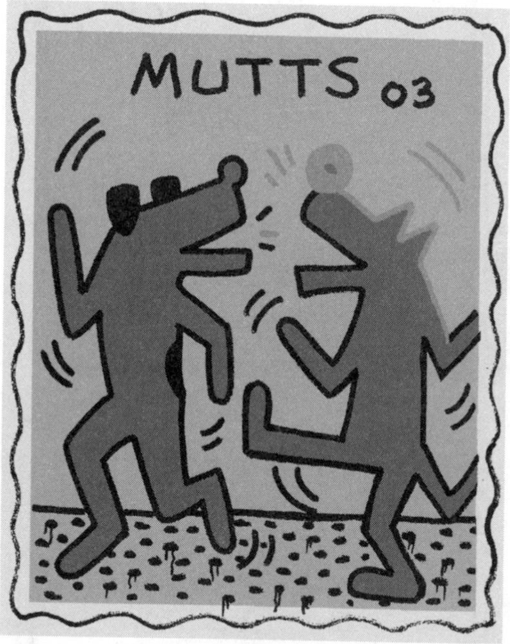
MUTTS 03

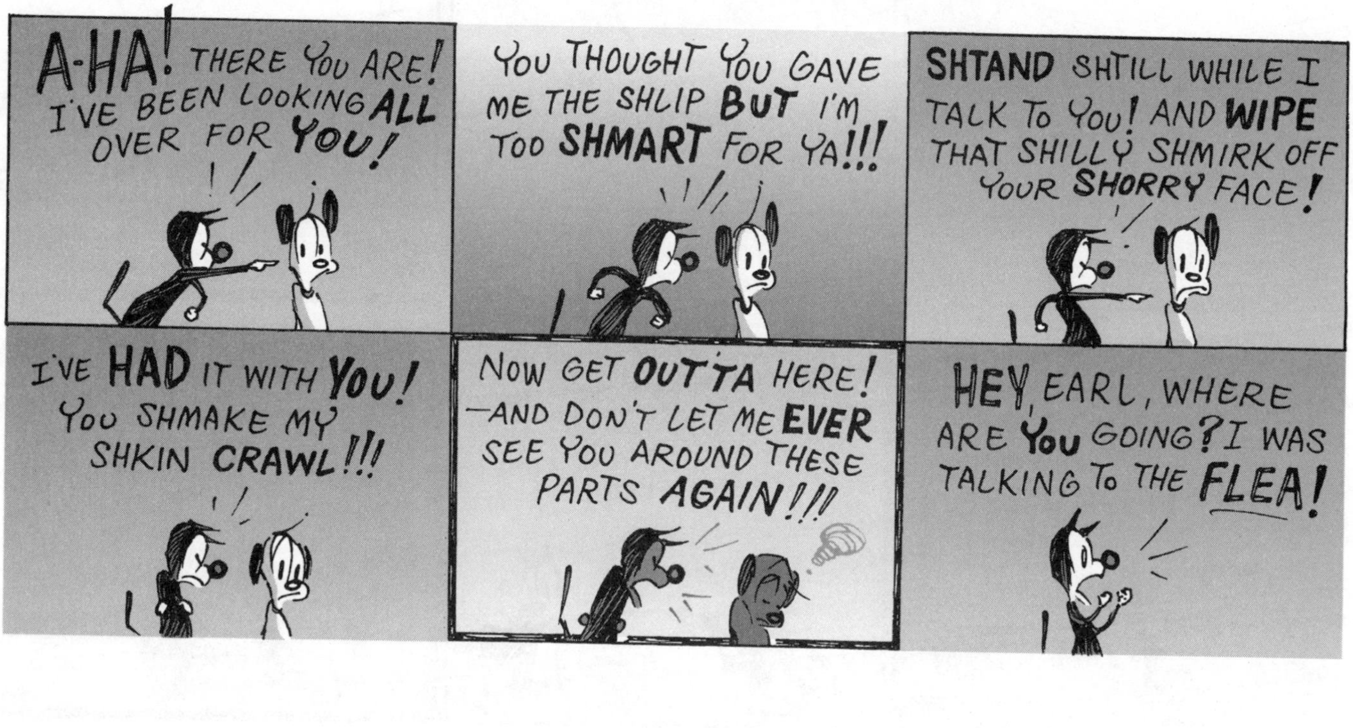
A-HA! THERE YOU ARE! I'VE BEEN LOOKING ALL OVER FOR YOU!
YOU THOUGHT YOU GAVE ME THE SHLIP BUT I'M TOO SHMART FOR YA!!!
SHTAND SHTILL WHILE I TALK TO YOU! AND WIPE THAT SHILLY SHMIRK OFF YOUR SHORRY FACE!
I'VE HAD IT WITH YOU! YOU SHMAKE MY SHKIN CRAWL!!!
NOW GET OUTTA HERE! —AND DON'T LET ME EVER SEE YOU AROUND THESE PARTS AGAIN!!!
HEY, EARL, WHERE ARE YOU GOING? I WAS TALKING TO THE FLEA!

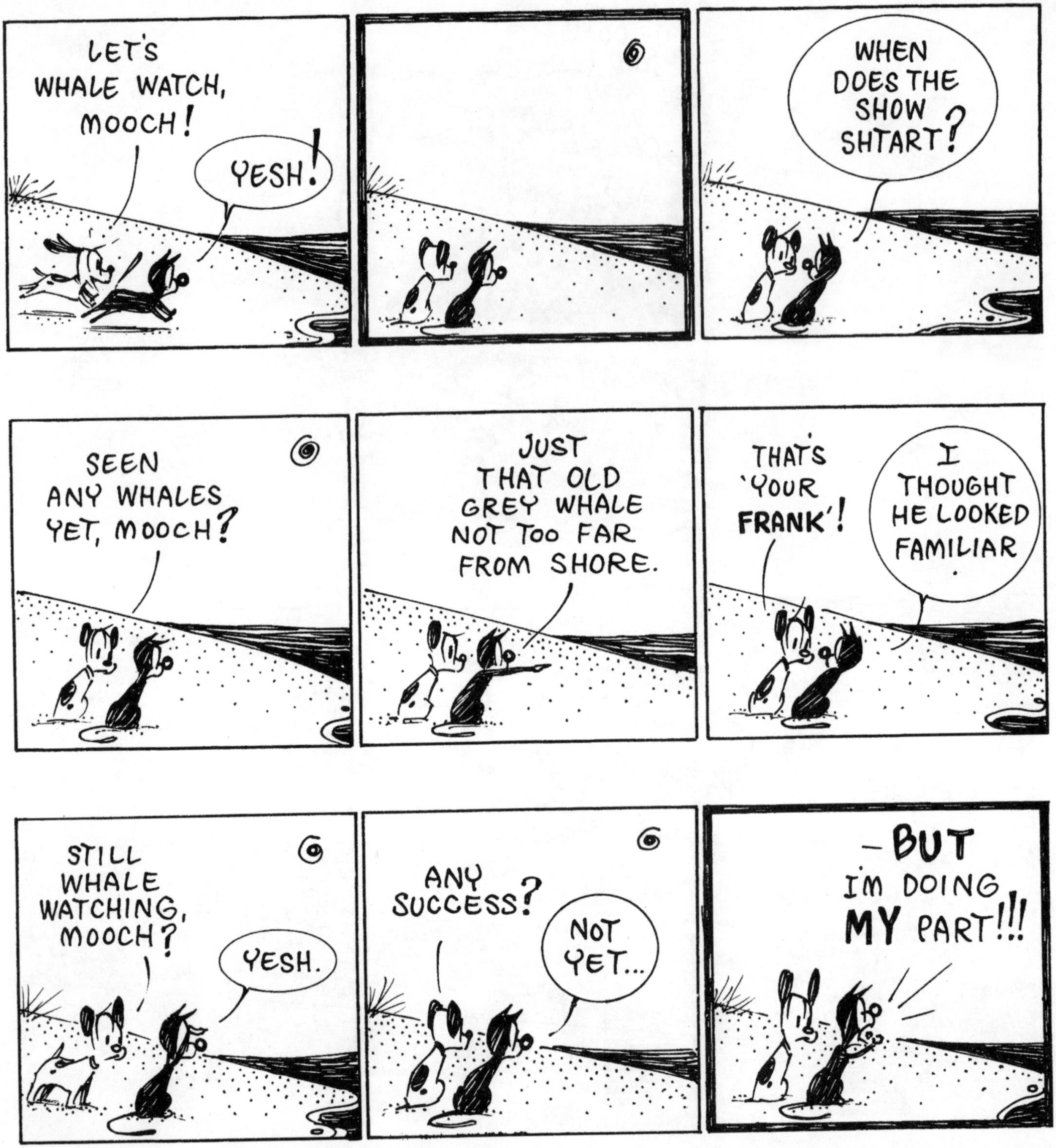
LET'S WHALE WATCH, MOOCH!
YESH!
WHEN DOES THE SHOW SHTART?
SEEN ANY WHALES YET, MOOCH?
JUST THAT OLD GREY WHALE NOT TOO FAR FROM SHORE.
THAT'S 'YOUR FRANK'!
I THOUGHT HE LOOKED FAMILIAR.
STILL WHALE WATCHING, MOOCH?
YESH.
ANY SUCCESS?
NOT YET...
–BUT I'M DOING MY PART!!!

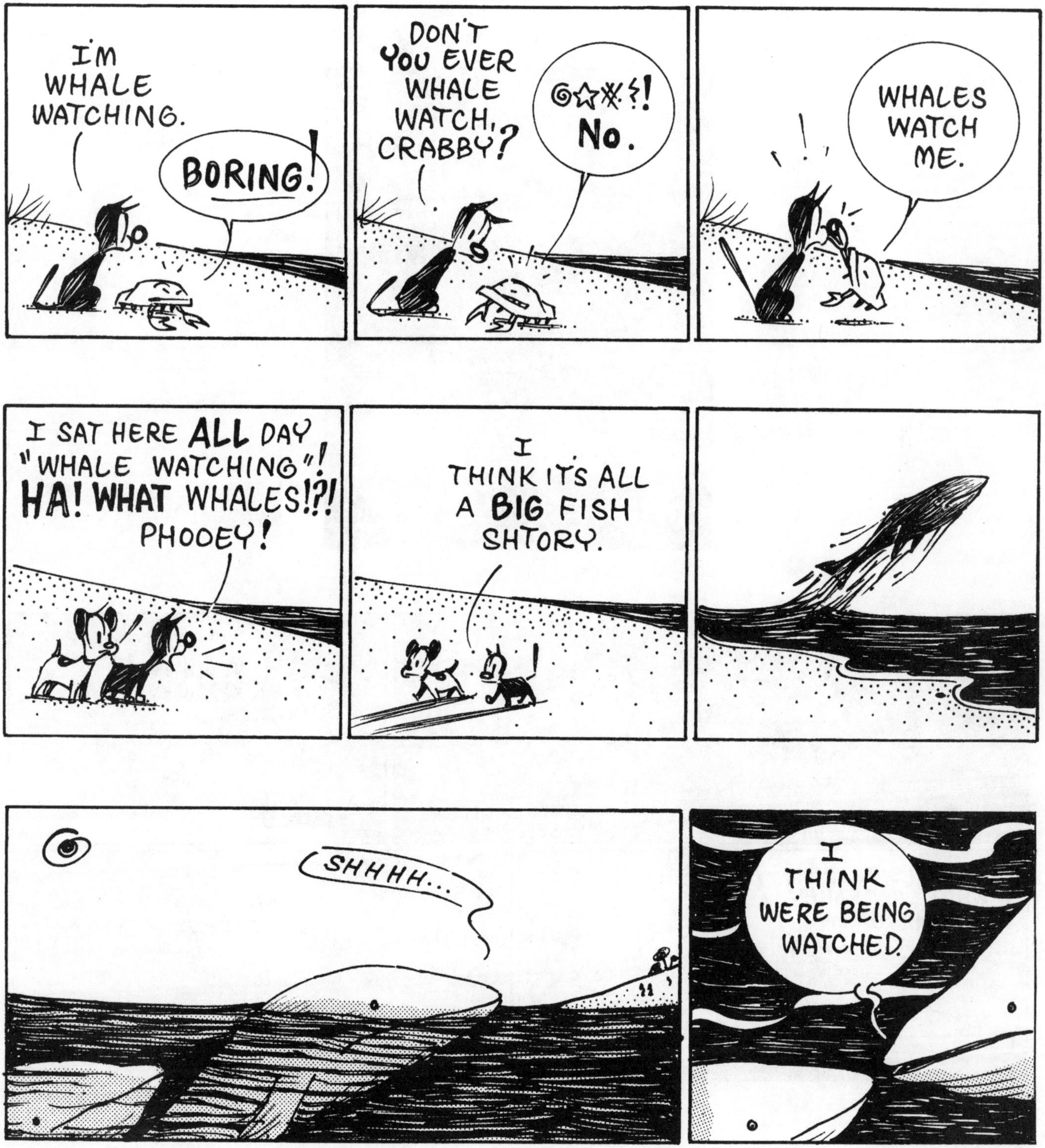
I'M WHALE WATCHING.
BORING!
DON'T YOU EVER WHALE WATCH, CRABBY?
@☆✻?! No.
WHALES WATCH ME.
I SAT HERE ALL DAY "WHALE WATCHING"! HA! WHAT WHALES!?! PHOOEY!
I THINK IT'S ALL A BIG FISH SHTORY.
SHHHH...
I THINK WE'RE BEING WATCHED.

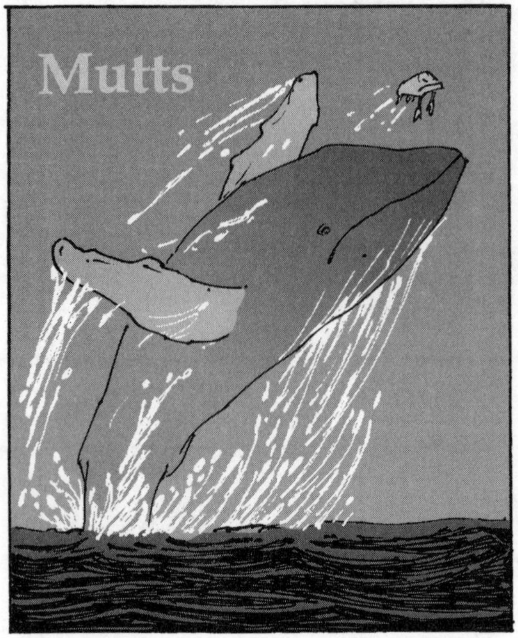
Mutts

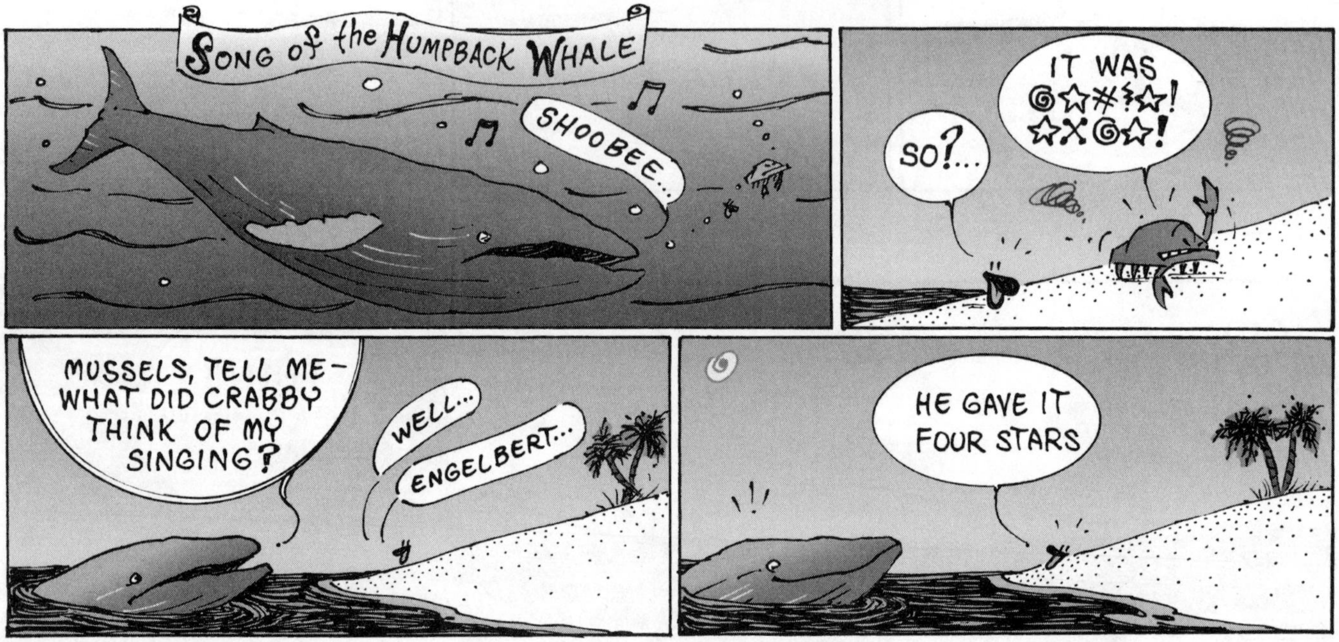
SONG of the HUMPBACK WHALE
SHOOBEE...
SO?...
IT WAS
MUSSELS, TELL ME– WHAT DID CRABBY THINK OF MY SINGING?
WELL...
ENGELBERT...
HE GAVE IT FOUR STARS

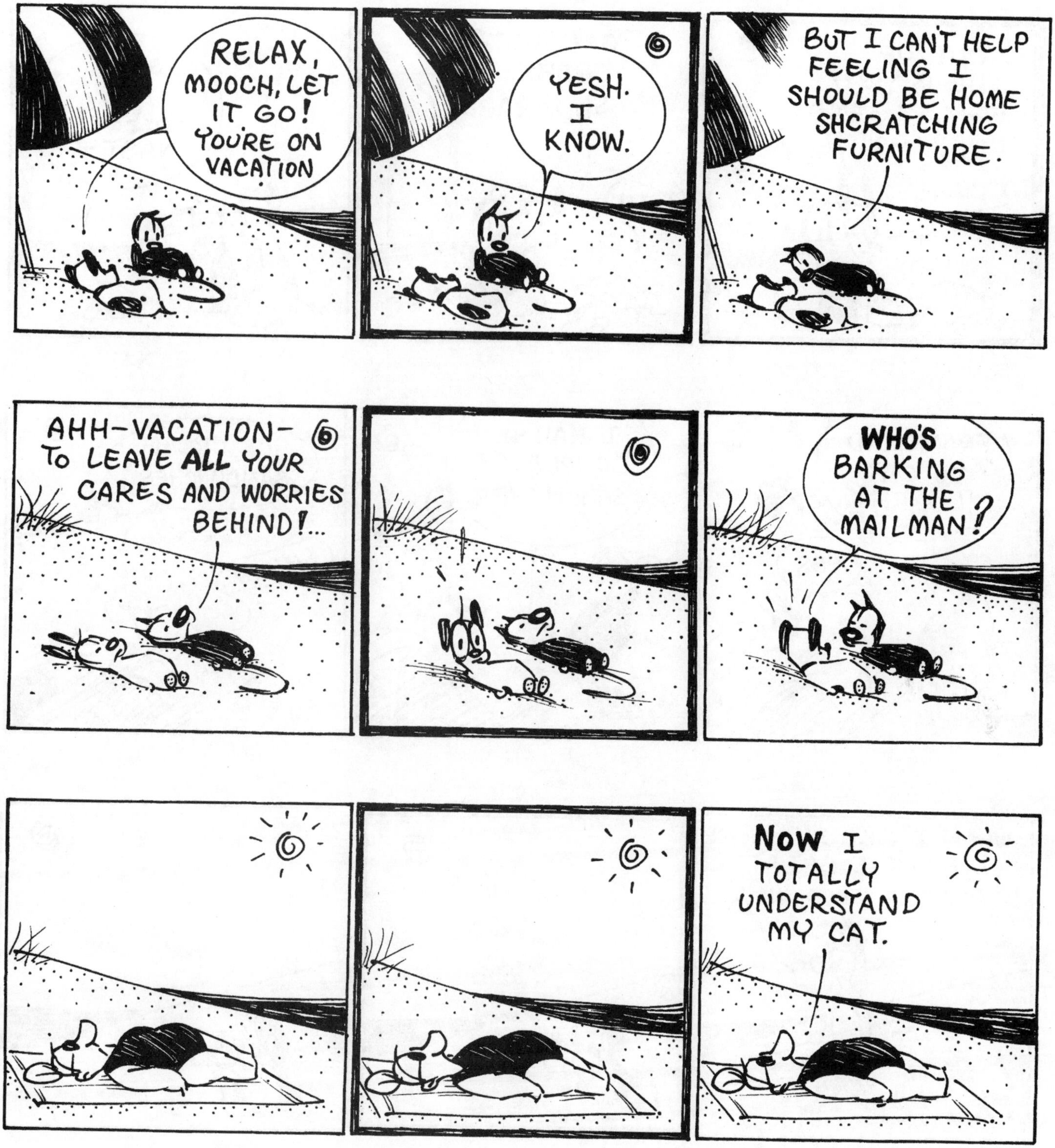
RELAX, MOOCH, LET IT GO! YOU'RE ON VACATION
YESH. I KNOW.
BUT I CAN'T HELP FEELING I SHOULD BE HOME SHCRATCHING FURNITURE.
AHH-VACATION- TO LEAVE **ALL** YOUR CARES AND WORRIES BEHIND!...
WHO'S BARKING AT THE MAILMAN?
NOW I TOTALLY UNDERSTAND MY CAT.

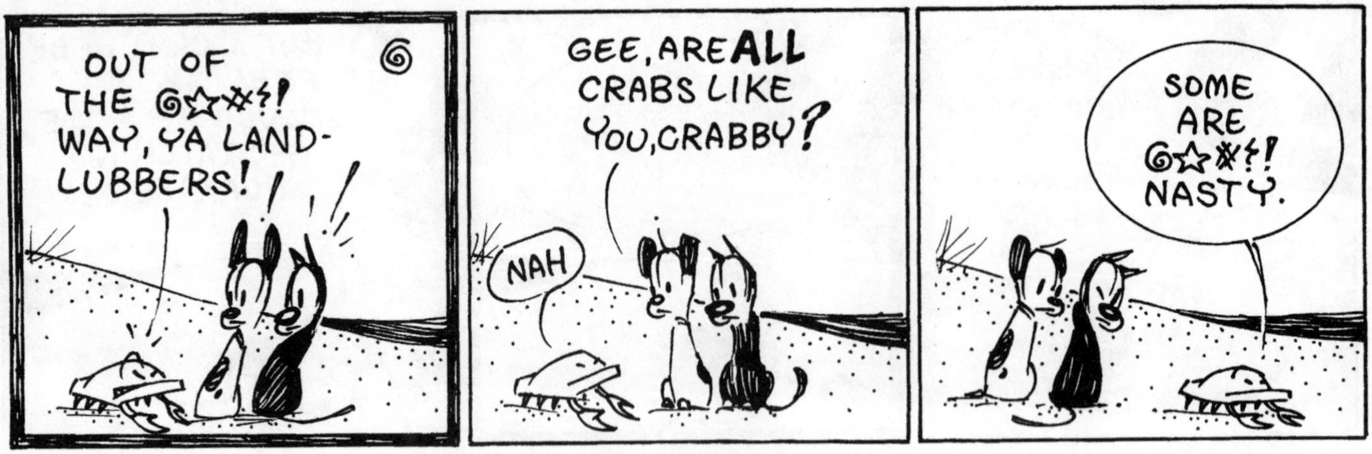
OUT OF THE G☆**?! WAY, YA LAND-LUBBERS!
GEE, ARE ALL CRABS LIKE YOU, CRABBY?
NAH
SOME ARE G☆**?! NASTY.

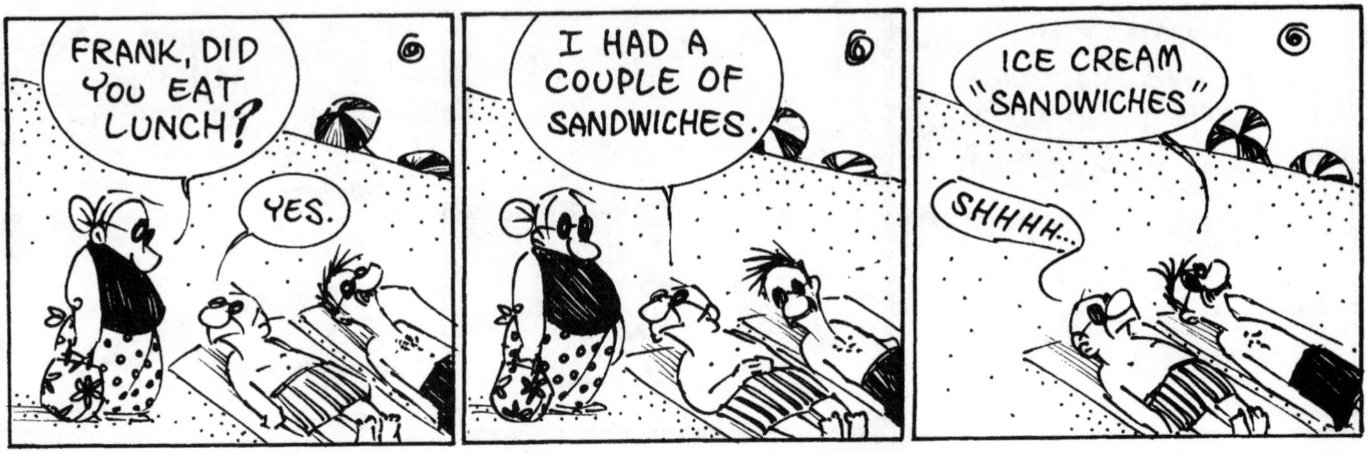
FRANK, DID YOU EAT LUNCH?
YES.
I HAD A COUPLE OF SANDWICHES.
ICE CREAM "SANDWICHES"
SHHHH...

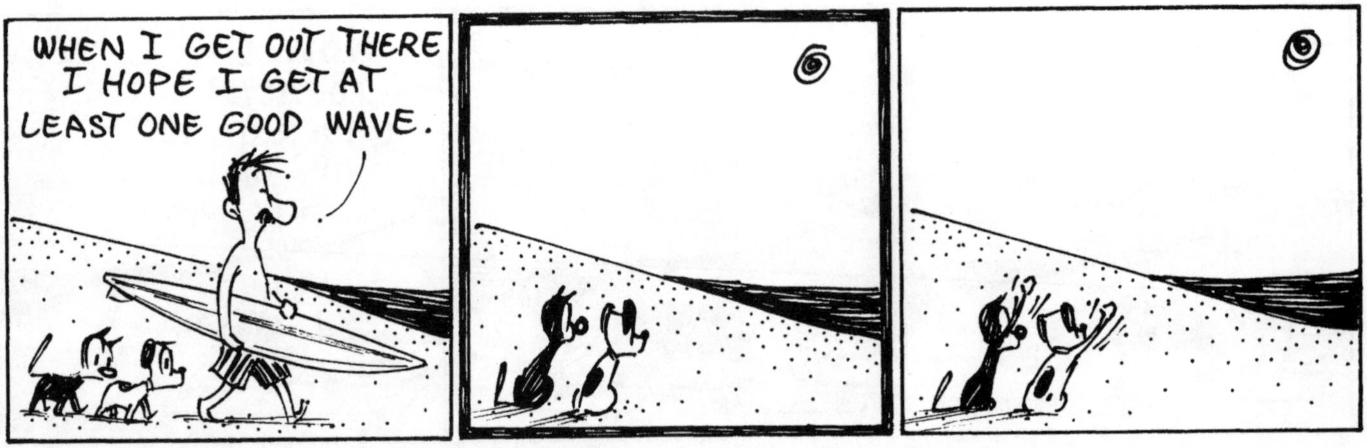
WHEN I GET OUT THERE I HOPE I GET AT LEAST ONE GOOD WAVE.

young
Mutts.
2¢
TRUE
LOVE
STORIES

DID I EVER TELL YOU ABOUT MY ENCOUNTER WITH "NESSIE"?
THE LOCH NESS MONSTER !?!
AAH... SHE WASN'T THAT BAD.
YEARS AGO, I WAS SUMMERING IN BONNIE OL' SCOTLAND WHEN I CAUGHT A GLIMPSE OF HER ELUSIVE BEAUTY...
I PLUNGED DEEP INTO THOSE DARK, MYSTERIOUS WATERS AFTER HER...
WE HAD NO PAST—WE HAD NO FUTURE—JUST THE MOMENT—I PROMISED—"WHAT HAPPENED THERE—STAYS THERE."—MY YOUNG 'SUMMER ROMANCE'.
HA! A SUMMER HOAX!
I HAVE A PHOTO!
IT'S ALL A BLUR!
JUST THE WAY I REMEMBER IT.
ARG!

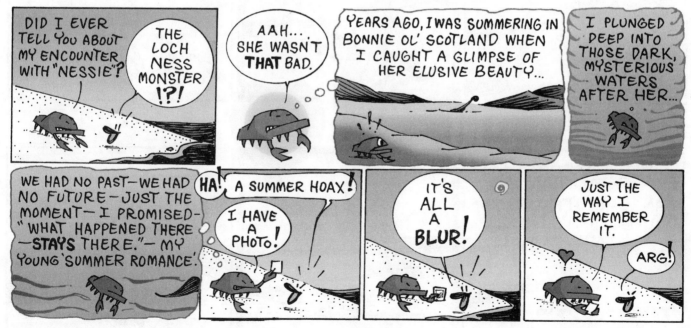

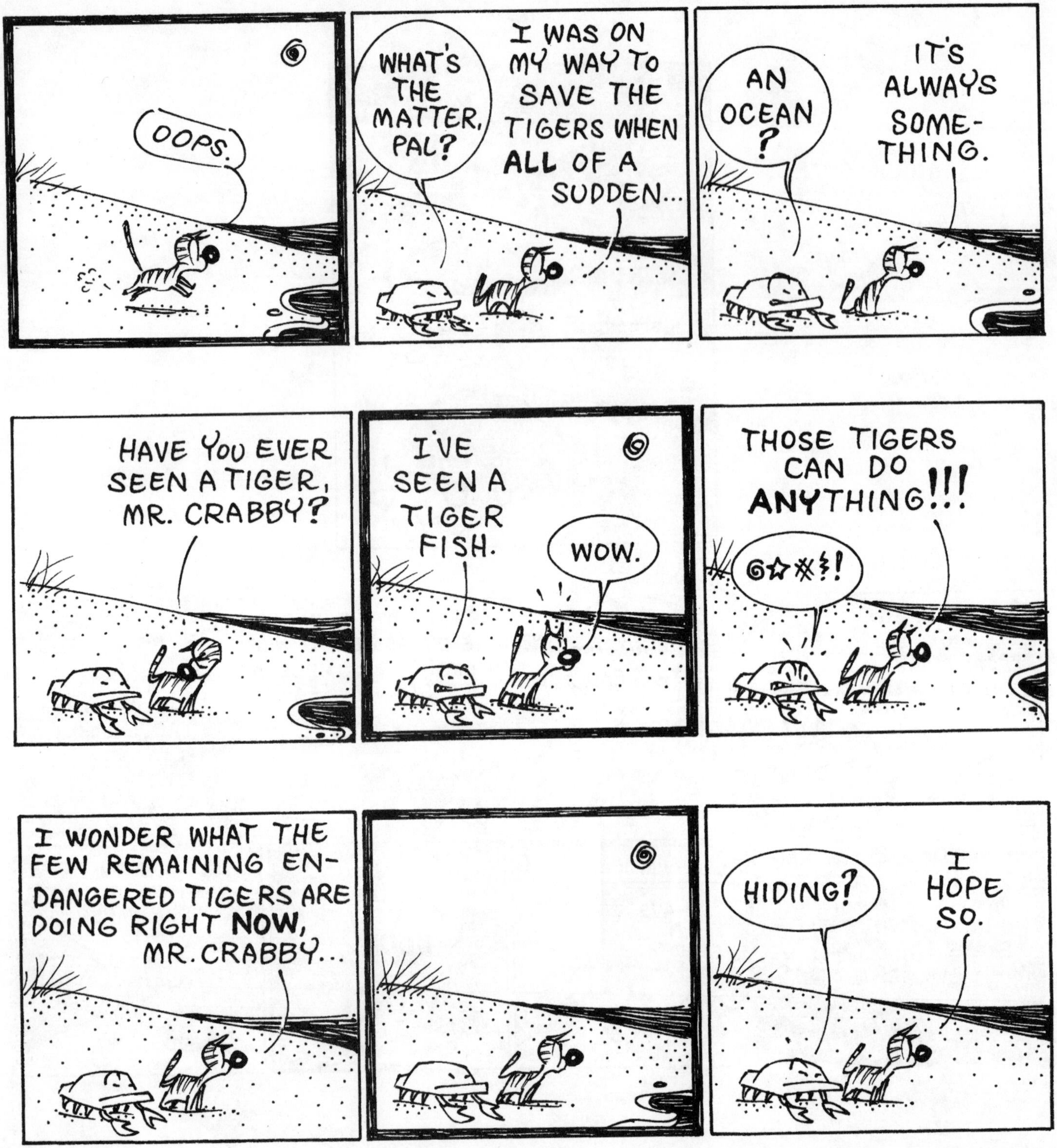
OOPS.
WHAT'S THE MATTER, PAL?
I WAS ON MY WAY TO SAVE THE TIGERS WHEN **ALL** OF A SUDDEN...
AN OCEAN?
IT'S ALWAYS SOME-THING.
HAVE YOU EVER SEEN A TIGER, MR. CRABBY?
I'VE SEEN A TIGER FISH.
WOW.
THOSE TIGERS CAN DO **ANY**THING!!!
I WONDER WHAT THE FEW REMAINING EN-DANGERED TIGERS ARE DOING RIGHT **NOW**, MR. CRABBY...
HIDING?
I HOPE SO.

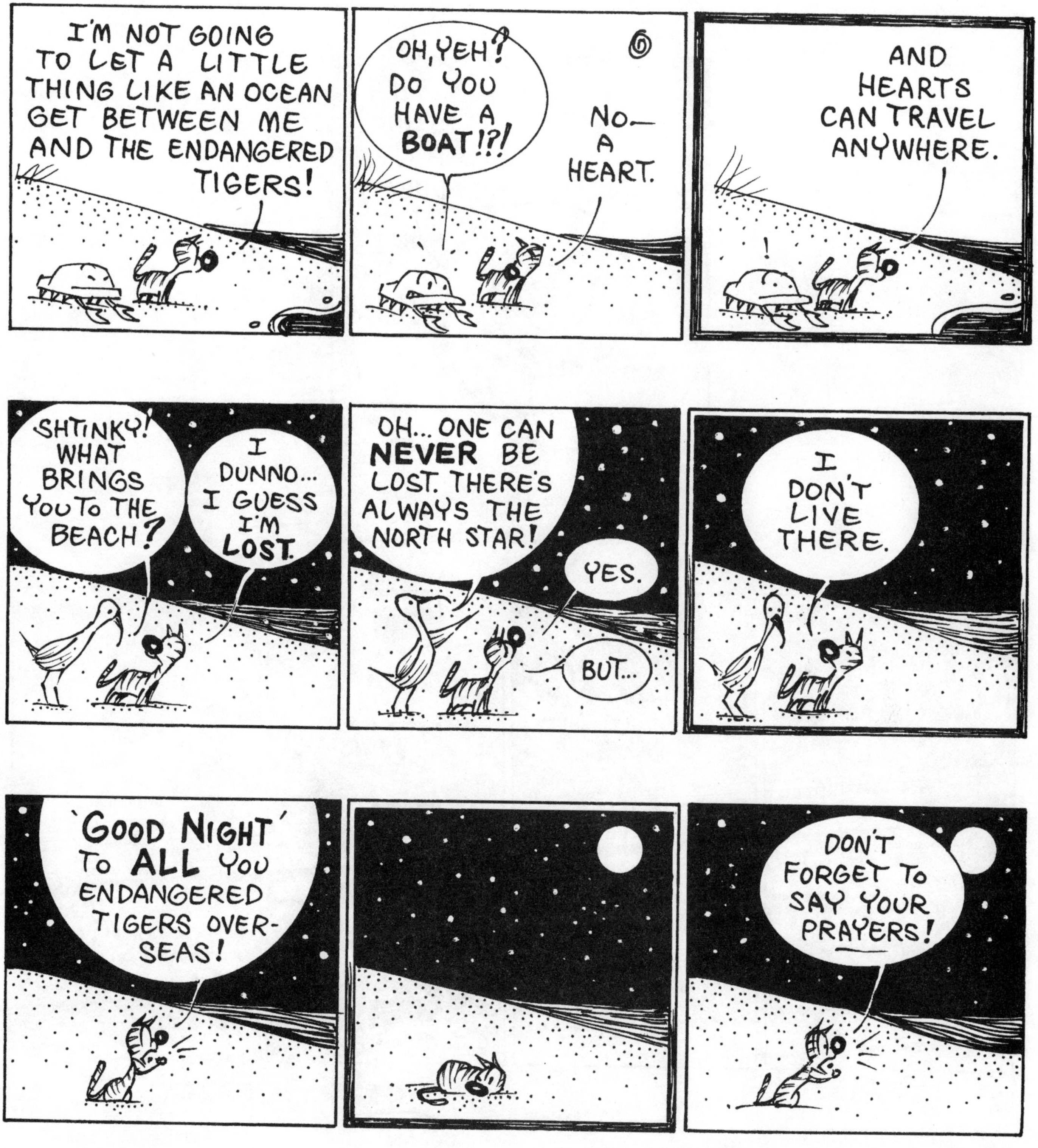
I'M NOT GOING TO LET A LITTLE THING LIKE AN OCEAN GET BETWEEN ME AND THE ENDANGERED TIGERS!
OH, YEH? DO YOU HAVE A BOAT!?!
NO— A HEART.
AND HEARTS CAN TRAVEL ANYWHERE.
SHTINKY! WHAT BRINGS YOU TO THE BEACH?
I DUNNO... I GUESS I'M LOST.
OH... ONE CAN NEVER BE LOST. THERE'S ALWAYS THE NORTH STAR!
YES.
BUT...
I DON'T LIVE THERE.
'GOOD NIGHT' TO ALL YOU ENDANGERED TIGERS OVER-SEAS!
DON'T FORGET TO SAY YOUR PRAYERS!

MUTTS
McDONNELL

THEY SAY IF YOU PUT A SEASHELL TO YOUR EAR YOU CAN HEAR THE OCEAN.
WOW.

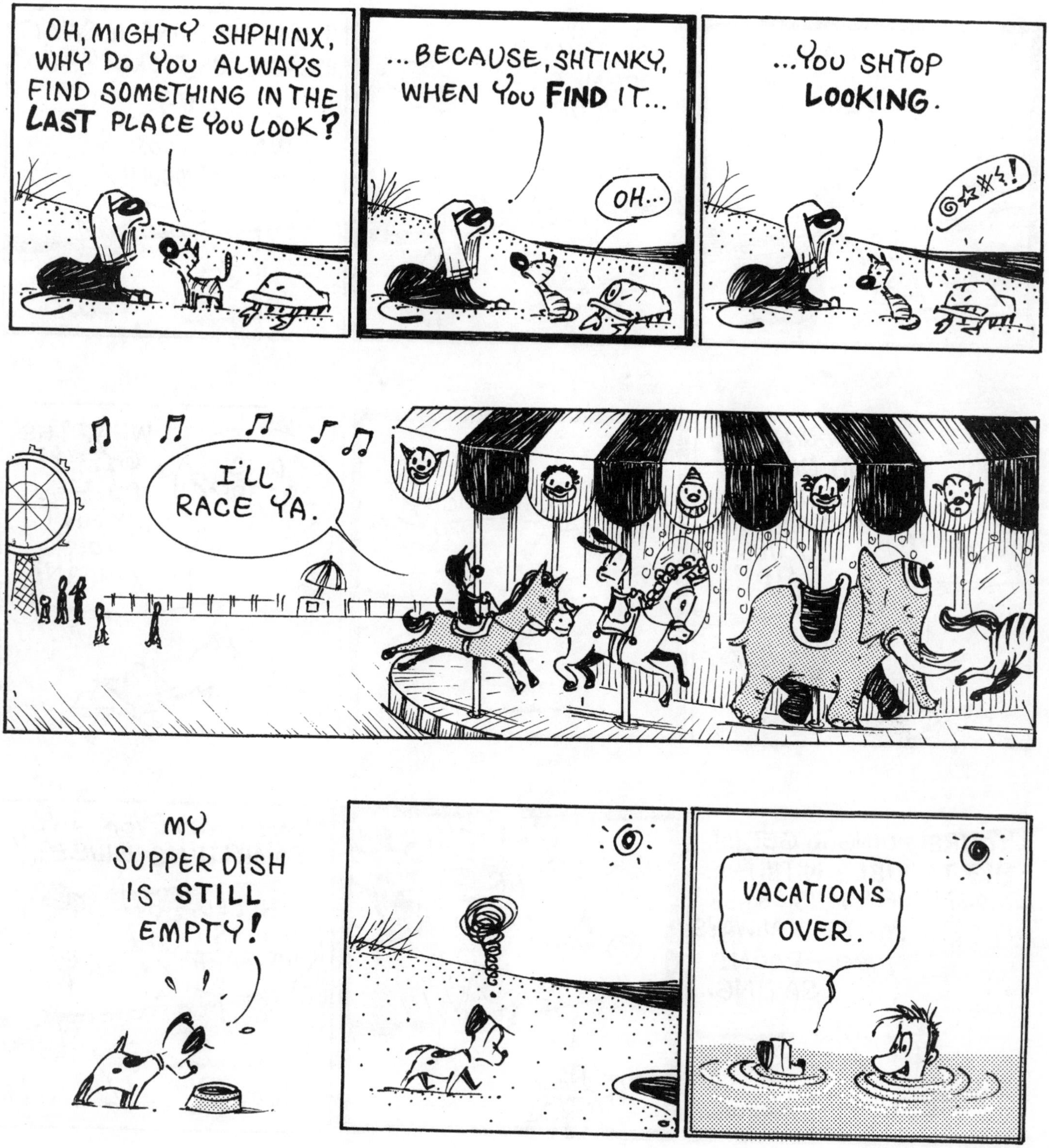
OH, MIGHTY SHPHINX, WHY DO YOU ALWAYS FIND SOMETHING IN THE **LAST** PLACE YOU LOOK?
...BECAUSE, SHTINKY, WHEN YOU **FIND** IT...
OH...
...YOU SHTOP **LOOKING**.
I'LL RACE YA.
MY SUPPER DISH IS **STILL** EMPTY!
VACATION'S OVER.

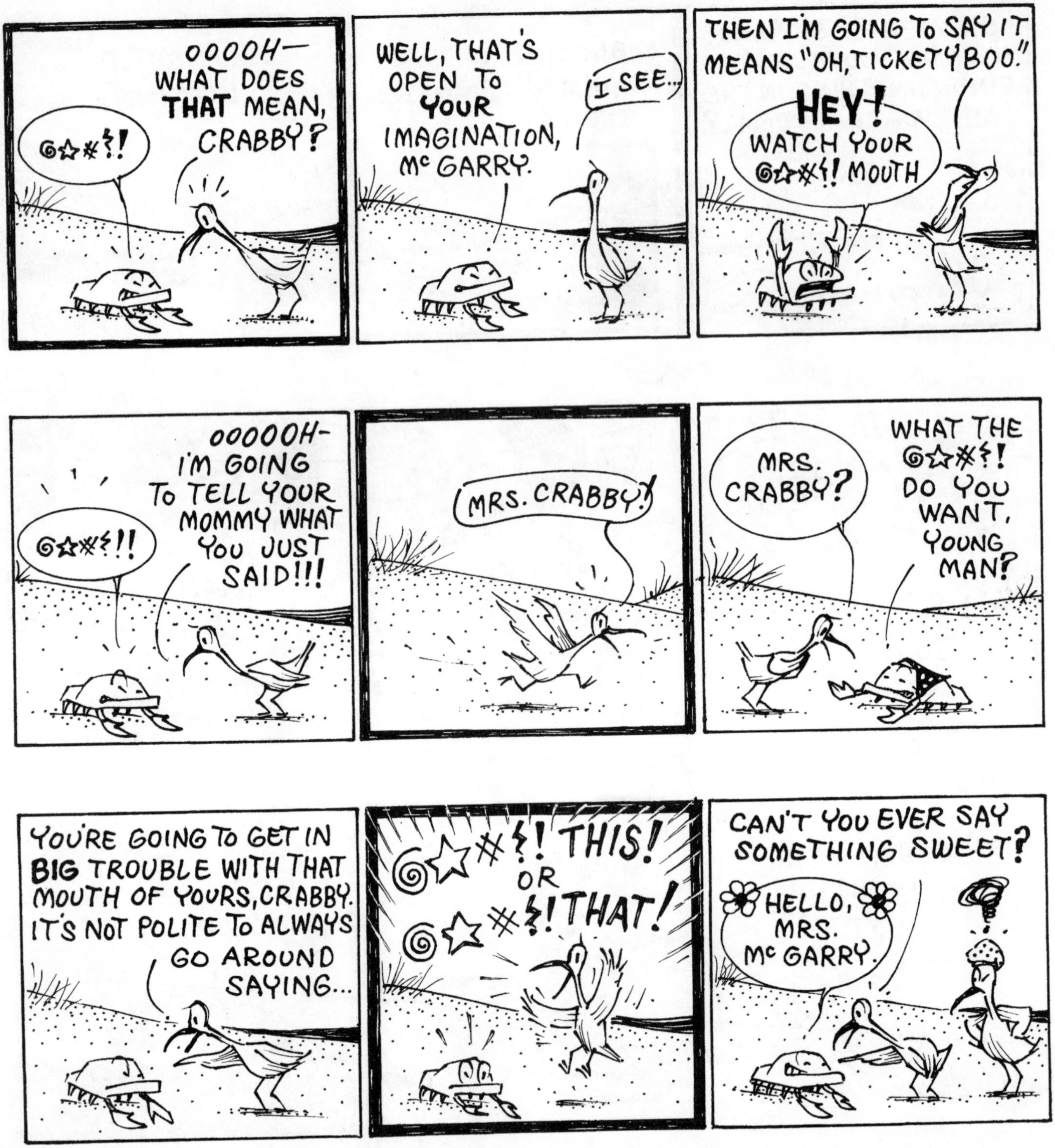
@☆#?!
OOOOH— WHAT DOES THAT MEAN, CRABBY?
WELL, THAT'S OPEN TO YOUR IMAGINATION, McGARRY.
I SEE...
THEN I'M GOING TO SAY IT MEANS "OH, TICKETYBOO."
HEY! WATCH YOUR @☆#?! MOUTH
@☆#?!!
OOOOOH- I'M GOING TO TELL YOUR MOMMY WHAT YOU JUST SAID!!!
MRS. CRABBY!
MRS. CRABBY?
WHAT THE @☆#?! DO YOU WANT, YOUNG MAN?
YOU'RE GOING TO GET IN BIG TROUBLE WITH THAT MOUTH OF YOURS, CRABBY. IT'S NOT POLITE TO ALWAYS GO AROUND SAYING...
@☆#?! THIS! OR @☆#?! THAT!
CAN'T YOU EVER SAY SOMETHING SWEET?
HELLO, MRS. McGARRY.

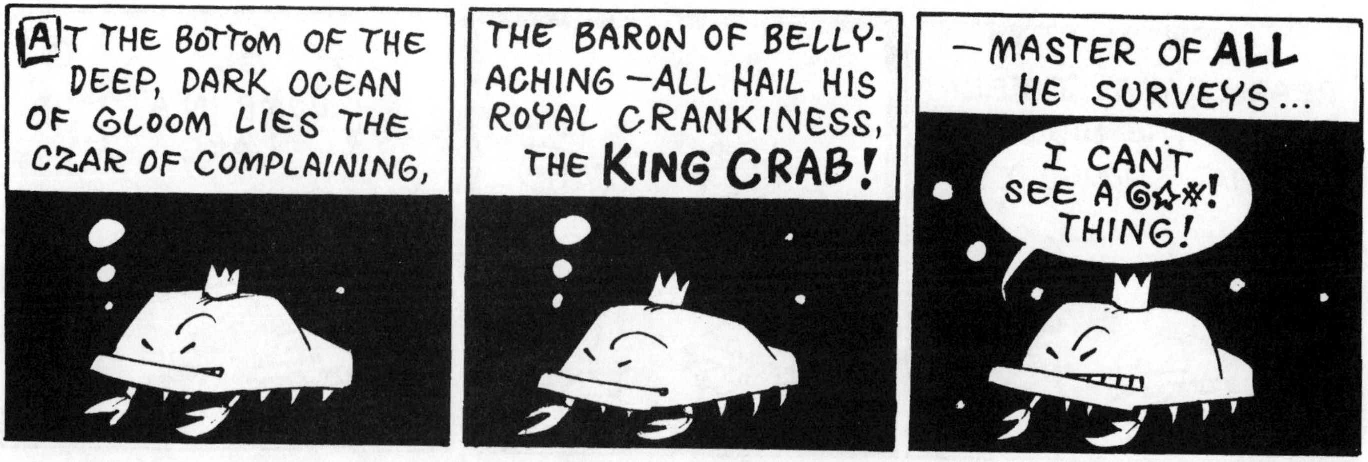
AT THE BOTTOM OF THE DEEP, DARK OCEAN OF GLOOM LIES THE CZAR OF COMPLAINING,
THE BARON OF BELLY-ACHING—ALL HAIL HIS ROYAL CRANKINESS, THE KING CRAB!
—MASTER OF ALL HE SURVEYS...
I CAN'T SEE A @☆*! THING!

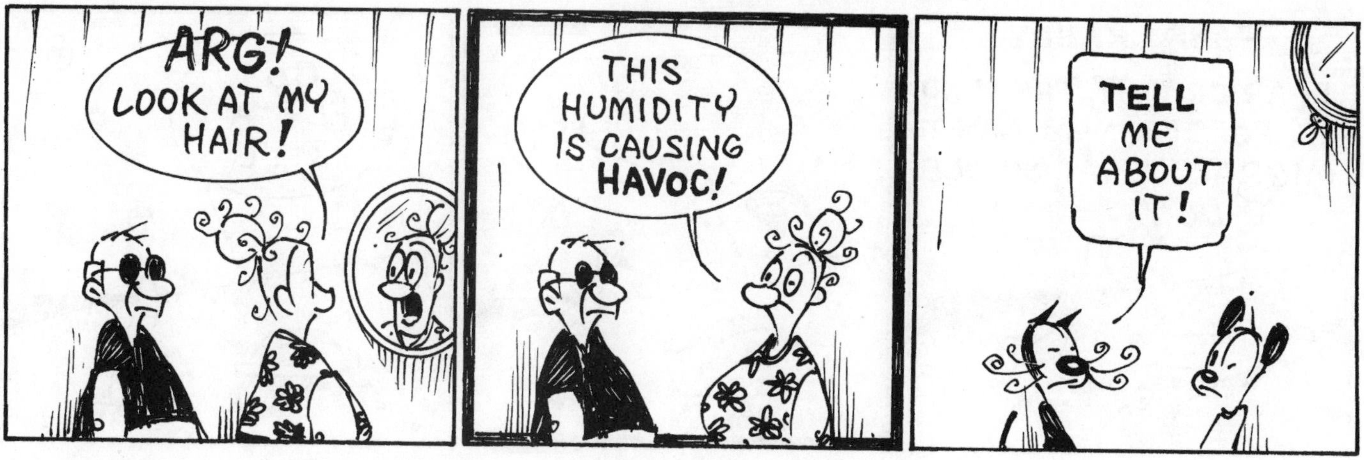
ARG! LOOK AT MY HAIR!
THIS HUMIDITY IS CAUSING HAVOC!
TELL ME ABOUT IT!

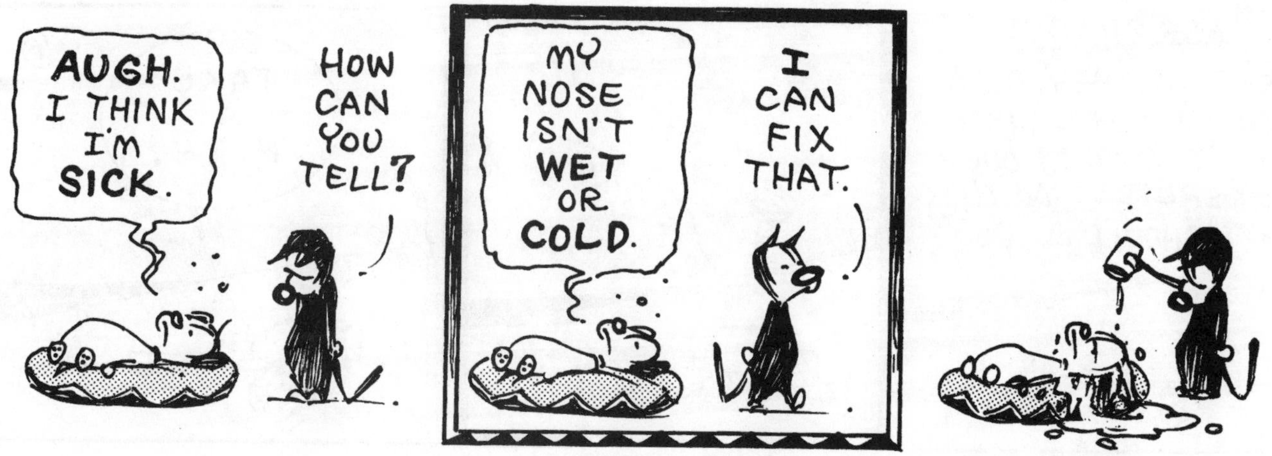
AUGH. I THINK I'M SICK.
HOW CAN YOU TELL?
MY NOSE ISN'T WET OR COLD.
I CAN FIX THAT.

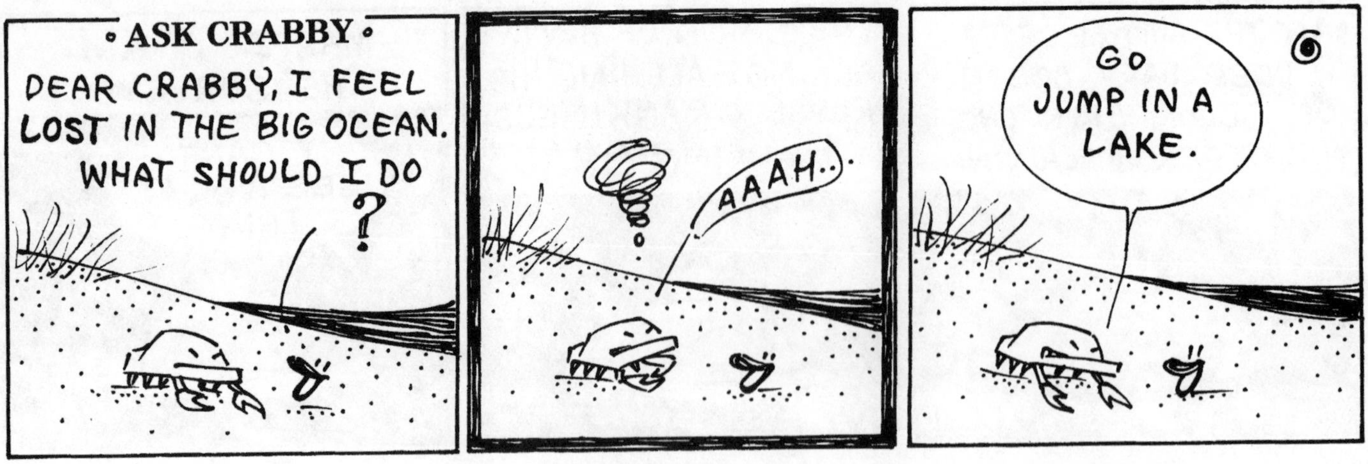
ASK CRABBY
DEAR CRABBY, I FEEL LOST IN THE BIG OCEAN. WHAT SHOULD I DO?
AAAH...
GO JUMP IN A LAKE.

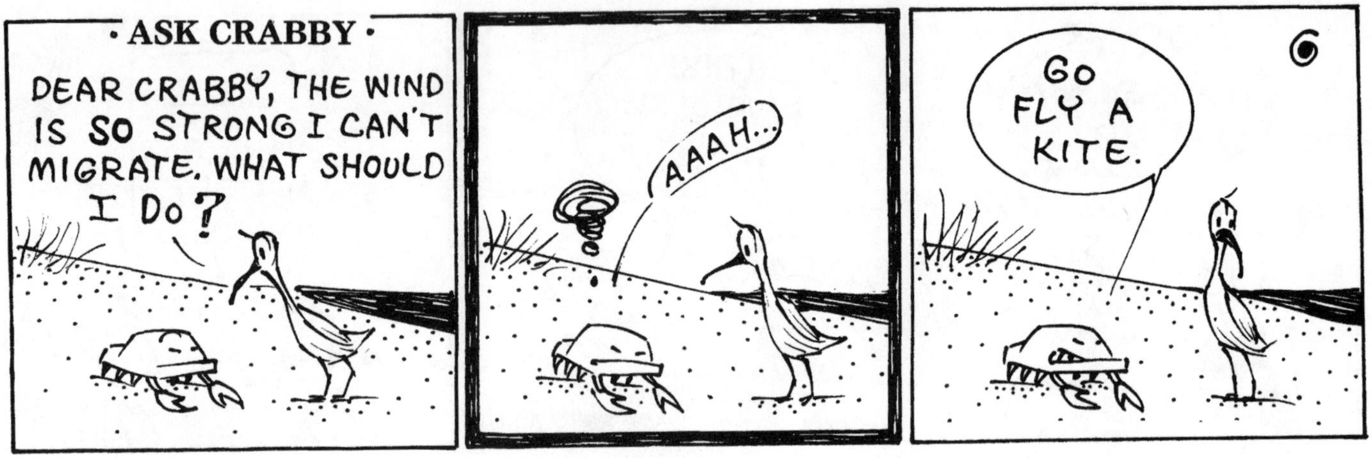
ASK CRABBY
DEAR CRABBY, THE WIND IS SO STRONG I CAN'T MIGRATE. WHAT SHOULD I DO?
AAAH...
GO FLY A KITE.

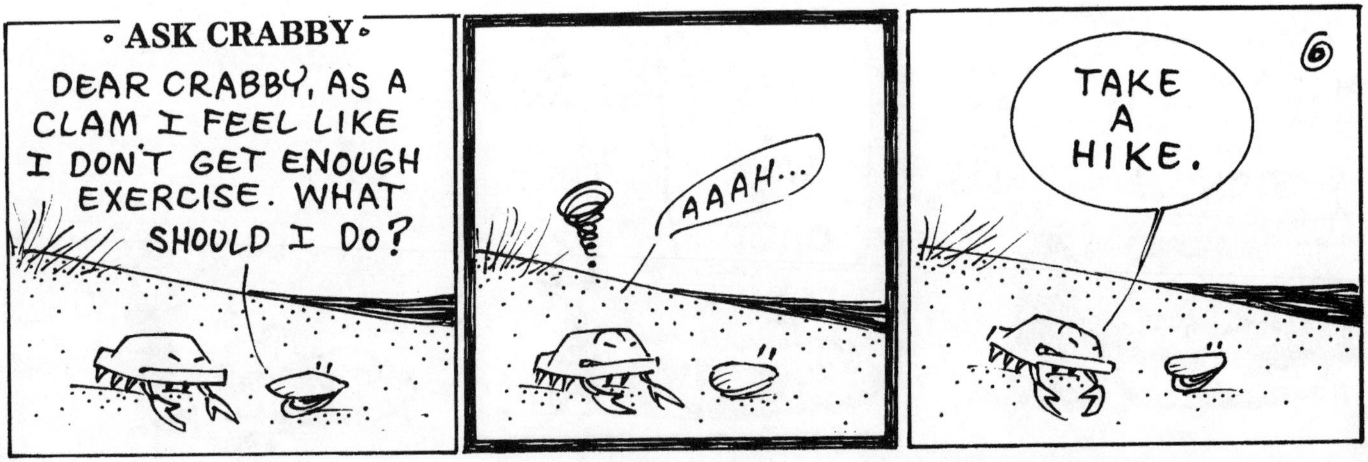
ASK CRABBY
DEAR CRABBY, AS A CLAM I FEEL LIKE I DON'T GET ENOUGH EXERCISE. WHAT SHOULD I DO?
AAAH...
TAKE A HIKE.

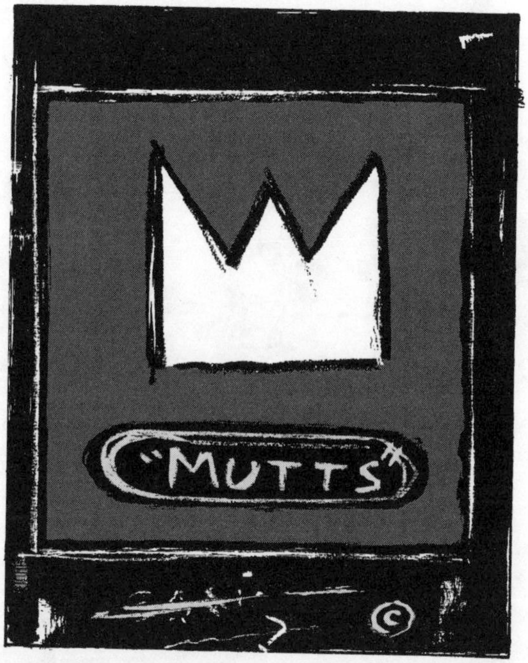
"MUTTS"

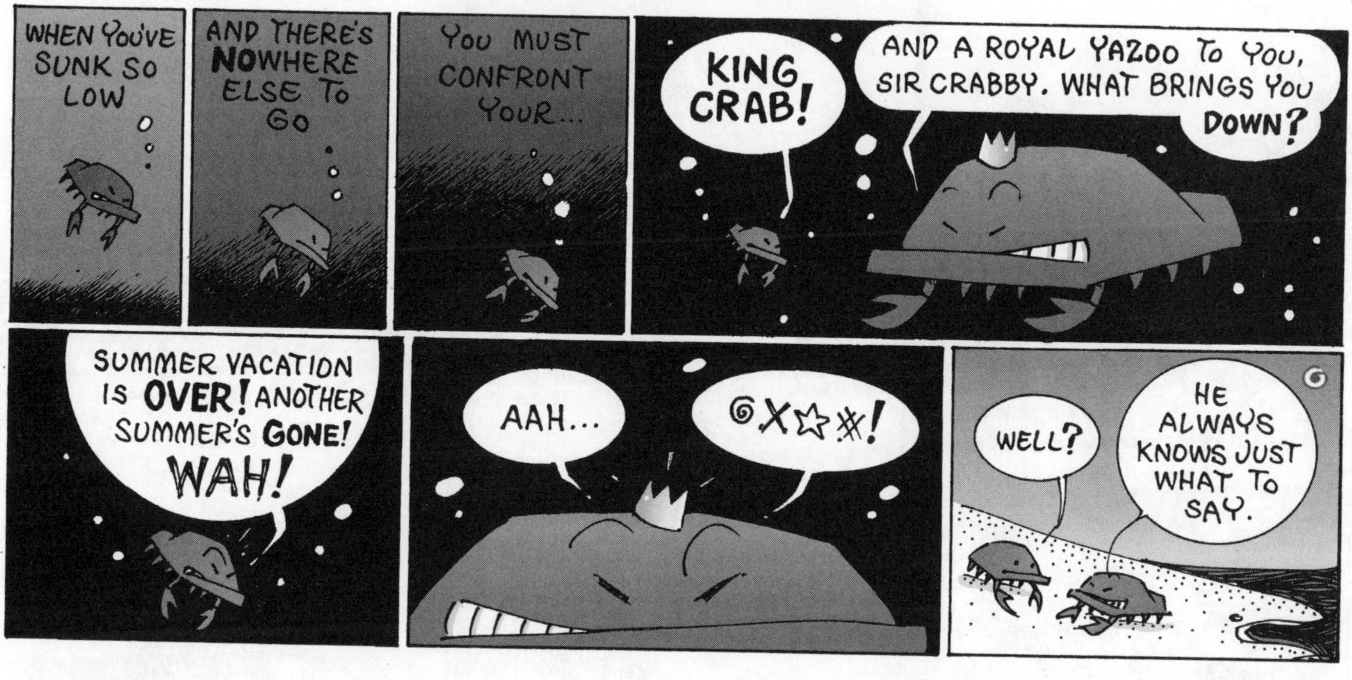
WHEN YOU'VE SUNK SO LOW
AND THERE'S NOWHERE ELSE TO GO
YOU MUST CONFRONT YOUR...
KING CRAB!
AND A ROYAL YAZOO TO YOU, SIR CRABBY. WHAT BRINGS YOU DOWN?
SUMMER VACATION IS OVER! ANOTHER SUMMER'S GONE! WAH!
AAH...
@X☆*!
WELL?
HE ALWAYS KNOWS JUST WHAT TO SAY.

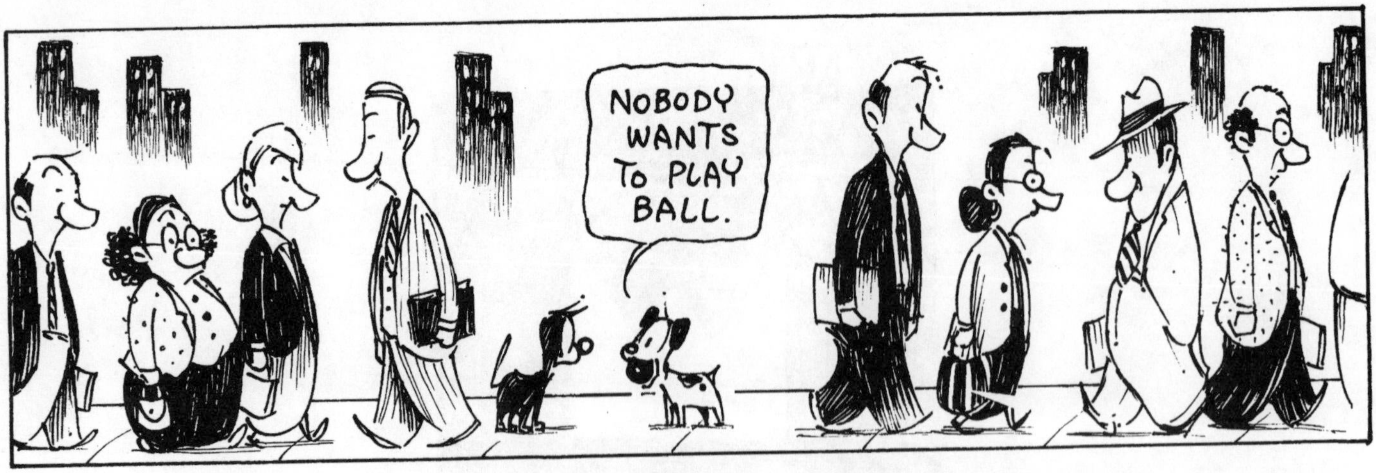
NOBODY WANTS TO PLAY BALL.

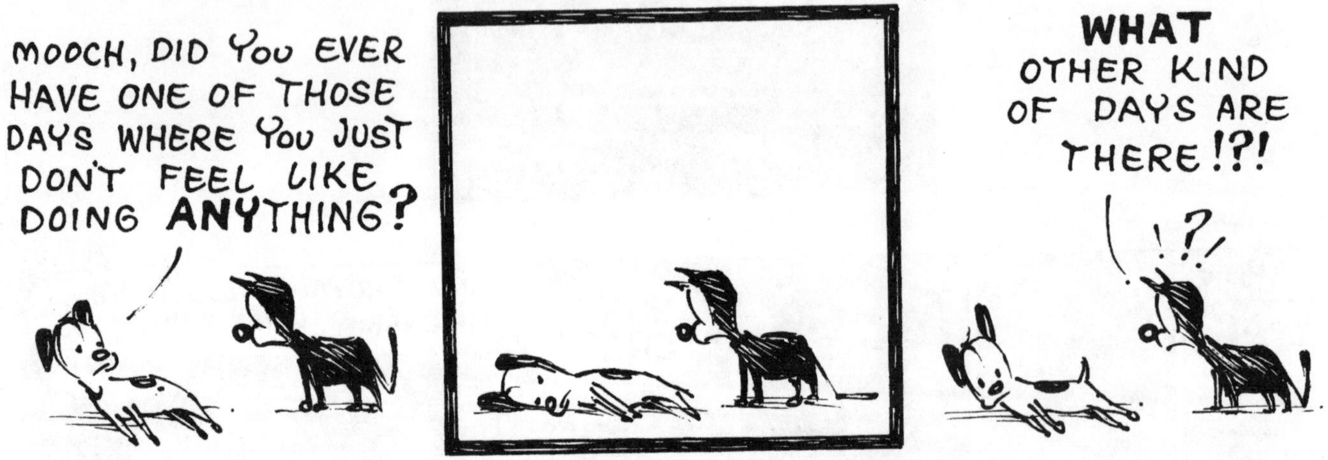
MOOCH, DID YOU EVER HAVE ONE OF THOSE DAYS WHERE YOU JUST DON'T FEEL LIKE DOING ANYTHING?
WHAT OTHER KIND OF DAYS ARE THERE!?!
!?!

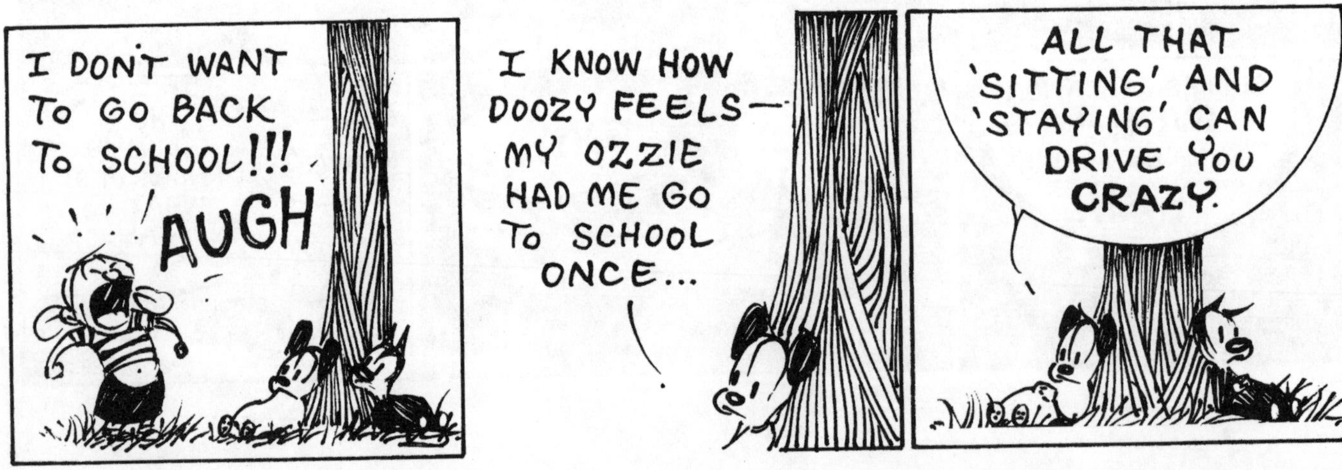
I DON'T WANT TO GO BACK TO SCHOOL!!!
AUGH
I KNOW HOW DOOZY FEELS— MY OZZIE HAD ME GO TO SCHOOL ONCE...
ALL THAT 'SITTING' AND 'STAYING' CAN DRIVE YOU CRAZY.

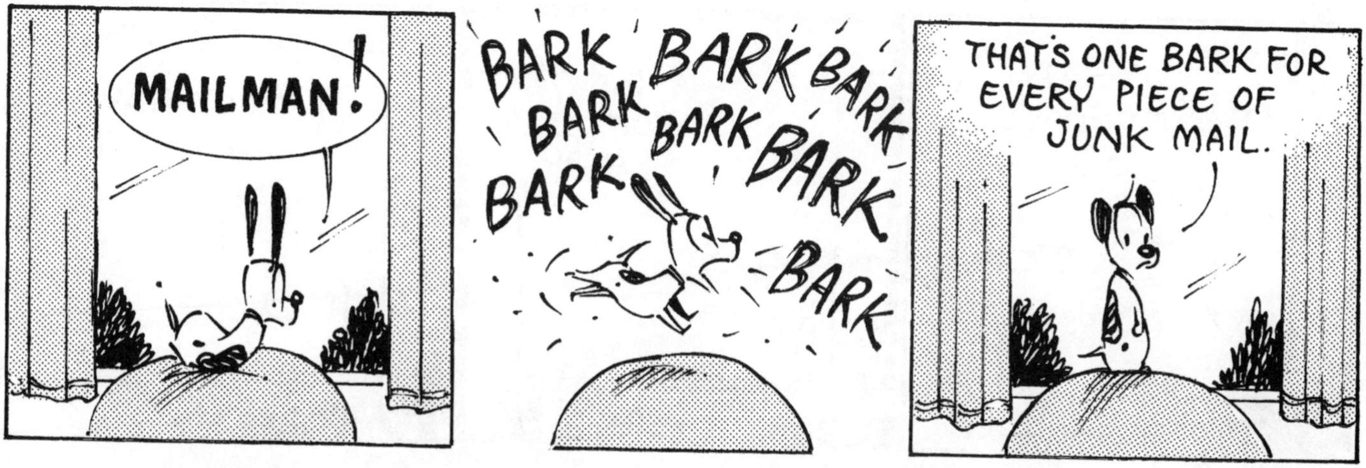
MAILMAN!
BARK BARK BARK BARK BARK BARK BARK BARK
THAT'S ONE BARK FOR EVERY PIECE OF JUNK MAIL.

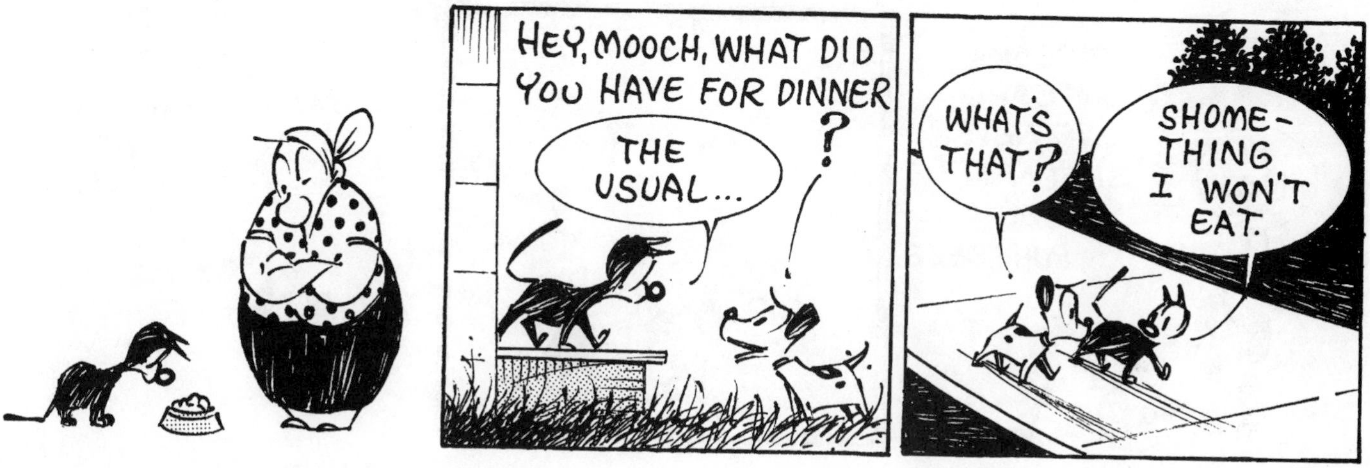
HEY, MOOCH, WHAT DID YOU HAVE FOR DINNER?
THE USUAL...
WHAT'S THAT?
SHOME-THING I WON'T EAT.

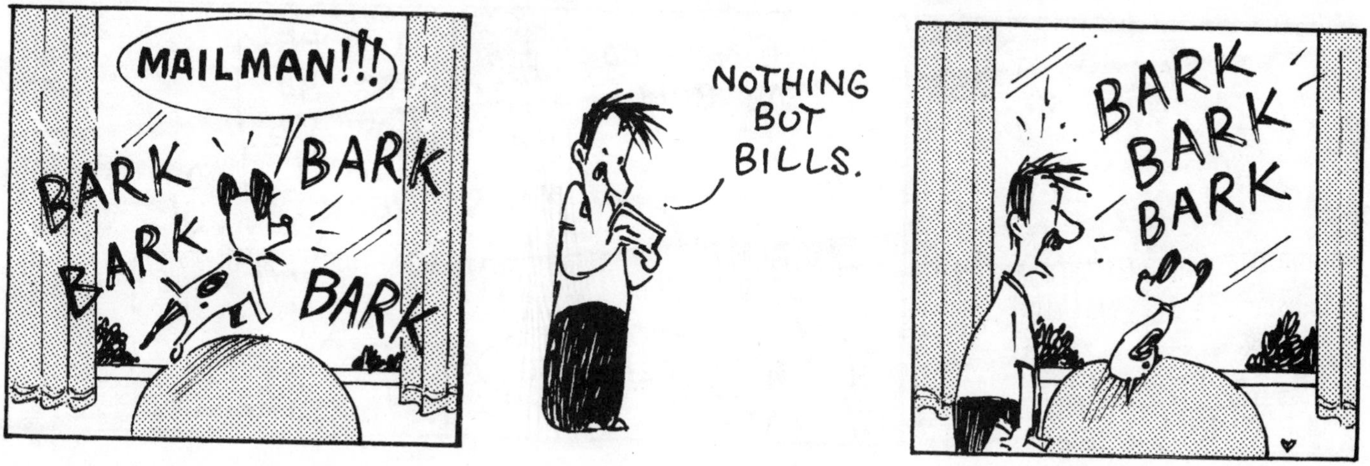
MAILMAN!!!
BARK BARK BARK BARK BARK
NOTHING BUT BILLS.
BARK BARK BARK

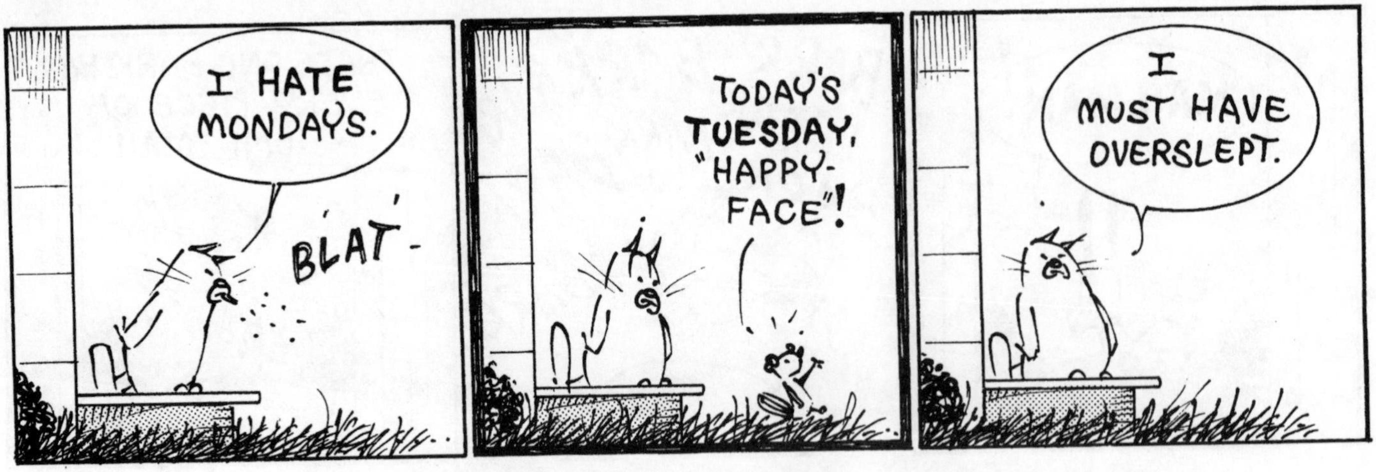
I HATE MONDAYS.
BLAT-
TODAY'S TUESDAY, "HAPPY-FACE"!
I MUST HAVE OVERSLEPT.

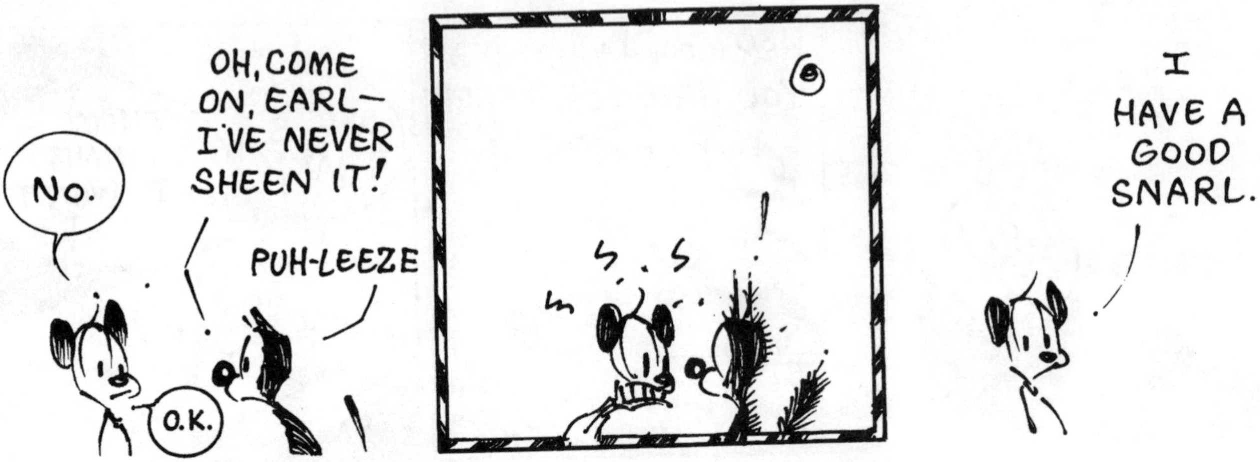
NO.
OH, COME ON, EARL- I'VE NEVER SHEEN IT!
O.K.
PUH-LEEZE
I HAVE A GOOD SNARL.

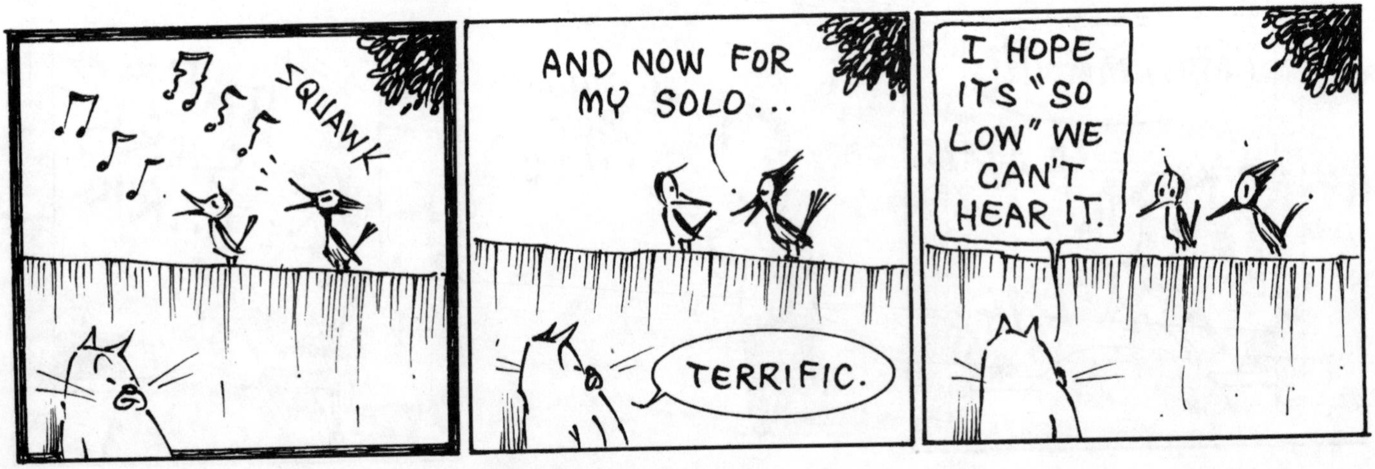
SQUAWK
AND NOW FOR MY SOLO...
TERRIFIC.
I HOPE IT'S "SO LOW" WE CAN'T HEAR IT.

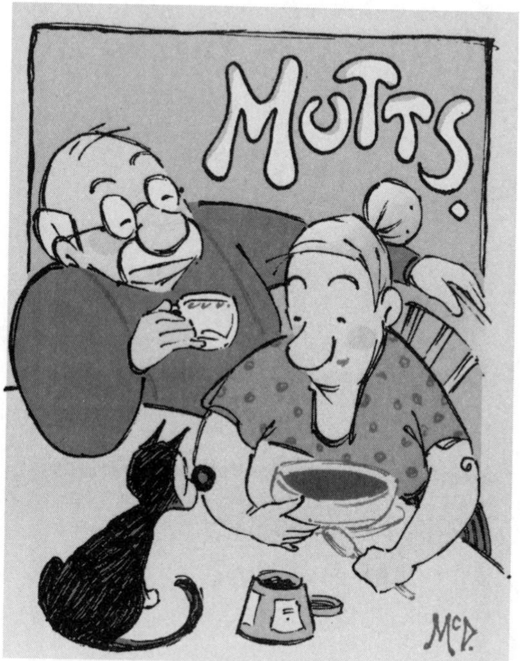
MUTTS

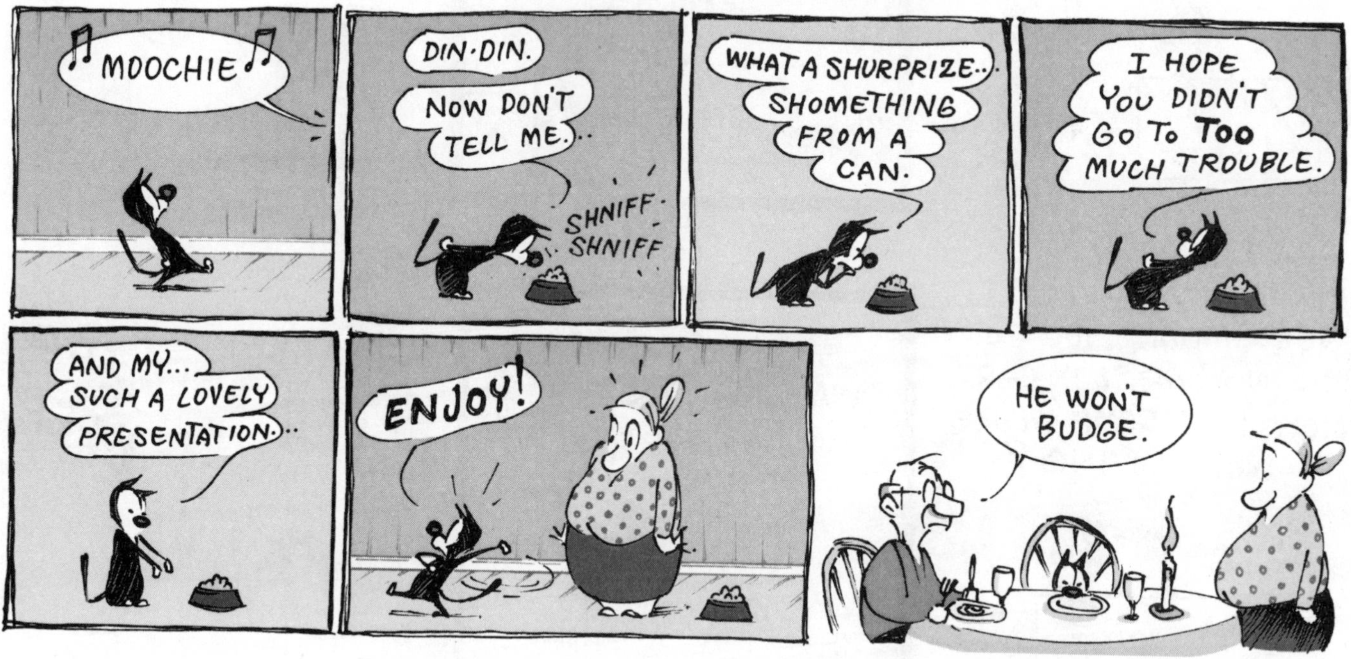
MOOCHIE
DIN·DIN.
NOW DON'T TELL ME...
SHNIFF SHNIFF
WHAT A SHURPRIZE...
SHOMETHING FROM A CAN.
I HOPE YOU DIDN'T GO TO TOO MUCH TROUBLE.
AND MY...
SUCH A LOVELY PRESENTATION...
ENJOY!
HE WON'T BUDGE.

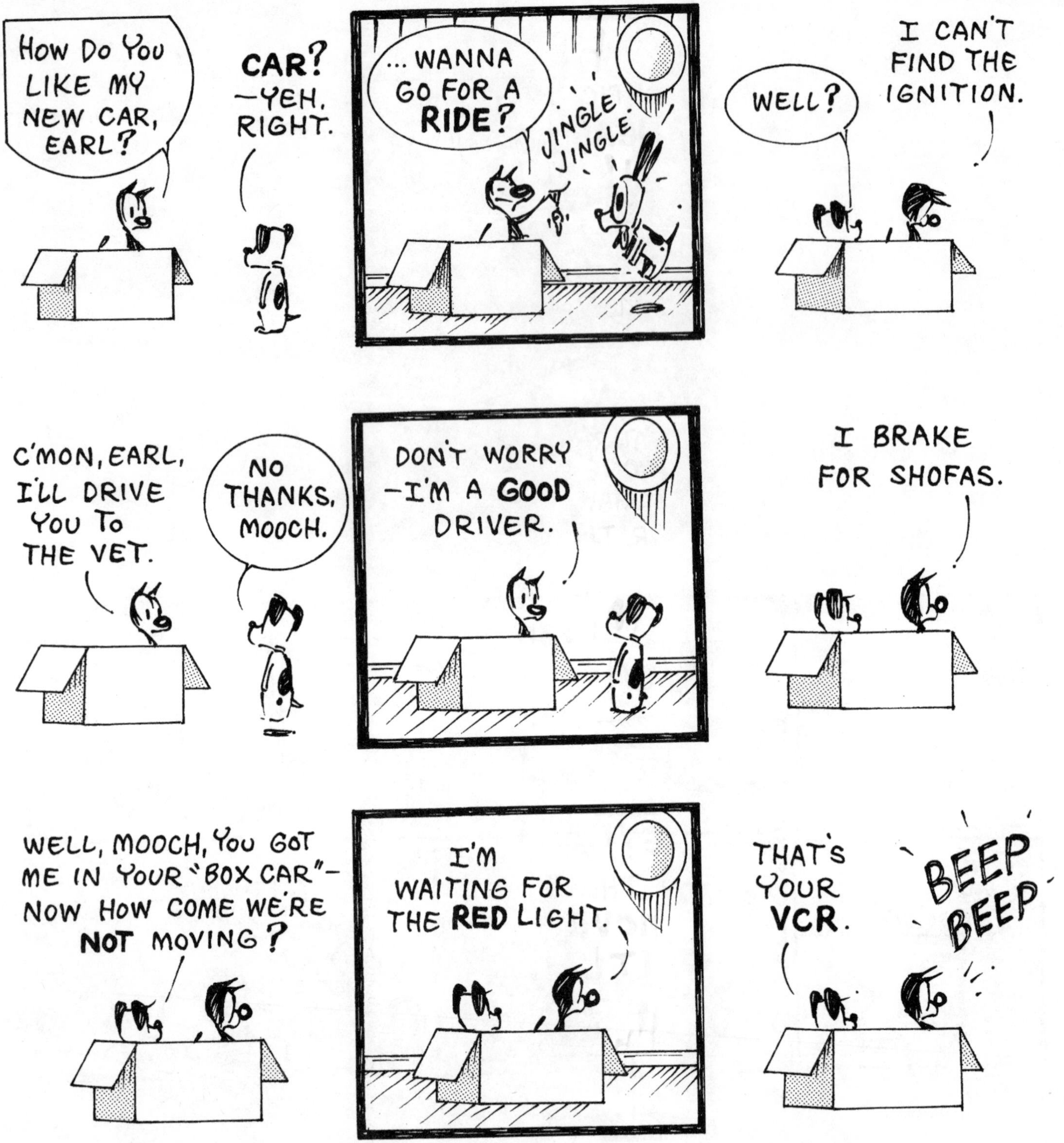
HOW DO YOU LIKE MY NEW CAR, EARL?
CAR? —YEH, RIGHT.
...WANNA GO FOR A RIDE?
JINGLE JINGLE
WELL?
I CAN'T FIND THE IGNITION.
C'MON, EARL, I'LL DRIVE YOU TO THE VET.
NO THANKS, MOOCH.
DON'T WORRY —I'M A GOOD DRIVER.
I BRAKE FOR SHOFAS.
WELL, MOOCH, YOU GOT ME IN YOUR "BOX CAR"— NOW HOW COME WE'RE NOT MOVING?
I'M WAITING FOR THE RED LIGHT.
THAT'S YOUR VCR.
BEEP BEEP

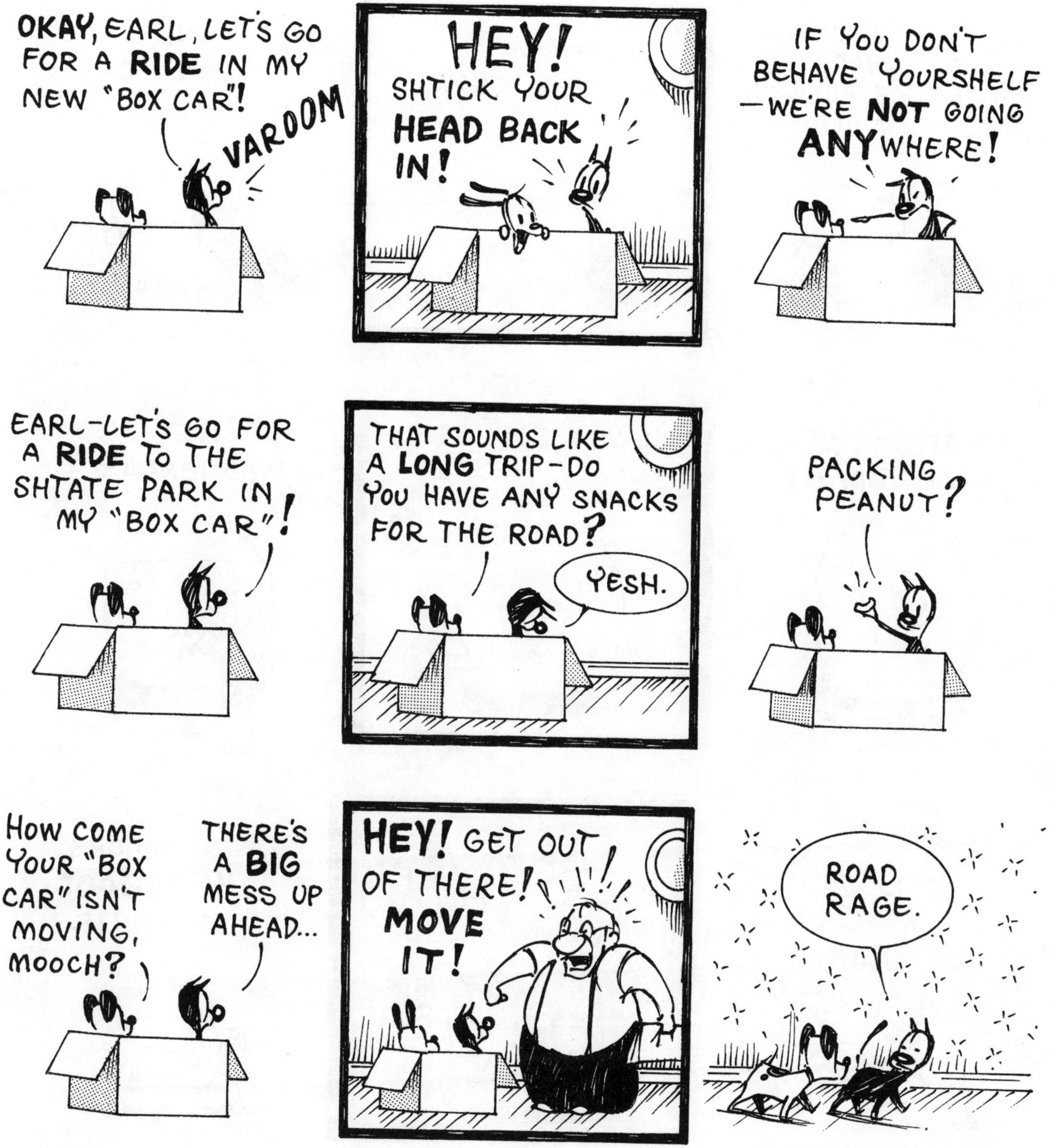
OKAY, EARL, LET'S GO FOR A RIDE IN MY NEW "BOX CAR"!
VAROOM
HEY! SHTICK YOUR HEAD BACK IN!
IF YOU DON'T BEHAVE YOURSHELF—WE'RE NOT GOING ANYWHERE!
EARL—LET'S GO FOR A RIDE TO THE SHTATE PARK IN MY "BOX CAR"!
THAT SOUNDS LIKE A LONG TRIP—DO YOU HAVE ANY SNACKS FOR THE ROAD?
YESH.
PACKING PEANUT?
HOW COME YOUR "BOX CAR" ISN'T MOVING, MOOCH?
THERE'S A BIG MESS UP AHEAD...
HEY! GET OUT OF THERE! MOVE IT!
ROAD RAGE.

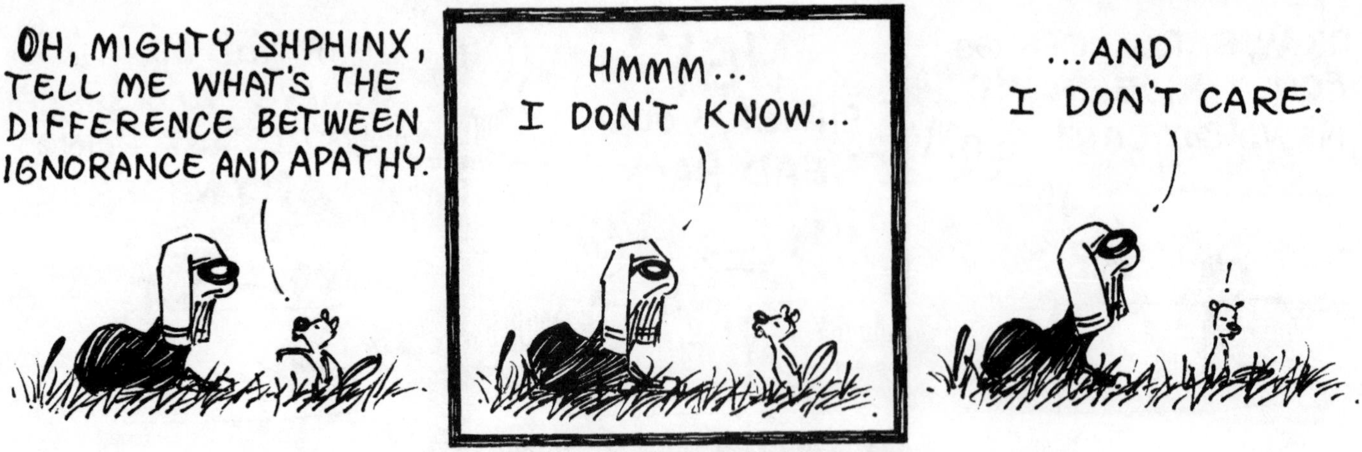
OH, MIGHTY SHPHINX, TELL ME WHAT'S THE DIFFERENCE BETWEEN IGNORANCE AND APATHY.
HMMM... I DON'T KNOW...
...AND I DON'T CARE.
!

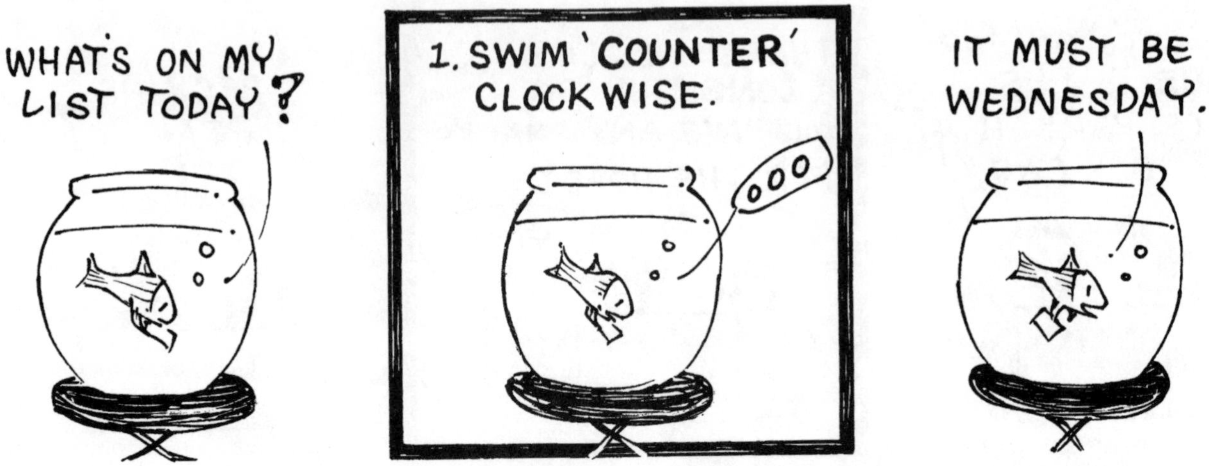
WHAT'S ON MY LIST TODAY?
1. SWIM 'COUNTER' CLOCKWISE.
OOO
IT MUST BE WEDNESDAY.

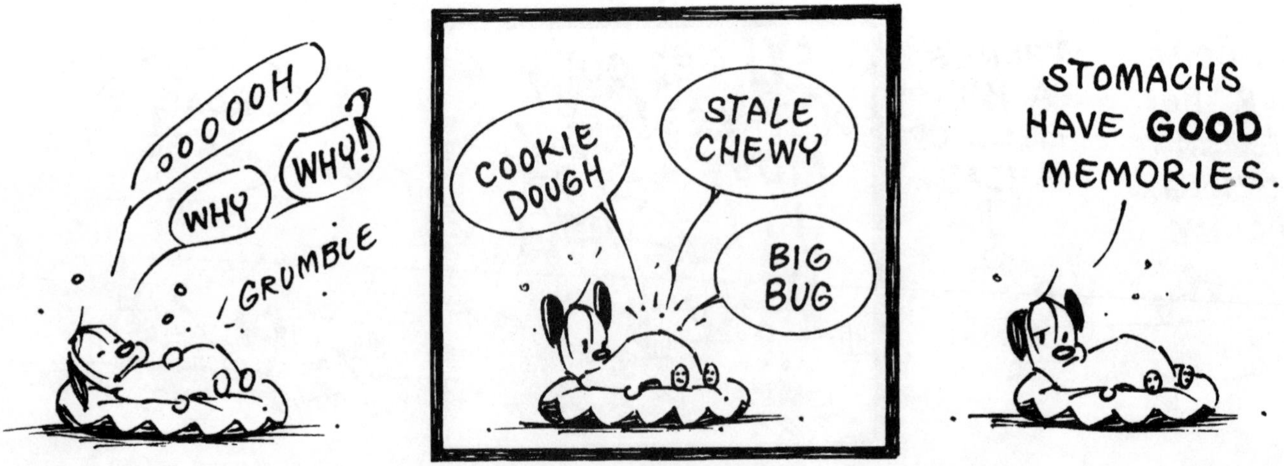
OOOOOH
WHY
WHY!
GRUMBLE
COOKIE DOUGH
STALE CHEWY
BIG BUG
STOMACHS HAVE GOOD MEMORIES.

THE GAME OF MUTTS

LET'S PLAY "KITTY"!
?
WE'LL HIDE IN SILLY PLACES
SING A LI'L KITTY SONG
MEOW MEOW MEOW
JUMP ON THE FURNITURE
RUN UP AND DOWN THE STAIRS WITH A KRAZY LOOK IN OUR EYES
SHNUB OUR DINNER
AND JUST... FLOP!
THAT'S A FUN GAME!
SURE. I PLAY IT ALL THE TIME.

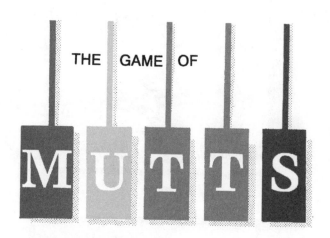

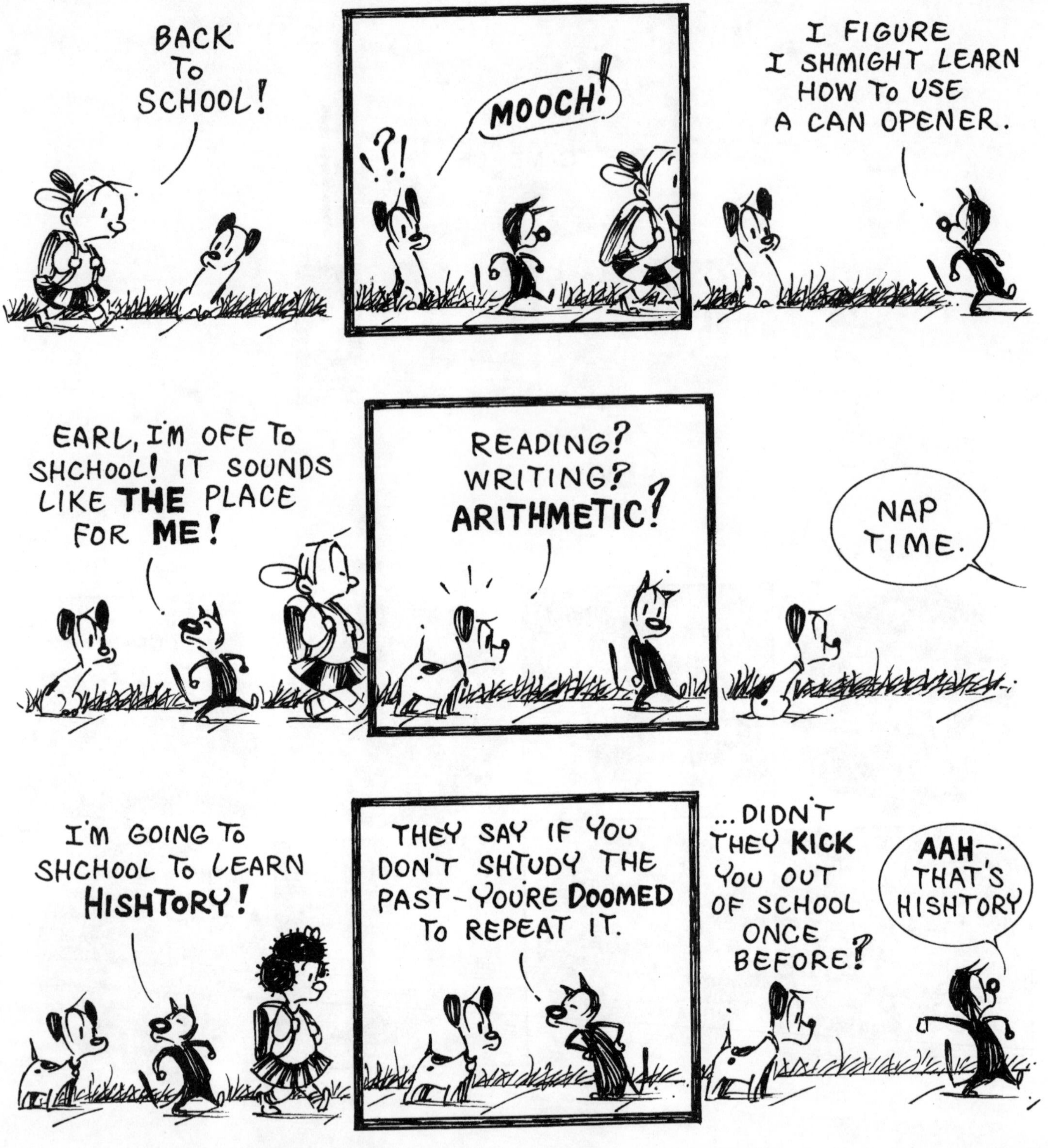
BACK TO SCHOOL!
MOOCH!
!?!
I FIGURE I SHMIGHT LEARN HOW TO USE A CAN OPENER.
EARL, I'M OFF TO SHCHOOL! IT SOUNDS LIKE **THE** PLACE FOR **ME**!
READING? WRITING? **ARITHMETIC**?
NAP TIME.
I'M GOING TO SHCHOOL TO LEARN **HISHTORY**!
THEY SAY IF YOU DON'T SHTUDY THE PAST - YOU'RE **DOOMED** TO REPEAT IT.
...DIDN'T THEY **KICK** YOU OUT OF SCHOOL ONCE BEFORE?
AAH— THAT'S HISHTORY

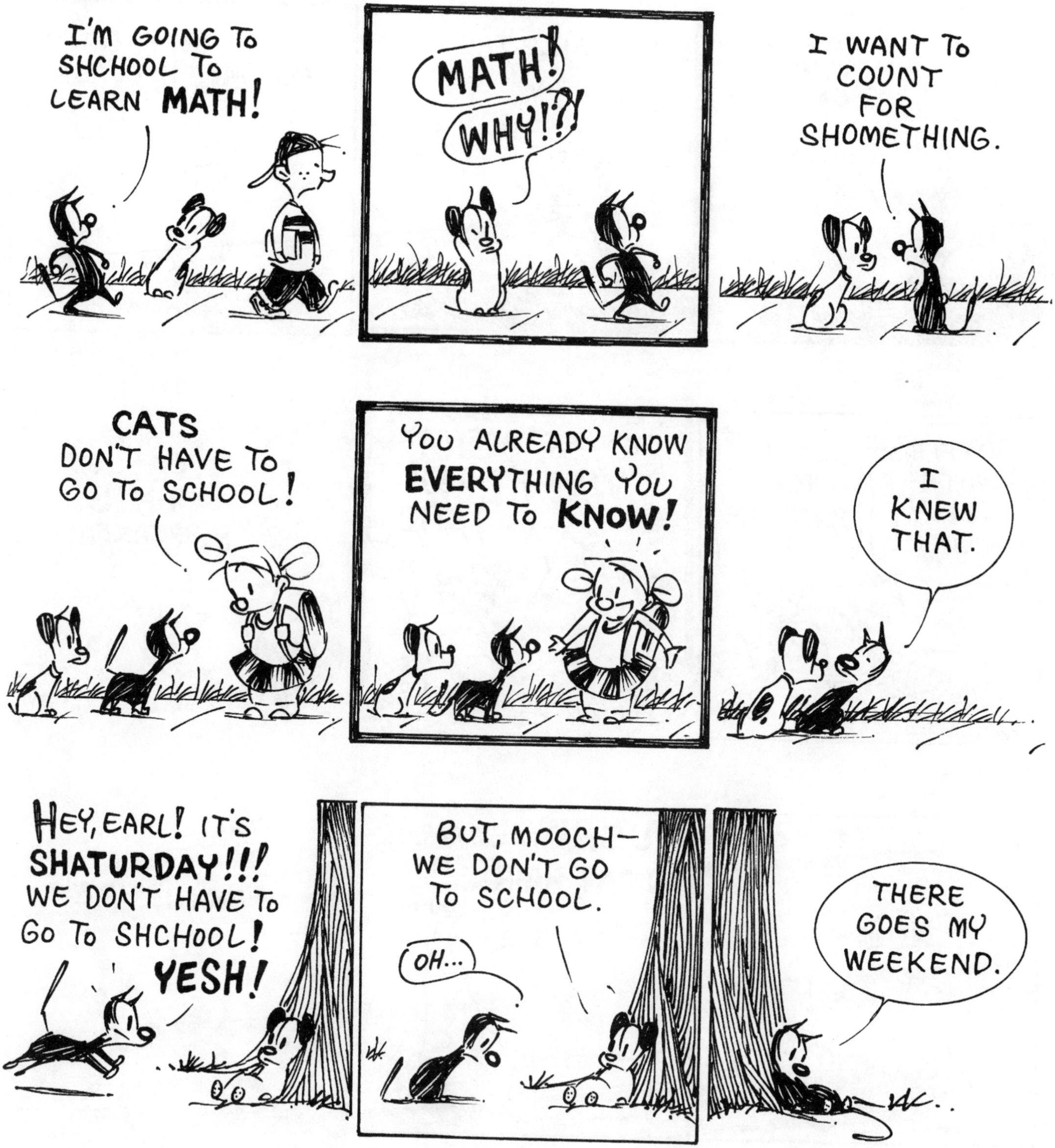
I'M GOING TO SHCHOOL TO LEARN MATH!
MATH!
WHY!?!
I WANT TO COUNT FOR SHOMETHING.
CATS DON'T HAVE TO GO TO SCHOOL!
YOU ALREADY KNOW EVERYTHING YOU NEED TO KNOW!
I KNEW THAT.
HEY, EARL! IT'S SHATURDAY!!! WE DON'T HAVE TO GO TO SHCHOOL!
YESH!
BUT, MOOCH— WE DON'T GO TO SCHOOL.
OH...
THERE GOES MY WEEKEND.

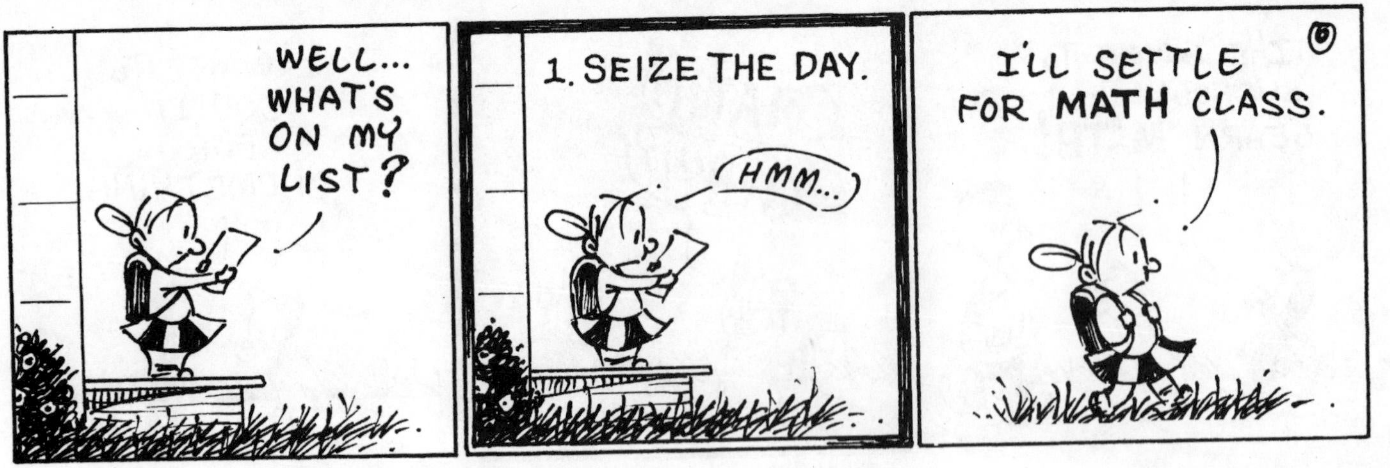
WELL... WHAT'S ON MY LIST?
1. SEIZE THE DAY.
HMM...
I'LL SETTLE FOR MATH CLASS.

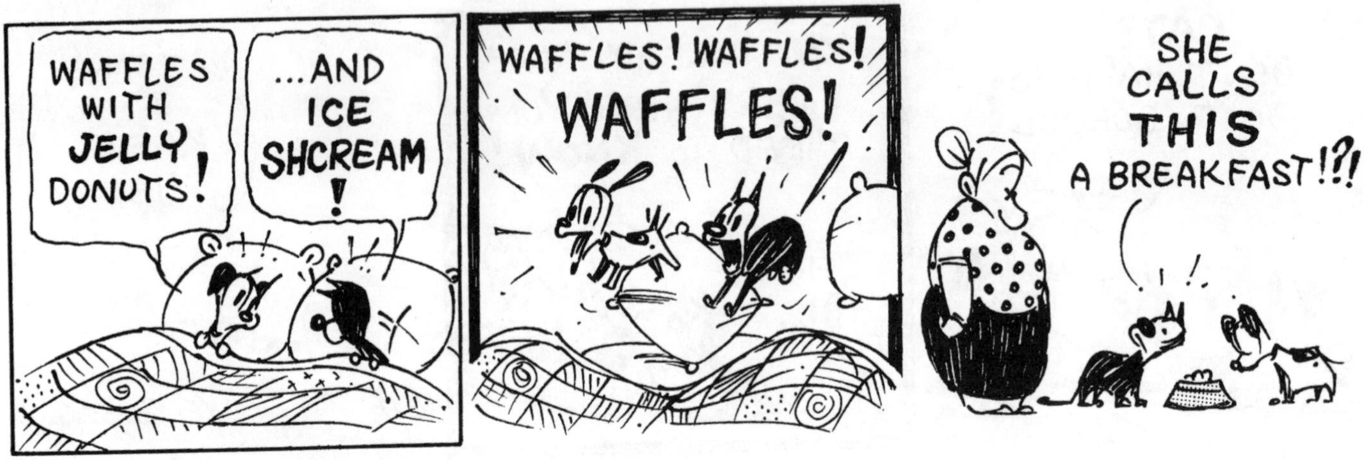
WAFFLES WITH JELLY DONUTS!
...AND ICE SHCREAM!
WAFFLES! WAFFLES!
WAFFLES!
SHE CALLS THIS A BREAKFAST!?!

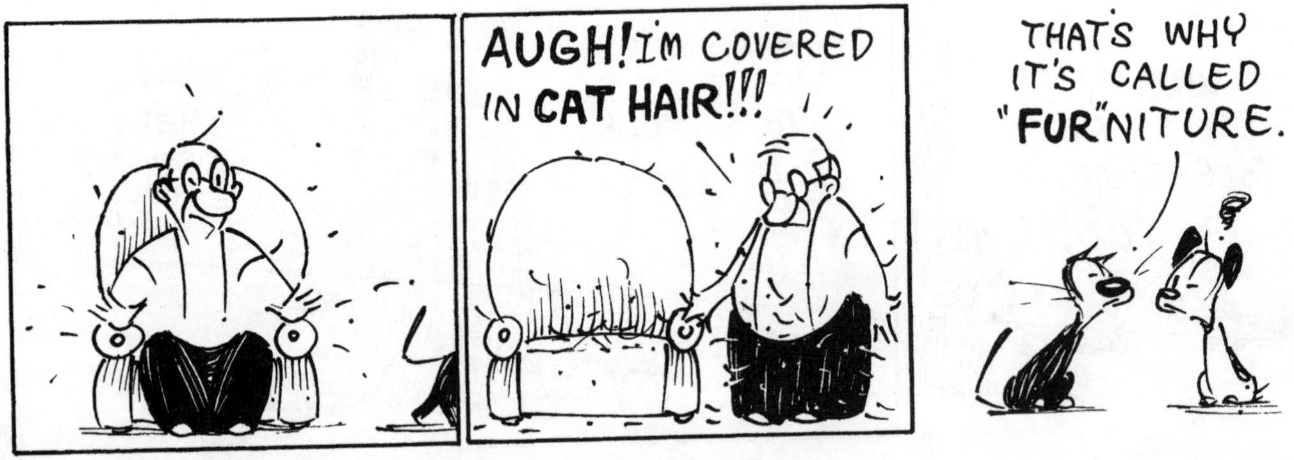
AUGH! I'M COVERED IN CAT HAIR!!!
THAT'S WHY IT'S CALLED "FUR"NITURE.

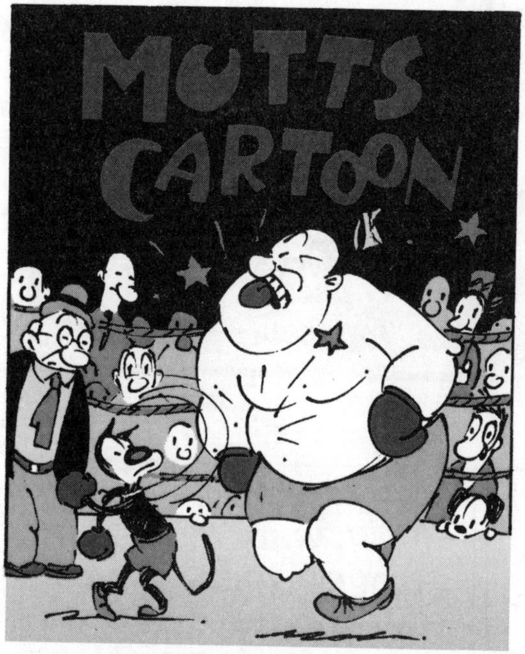
MUTTS
CARTOON

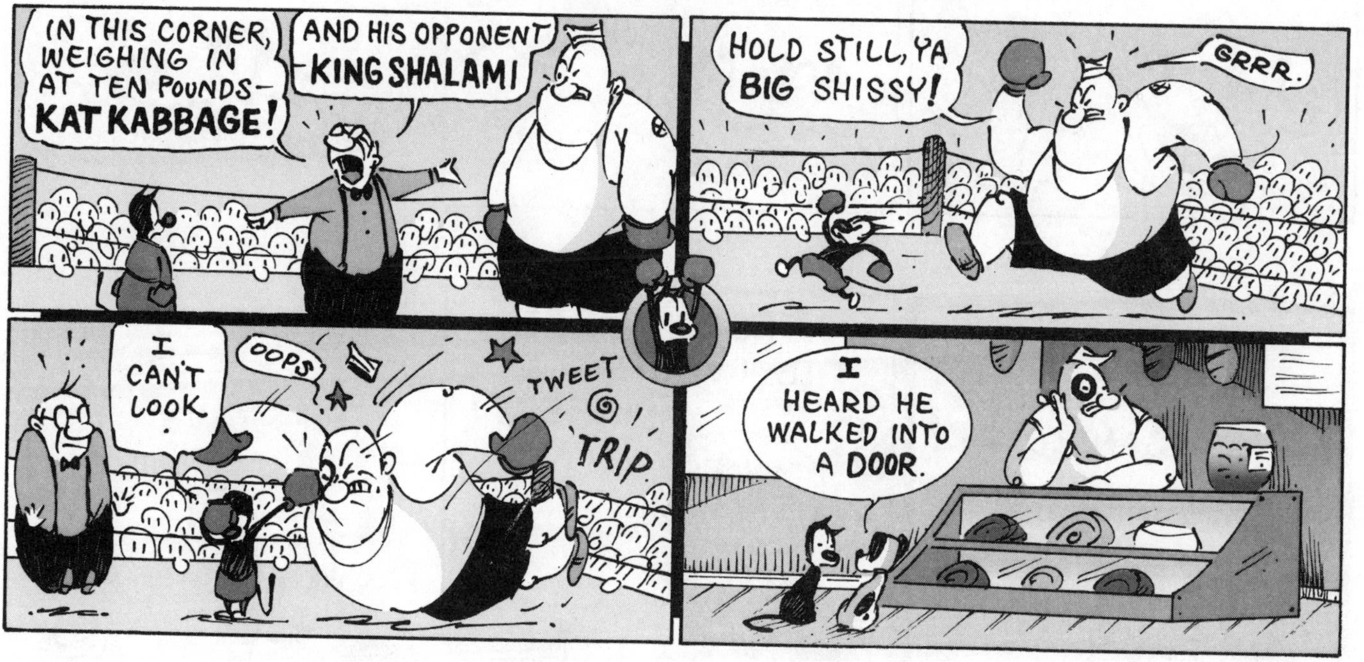
IN THIS CORNER, WEIGHING IN AT TEN POUNDS- KAT KABBAGE!
AND HIS OPPONENT KING SHALAMI
HOLD STILL, YA BIG SHISSY!
GRRR.
I CAN'T LOOK.
OOPS
TWEET
TRIP
I HEARD HE WALKED INTO A DOOR.

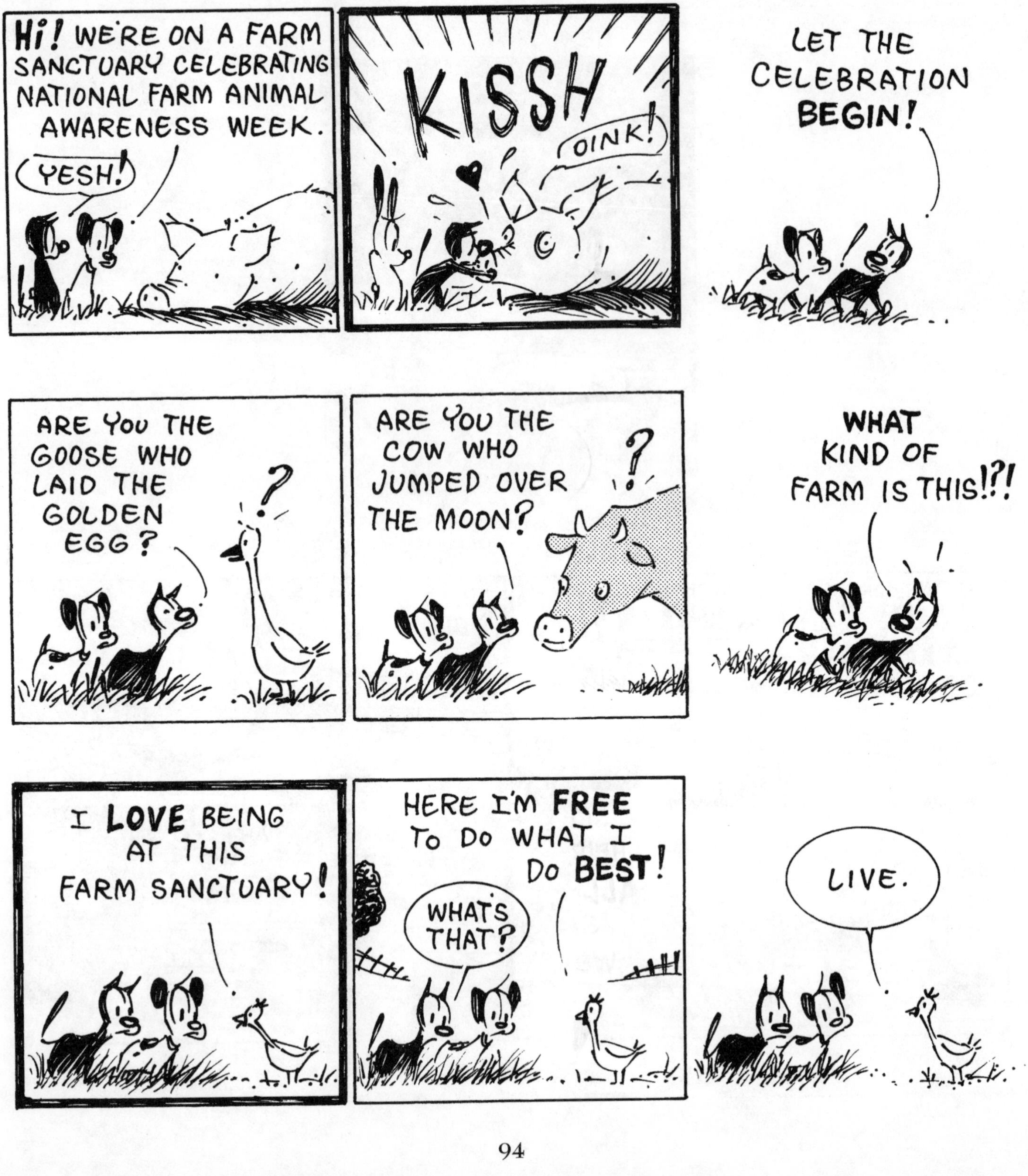
HI! WE'RE ON A FARM SANCTUARY CELEBRATING NATIONAL FARM ANIMAL AWARENESS WEEK.
YESH!
KISSH
OINK!
LET THE CELEBRATION BEGIN!
ARE YOU THE GOOSE WHO LAID THE GOLDEN EGG?
?
ARE YOU THE COW WHO JUMPED OVER THE MOON?
?
WHAT KIND OF FARM IS THIS!?!
I LOVE BEING AT THIS FARM SANCTUARY!
HERE I'M FREE TO DO WHAT I DO BEST!
WHAT'S THAT?
LIVE.

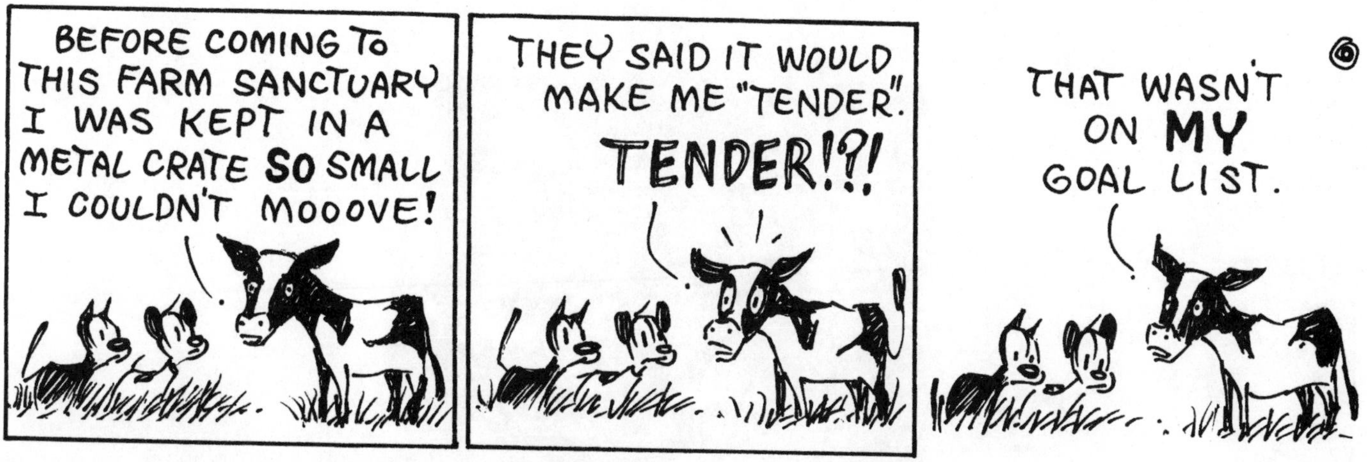
BEFORE COMING TO THIS FARM SANCTUARY I WAS KEPT IN A METAL CRATE SO SMALL I COULDN'T MOOOVE!
THEY SAID IT WOULD MAKE ME "TENDER".
TENDER!?!
THAT WASN'T ON MY GOAL LIST.

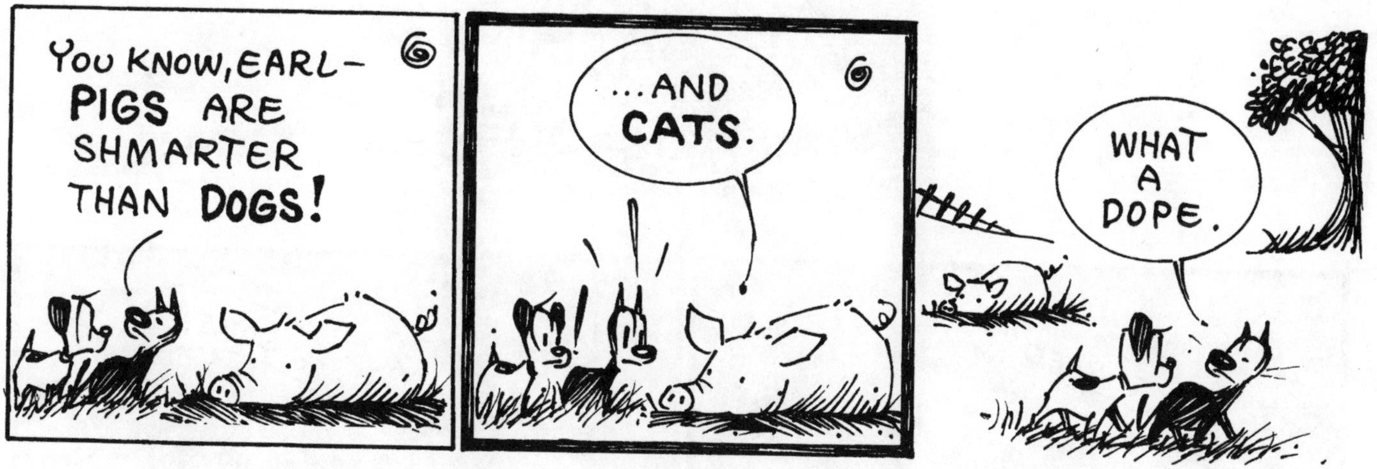
YOU KNOW, EARL- PIGS ARE SHMARTER THAN DOGS!
...AND CATS.
WHAT A DOPE.

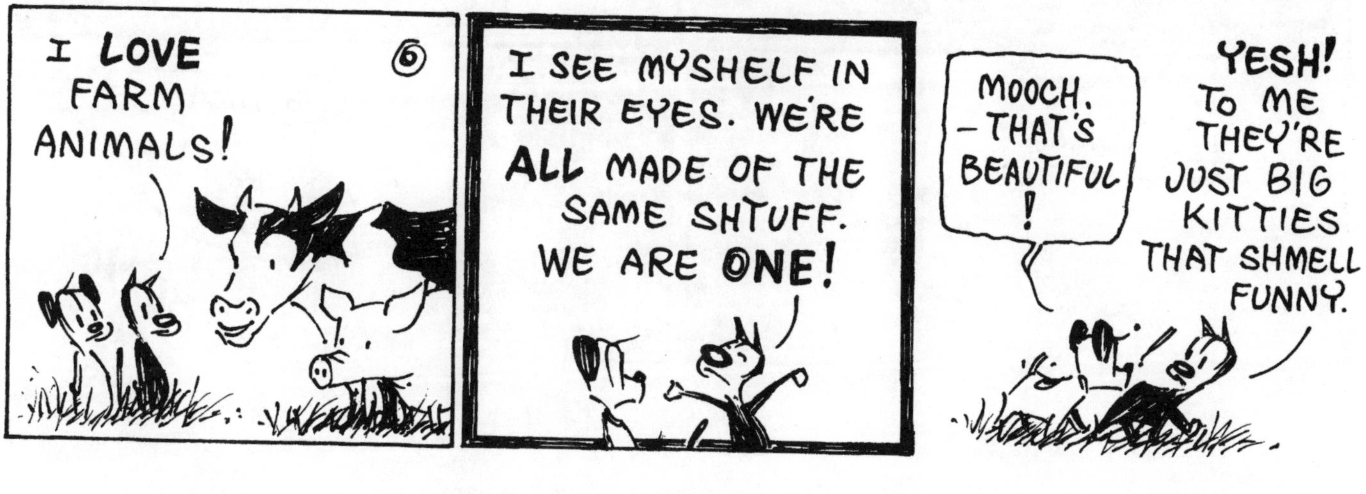
I LOVE FARM ANIMALS!
I SEE MYSHELF IN THEIR EYES. WE'RE ALL MADE OF THE SAME SHTUFF. WE ARE ONE!
MOOCH. - THAT'S BEAUTIFUL!
YESH! TO ME THEY'RE JUST BIG KITTIES THAT SHMELL FUNNY.

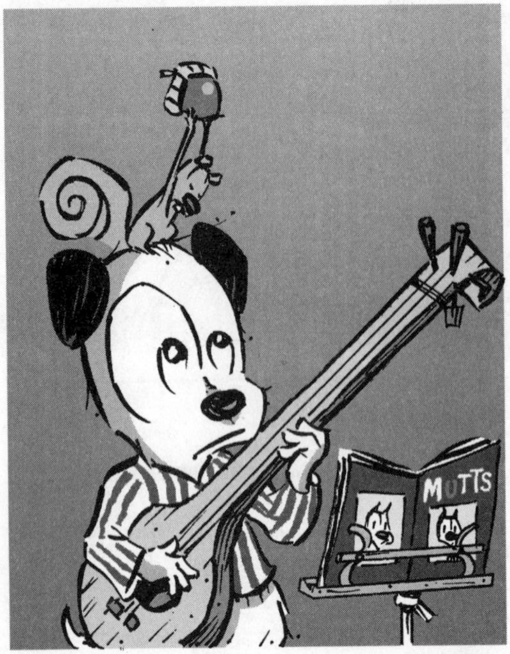
MUTTS

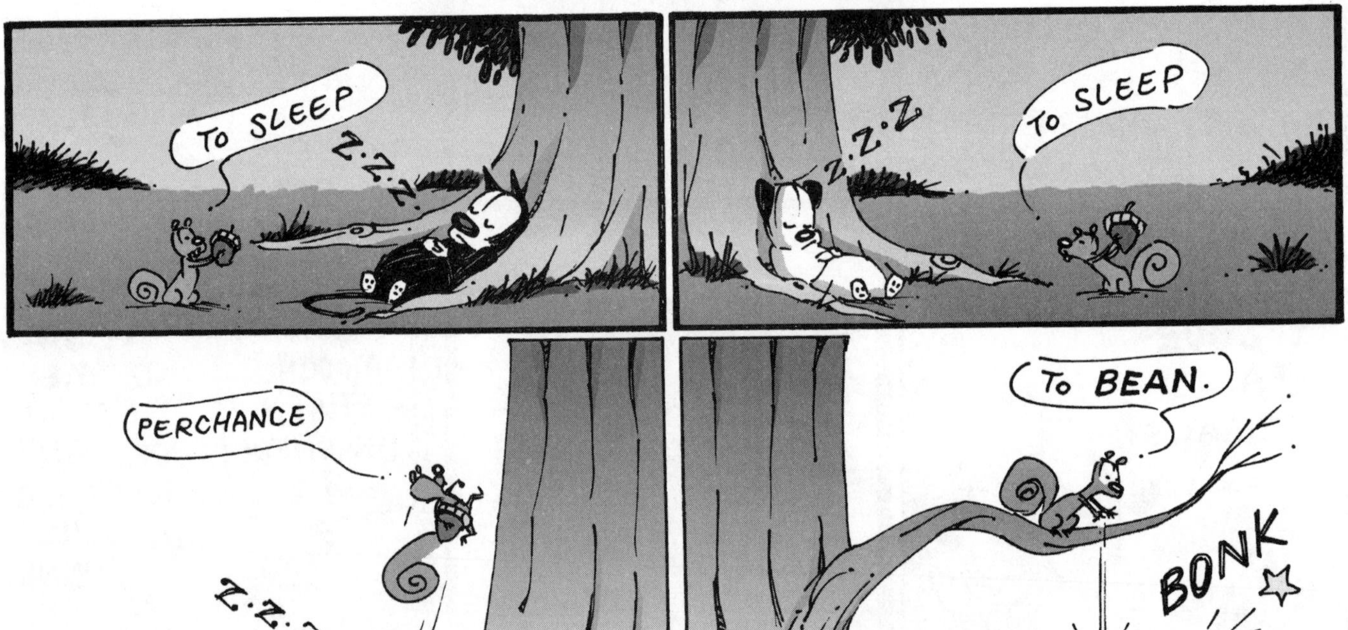
To SLEEP
Z.Z.Z
Z.Z.Z
To SLEEP
PERCHANCE
Z.Z.Z
To BEAN.
BONK

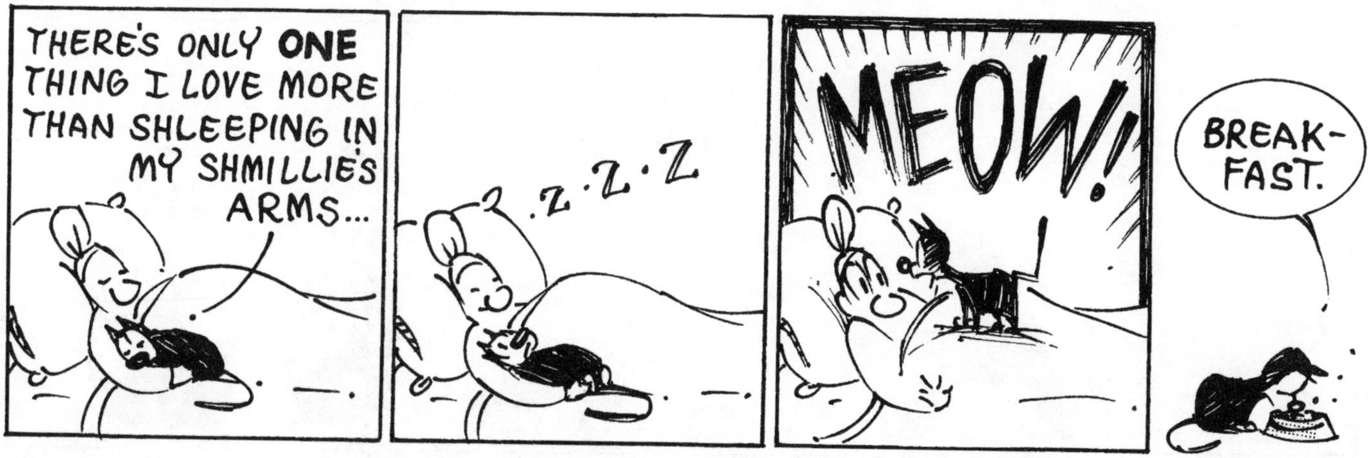
THERE'S ONLY **ONE** THING I LOVE MORE THAN SHLEEPING IN MY SHMILLIE'S ARMS...
Z·Z·Z·Z
MEOW!
BREAK-FAST.

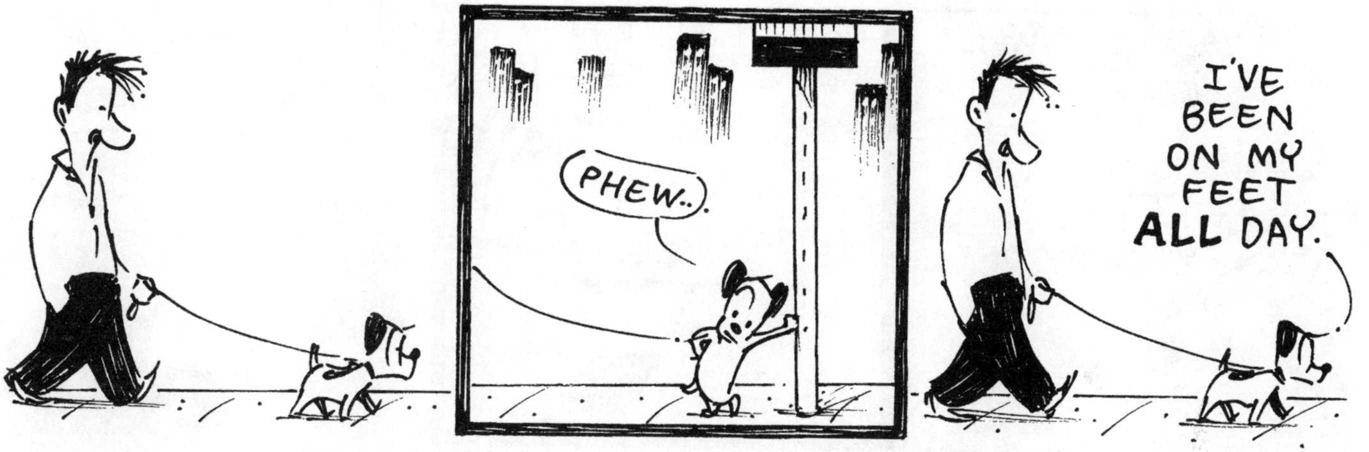
PHEW..
I'VE BEEN ON MY FEET **ALL** DAY.

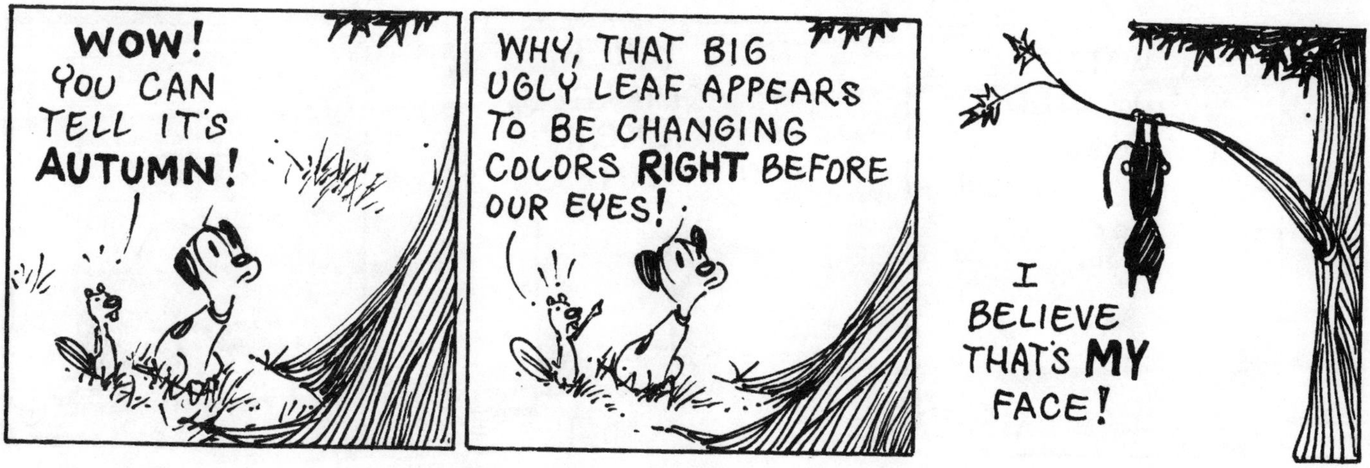
WOW! YOU CAN TELL IT'S **AUTUMN!**
WHY, THAT BIG UGLY LEAF APPEARS TO BE CHANGING COLORS **RIGHT** BEFORE OUR EYES!
I BELIEVE THAT'S **MY** FACE!

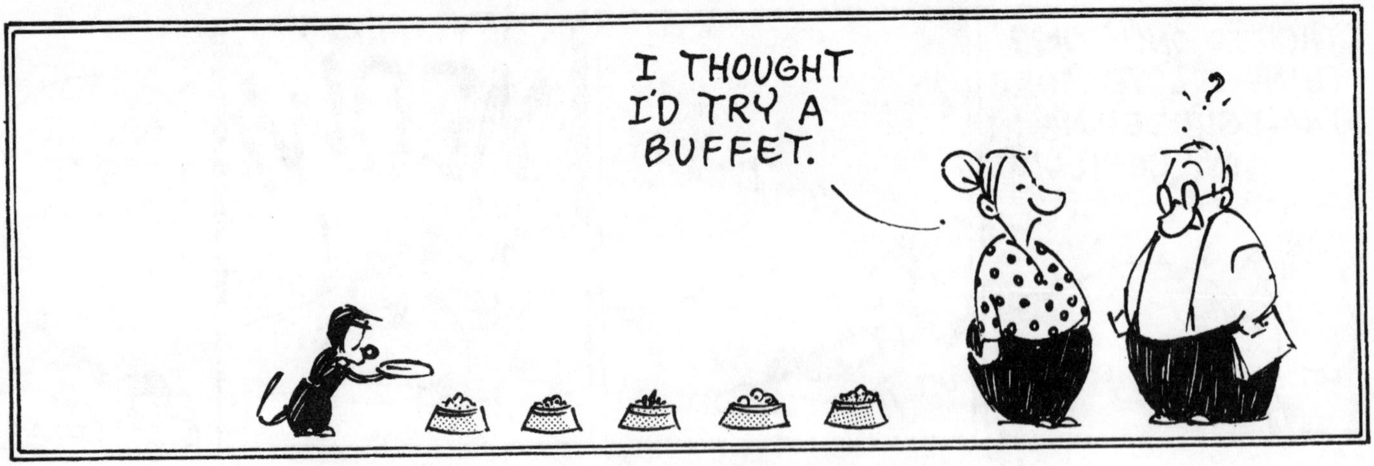
I THOUGHT I'D TRY A BUFFET.
?

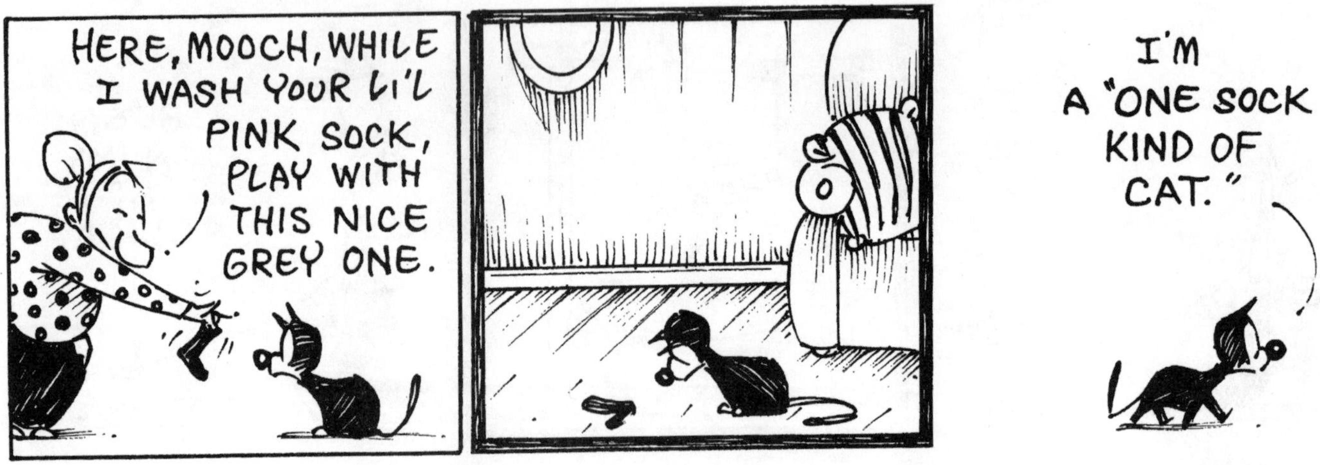
HERE, MOOCH, WHILE I WASH YOUR LI'L PINK SOCK, PLAY WITH THIS NICE GREY ONE.
I'M A "ONE SOCK KIND OF CAT."

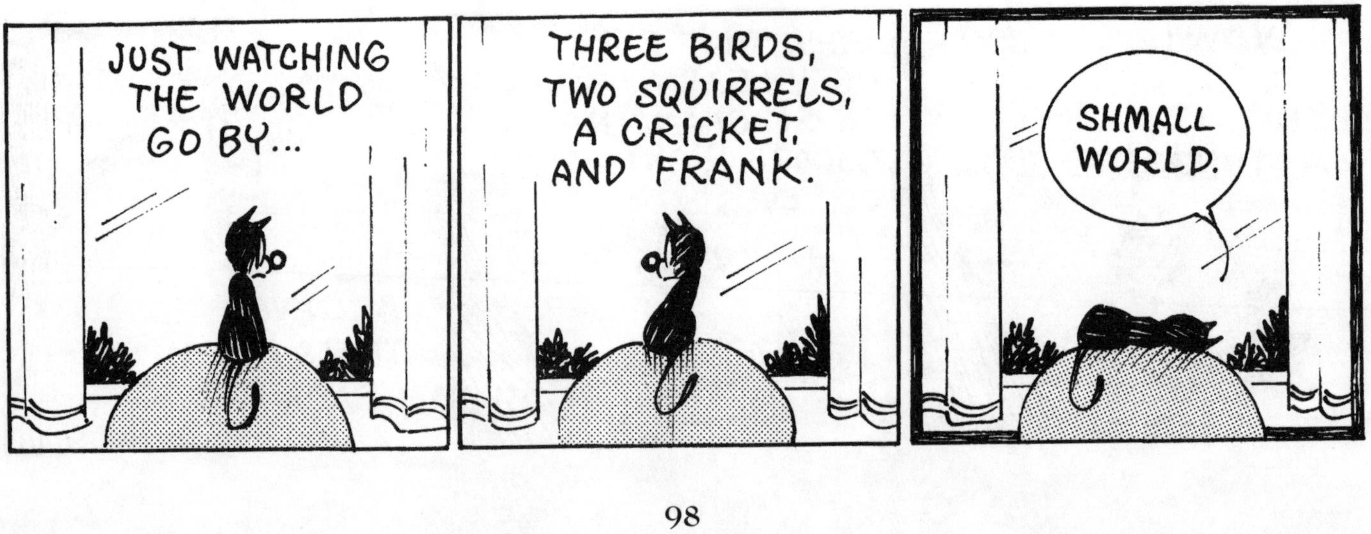
JUST WATCHING THE WORLD GO BY...
THREE BIRDS, TWO SQUIRRELS, A CRICKET, AND FRANK.
SHMALL WORLD.

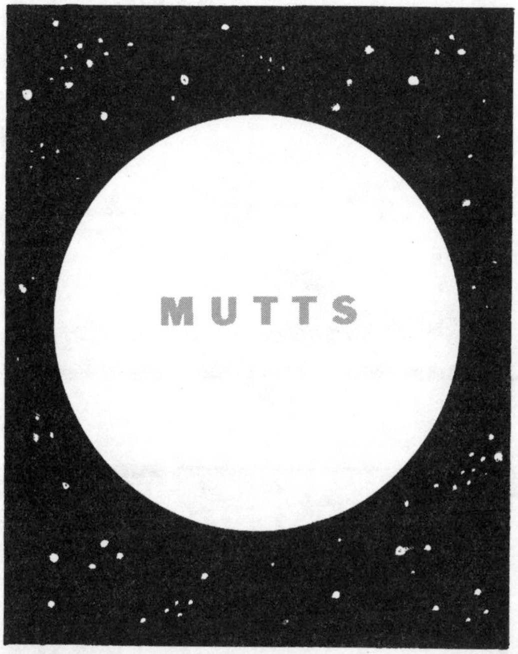
MUTTS

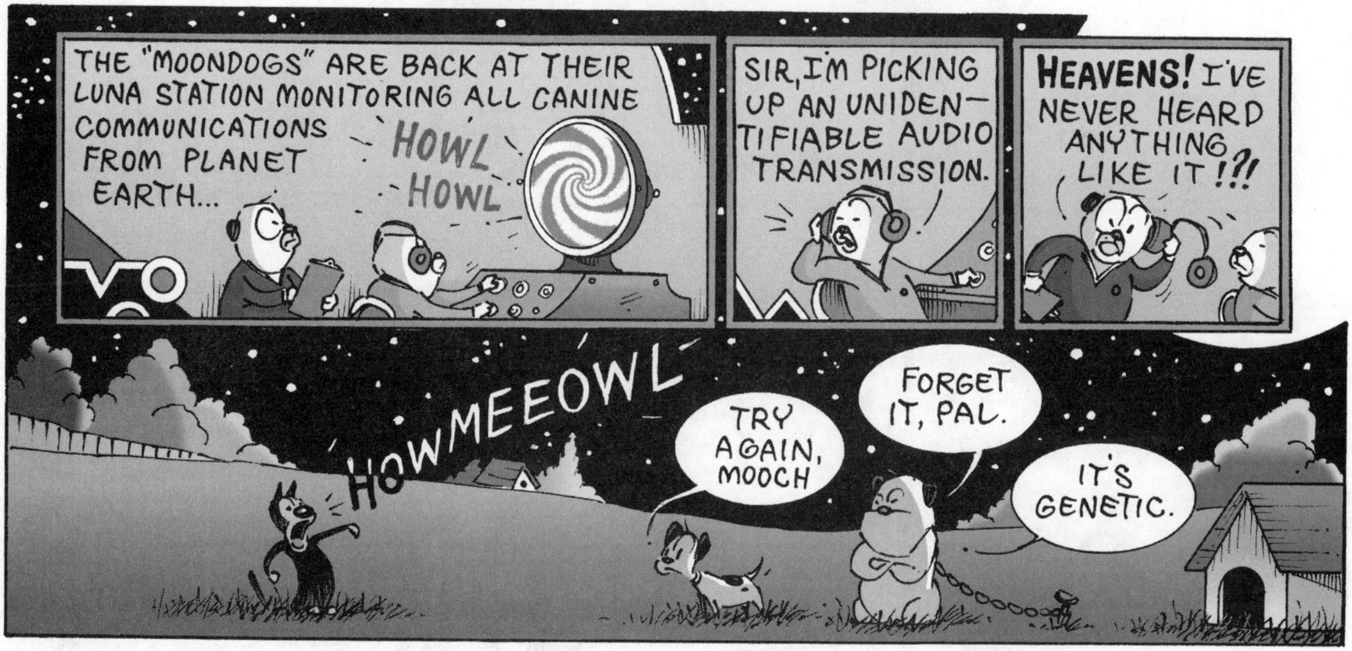
THE "MOONDOGS" ARE BACK AT THEIR LUNA STATION MONITORING ALL CANINE COMMUNICATIONS FROM PLANET EARTH...
HOWL
HOWL
SIR, I'M PICKING UP AN UNIDEN-TIFIABLE AUDIO TRANSMISSION.
HEAVENS! I'VE NEVER HEARD ANYTHING LIKE IT !?!
HOWMEEOWL
TRY AGAIN, MOOCH
FORGET IT, PAL.
IT'S GENETIC.

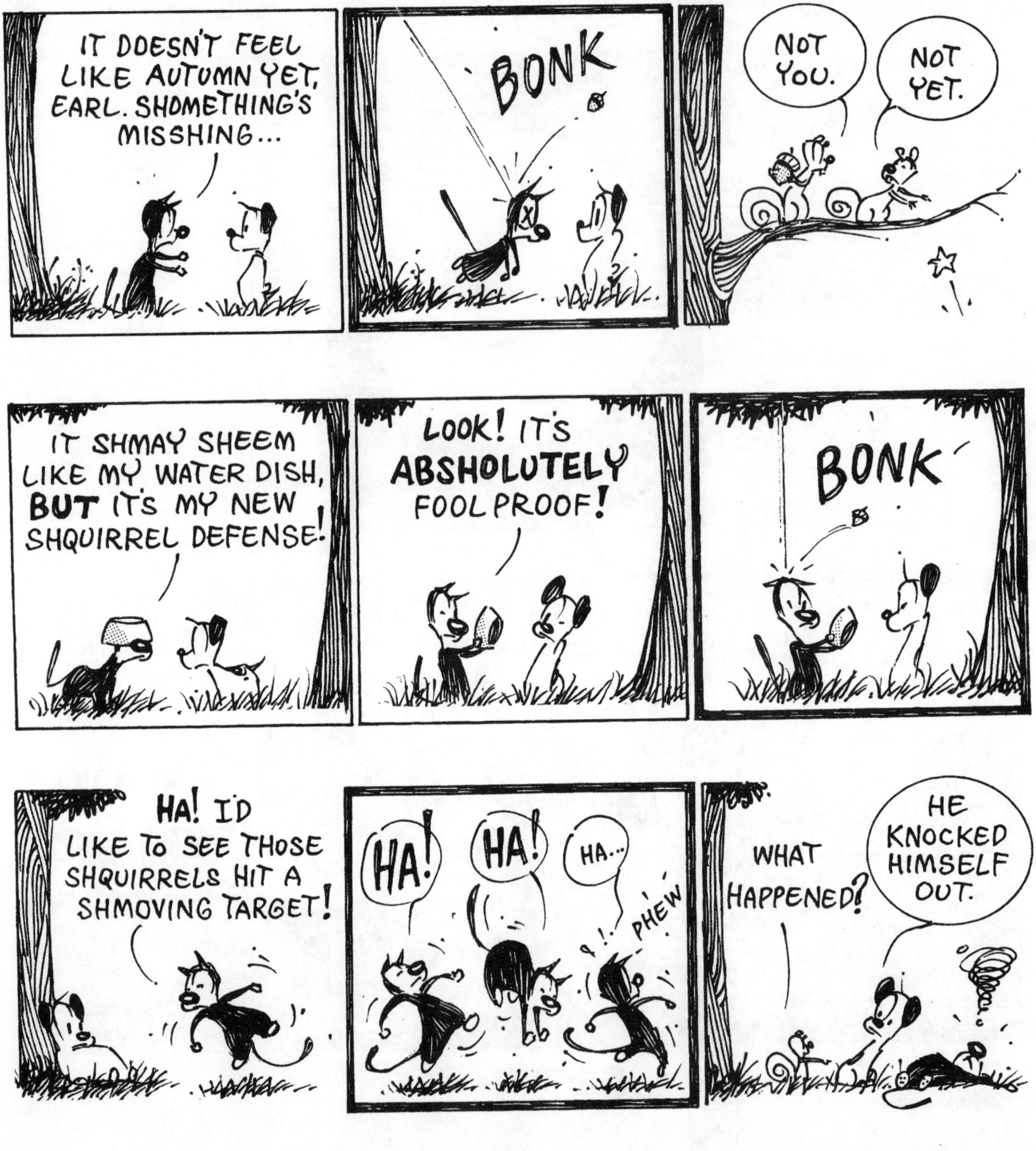
IT DOESN'T FEEL LIKE AUTUMN YET, EARL. SHOMETHING'S MISSHING...
BONK
NOT YOU.
NOT YET.
IT SHMAY SHEEM LIKE MY WATER DISH, BUT IT'S MY NEW SHQUIRREL DEFENSE!
LOOK! IT'S ABSHOLUTELY FOOLPROOF!
BONK
HA! I'D LIKE TO SEE THOSE SHQUIRRELS HIT A SHMOVING TARGET!
HA!
HA!
HA...
PHEW
WHAT HAPPENED?
HE KNOCKED HIMSELF OUT.

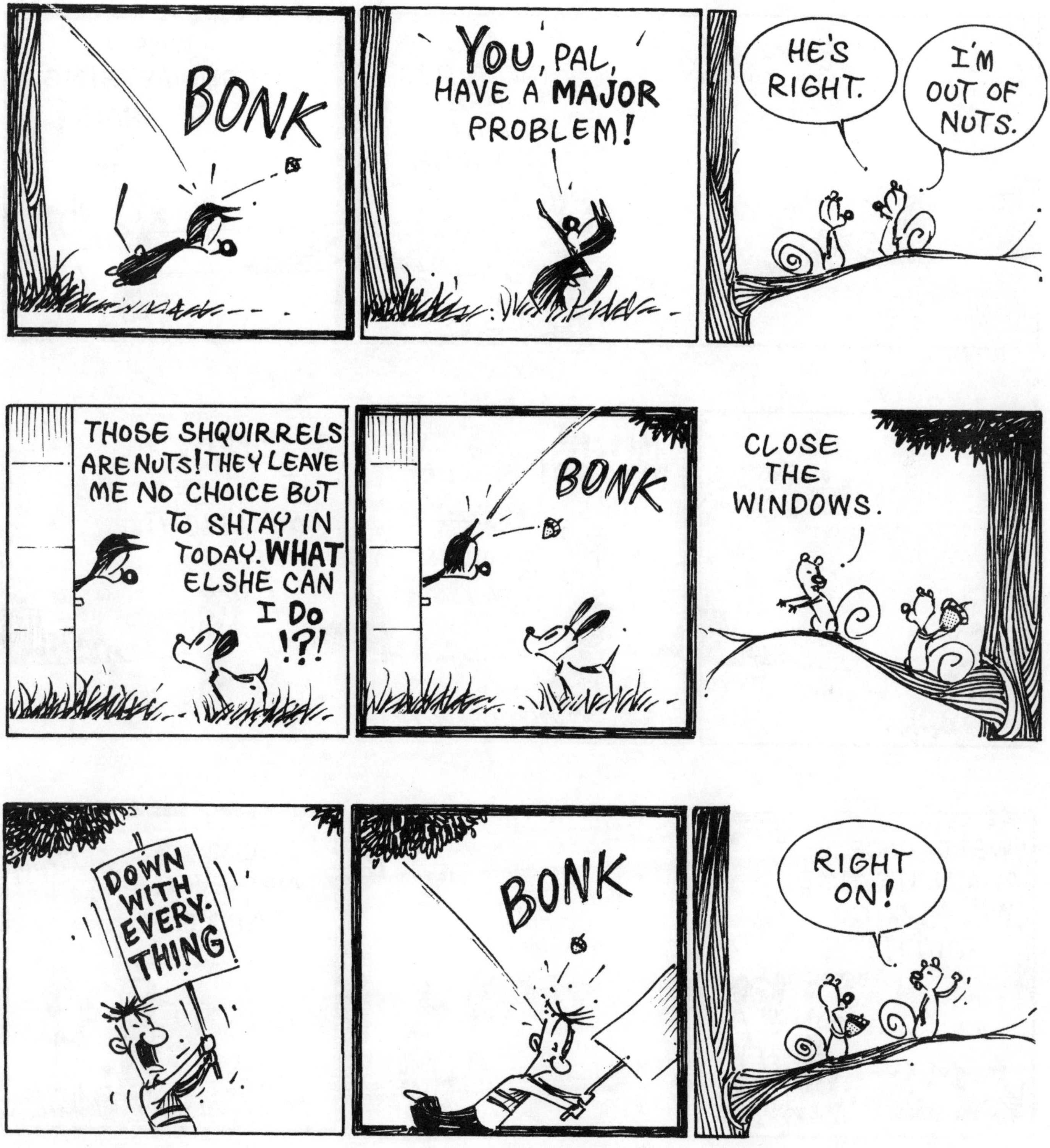
BONK
YOU, PAL, HAVE A MAJOR PROBLEM!
HE'S RIGHT.
I'M OUT OF NUTS.
THOSE SHQUIRRELS ARE NUTS! THEY LEAVE ME NO CHOICE BUT TO SHTAY IN TODAY. WHAT ELSHE CAN I DO !?!
BONK
CLOSE THE WINDOWS.
DOWN WITH EVERYTHING
BONK
RIGHT ON!

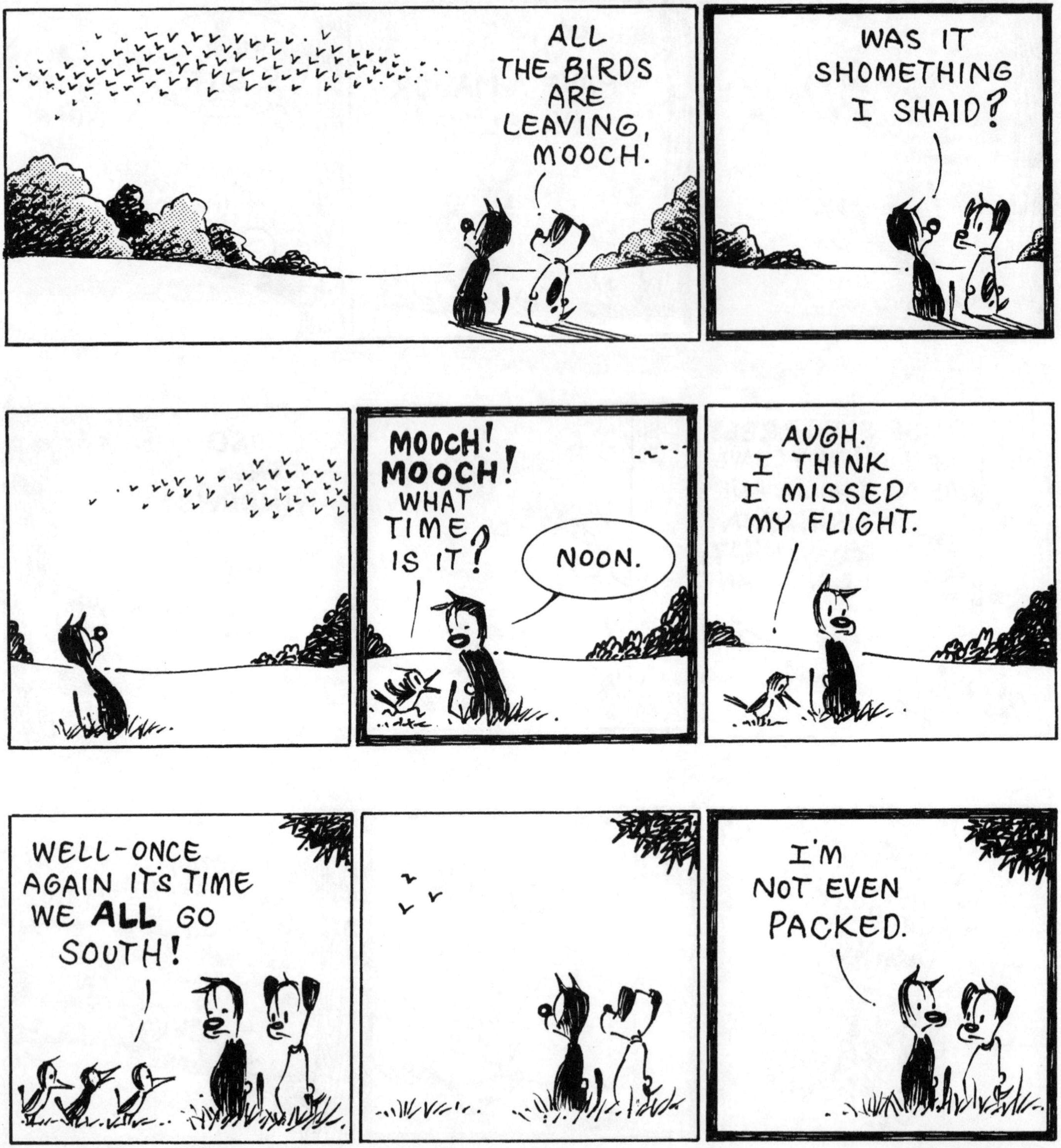
ALL THE BIRDS ARE LEAVING, MOOCH.
WAS IT SHOMETHING I SHAID?
MOOCH! **MOOCH!** WHAT TIME IS IT?
NOON.
AUGH. I THINK I MISSED MY FLIGHT.
WELL-ONCE AGAIN IT'S TIME WE **ALL** GO SOUTH!
I'M NOT EVEN PACKED.

SOUTH
SOUTH
SOUTH
SOUTH
SOUTH
NOT **ONE** ORIGINAL THOUGHT IN THE WHOLE BUNCH.
WE'RE FLYING DOWN TO THE HOT BEACHES OF CANCUN TO GET CRAZY AND PARTY **ALL** WINTER LONG!!!
YOU GO, GIRL!
PARTY!
BIRDS GONE WILD.
SOUTH!
BUT **HOW** DO YOU KNOW WHEN YOU'VE REACHED YOUR DESHTINATION
?
IT **FEELS** RIGHT.
I KNOW **JUST** WHAT YOU MEAN.
ZIP
PURR...

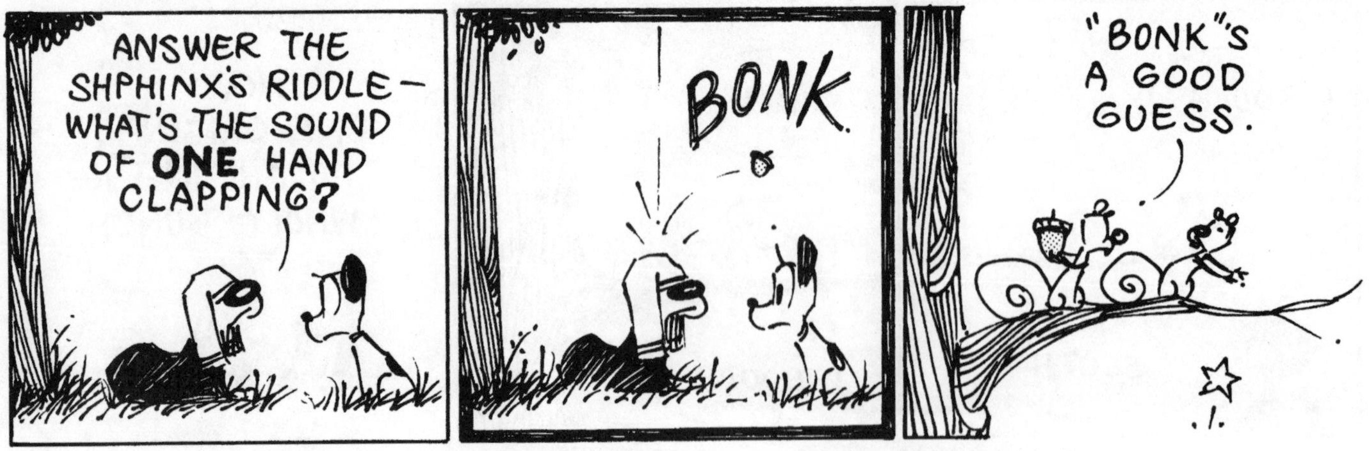
ANSWER THE SHPHINX'S RIDDLE— WHAT'S THE SOUND OF **ONE** HAND CLAPPING?
BONK
"BONK"'S A GOOD GUESS.

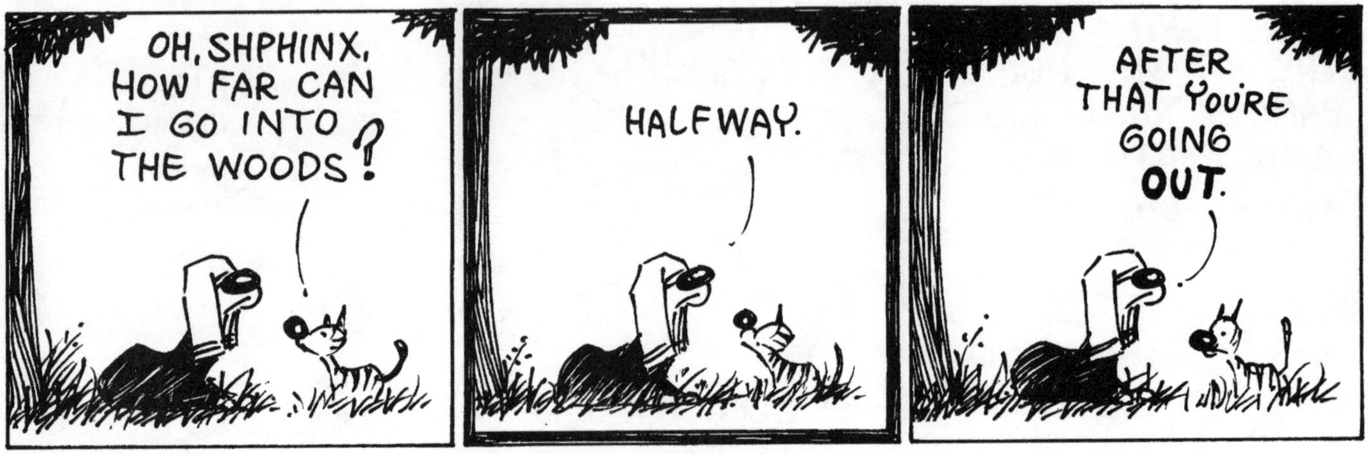
OH, SHPHINX, HOW FAR CAN I GO INTO THE WOODS?
HALFWAY.
AFTER THAT YOU'RE GOING **OUT**.

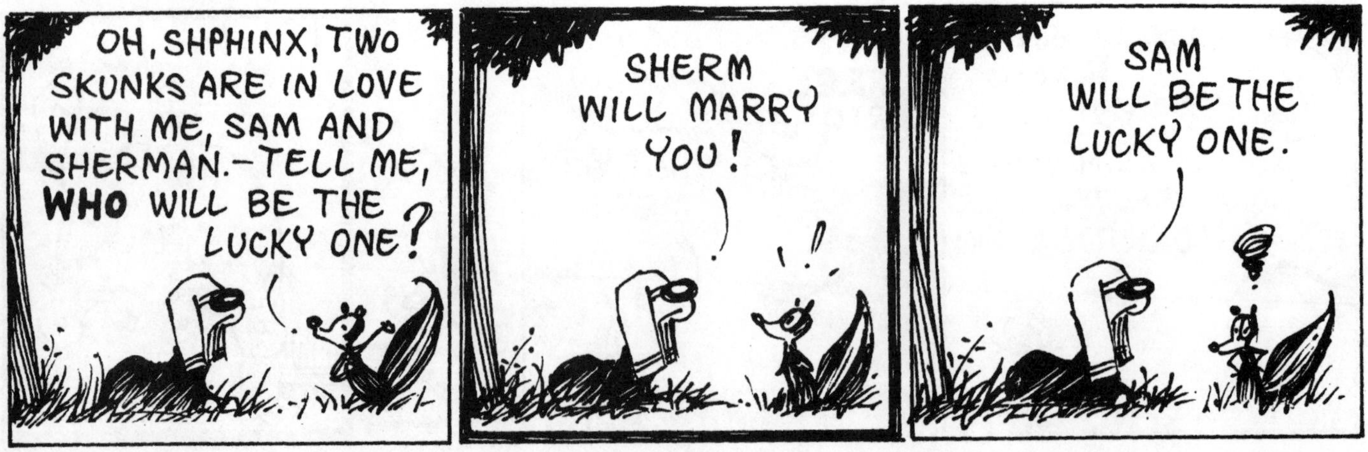
OH, SHPHINX, TWO SKUNKS ARE IN LOVE WITH ME, SAM AND SHERMAN.—TELL ME, **WHO** WILL BE THE LUCKY ONE?
SHERM WILL MARRY YOU!
SAM WILL BE THE LUCKY ONE.

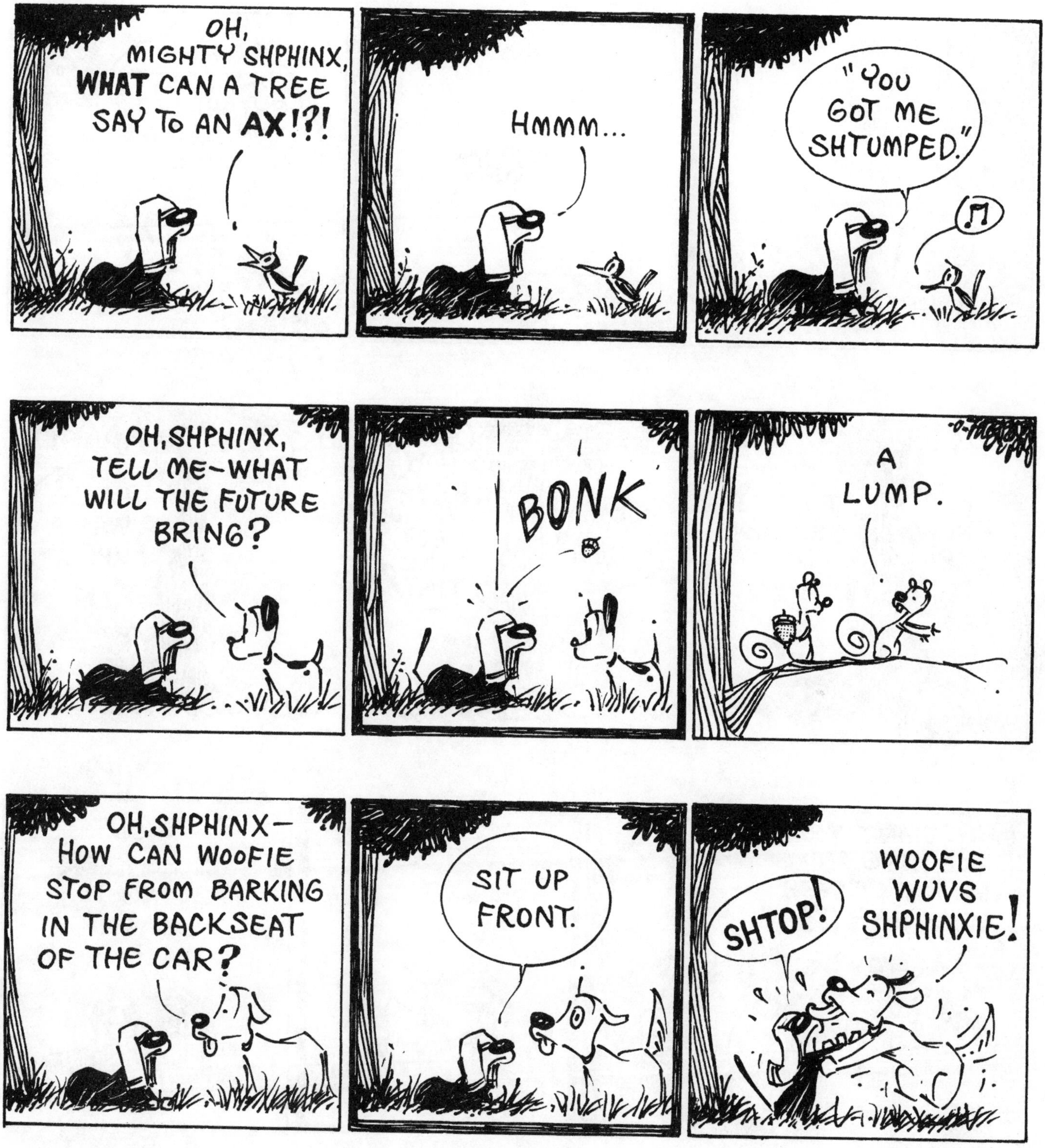
OH, MIGHTY SHPHINX, WHAT CAN A TREE SAY TO AN AX!?!
HMMM...
"YOU GOT ME SHTUMPED."
OH, SHPHINX, TELL ME–WHAT WILL THE FUTURE BRING?
BONK
A LUMP.
OH, SHPHINX– HOW CAN WOOFIE STOP FROM BARKING IN THE BACKSEAT OF THE CAR?
SIT UP FRONT.
SHTOP!
WOOFIE WUVS SHPHINXIE!

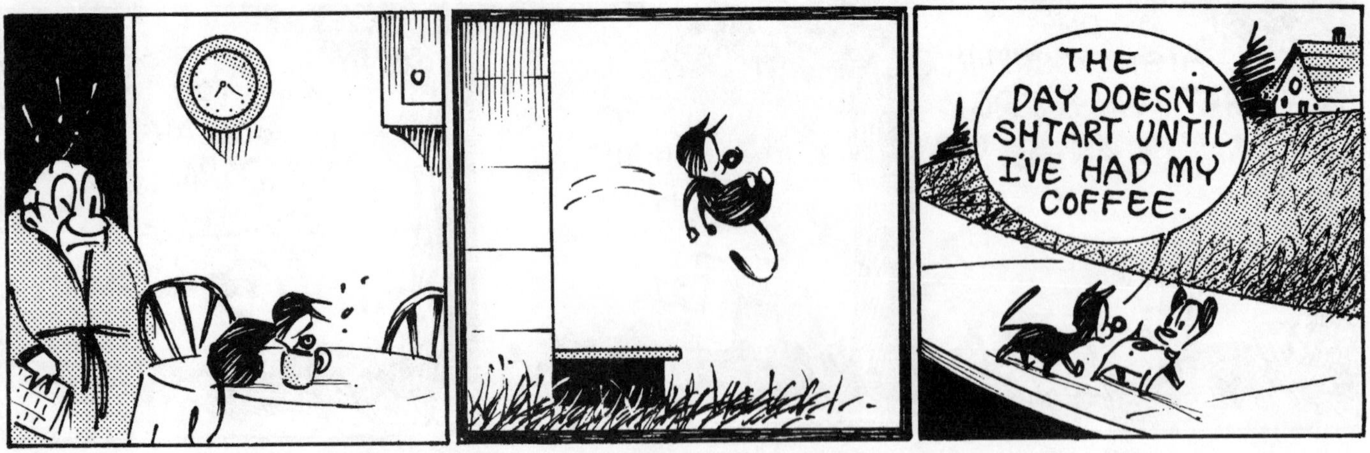
THE DAY DOESN'T SHTART UNTIL I'VE HAD MY COFFEE.

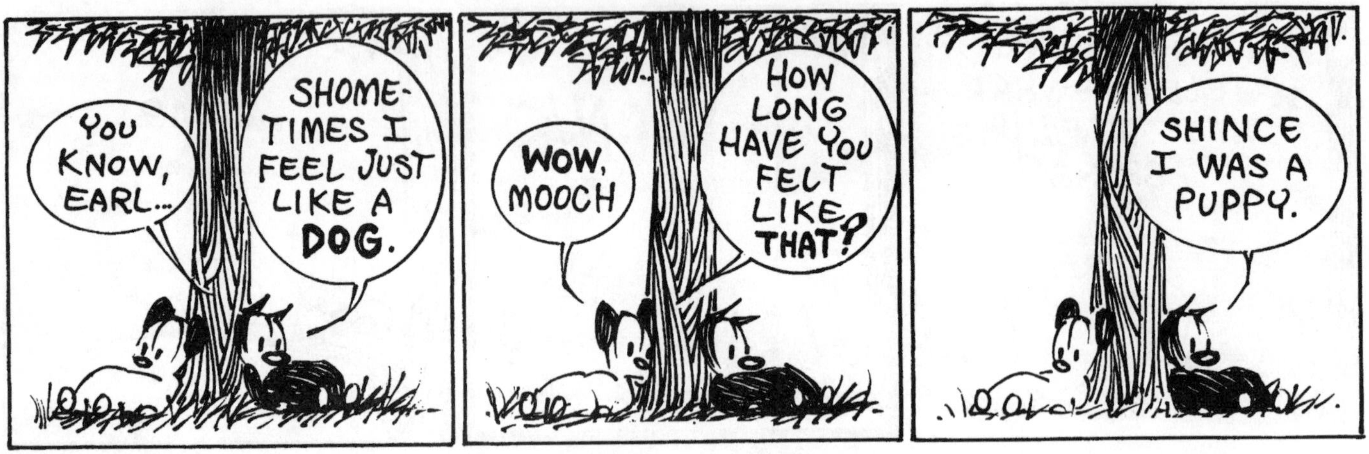
YOU KNOW, EARL...
SHOME-TIMES I FEEL JUST LIKE A DOG.
WOW, MOOCH
HOW LONG HAVE YOU FELT LIKE THAT?
SHINCE I WAS A PUPPY.

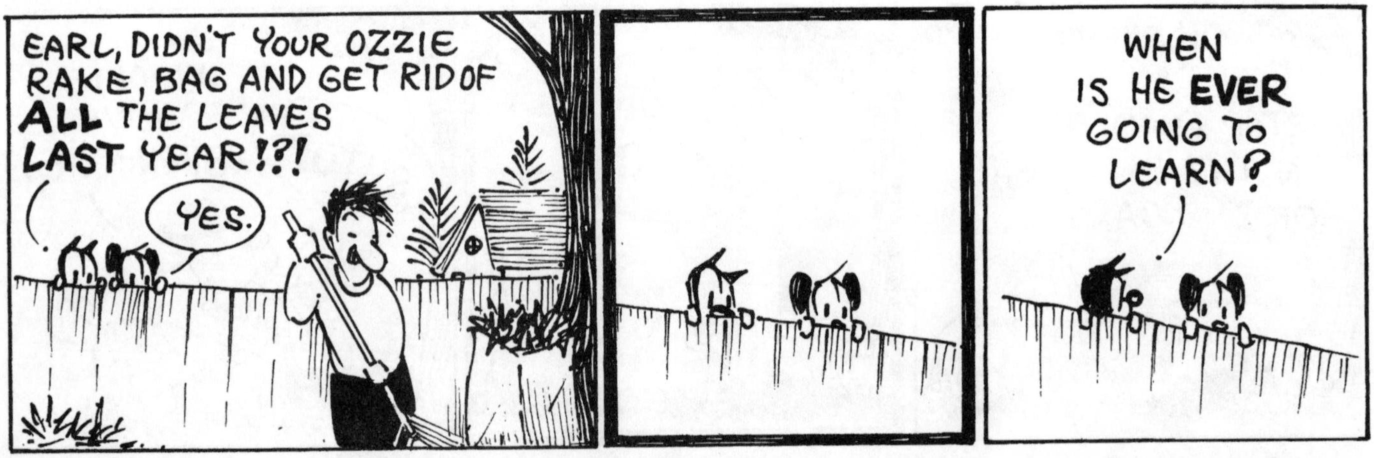
EARL, DIDN'T YOUR OZZIE RAKE, BAG AND GET RID OF ALL THE LEAVES LAST YEAR!?!
YES.
WHEN IS HE EVER GOING TO LEARN?

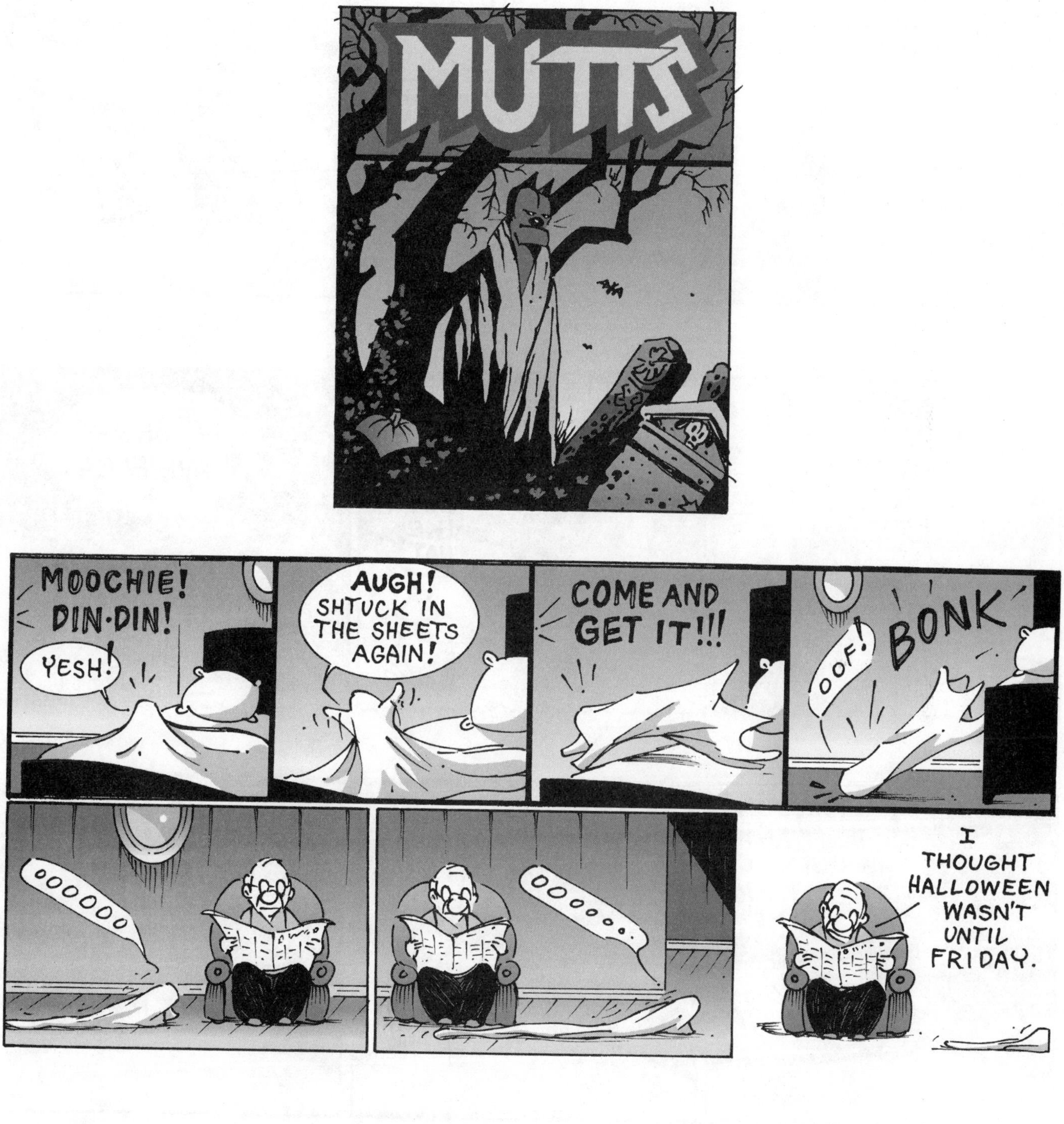
MUTTS
MOOCHIE! DIN-DIN!
YESH!
AUGH! SHTUCK IN THE SHEETS AGAIN!
COME AND GET IT!!!
OOF!
BONK
OOOOOO
OOOOOO
I THOUGHT HALLOWEEN WASN'T UNTIL FRIDAY.

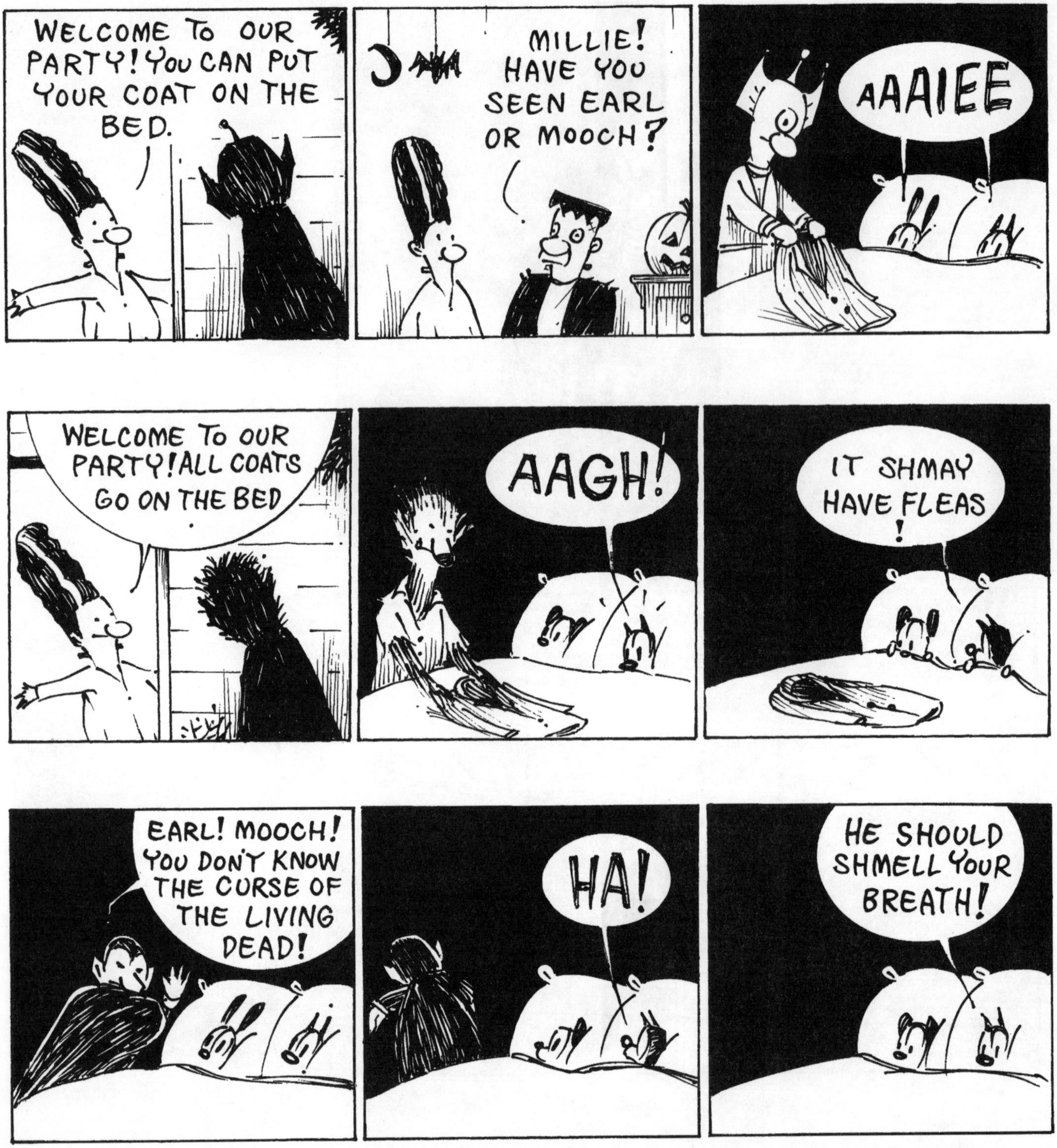
WELCOME TO OUR PARTY! YOU CAN PUT YOUR COAT ON THE BED.
MILLIE! HAVE YOU SEEN EARL OR MOOCH?
AAAIEE
WELCOME TO OUR PARTY! ALL COATS GO ON THE BED
AAGH!
IT SHMAY HAVE FLEAS!
EARL! MOOCH! YOU DON'T KNOW THE CURSE OF THE LIVING DEAD!
HA!
HE SHOULD SHMELL YOUR BREATH!

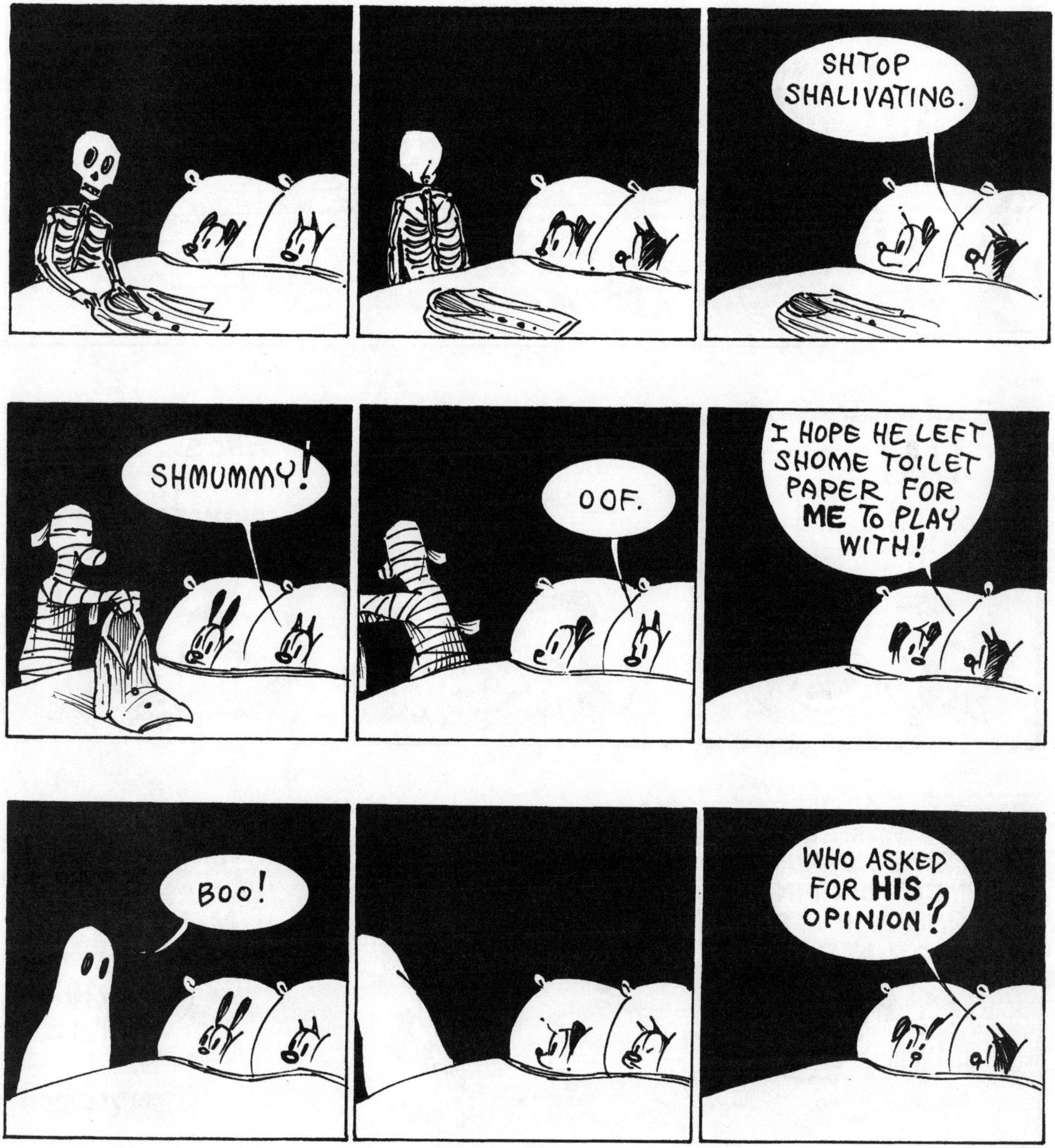
SHTOP SHALIVATING.
SHMUMMY!
OOF.
I HOPE HE LEFT SHOME TOILET PAPER FOR **ME** TO PLAY WITH!
BOO!
WHO ASKED FOR **HIS** OPINION?

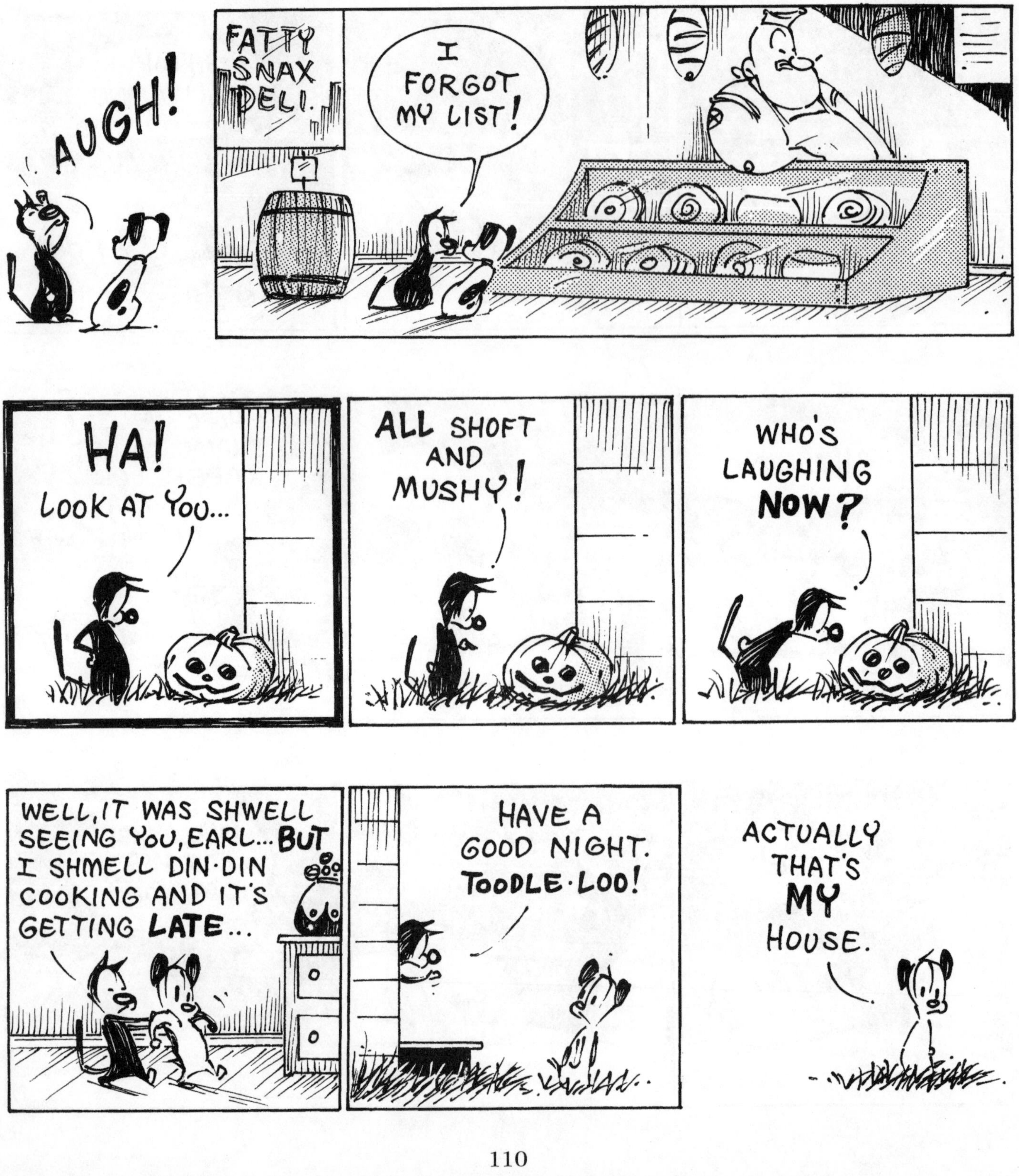
AUGH!
FATTY SNAX DELI
I FORGOT MY LIST!
HA! LOOK AT YOU...
ALL SHOFT AND MUSHY!
WHO'S LAUGHING NOW?
WELL, IT WAS SHWELL SEEING YOU, EARL... BUT I SHMELL DIN·DIN COOKING AND IT'S GETTING LATE...
HAVE A GOOD NIGHT. TOODLE·LOO!
ACTUALLY THAT'S MY HOUSE.

·MUTTS·
~BY·McDONNELL~

SHELTER STORY NEWS
Beau: Found wandering the streets. Help him find a home.
Peanut: Lost and forgotten, a tiny kitten with a big heart.
Chickpea and her brother: Surrendered littermates.
Uma: Dropped off. Give her a second chance.
Rosie: Abandoned, rescued and waiting.
Stanley: Lived under a truck. Loves everybody.
I'LL TAKE 'EM ALL!

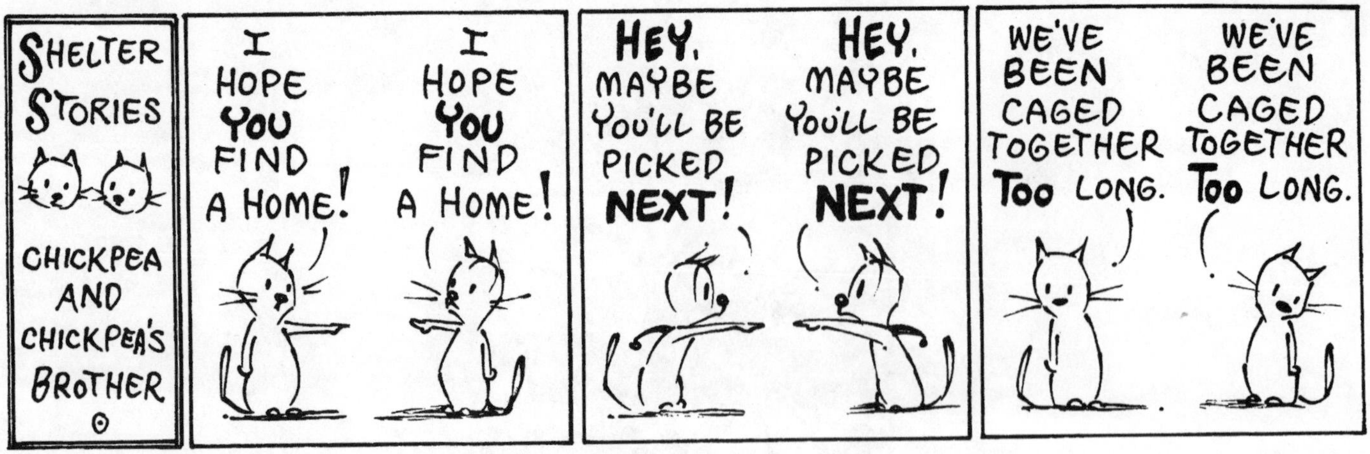
SHELTER STORIES
CHICKPEA AND CHICKPEA'S BROTHER
I HOPE **YOU** FIND A HOME!
I HOPE **YOU** FIND A HOME!
HEY, MAYBE YOU'LL BE PICKED **NEXT**!
HEY, MAYBE YOU'LL BE PICKED **NEXT**!
WE'VE BEEN CAGED TOGETHER **TOO** LONG.
WE'VE BEEN CAGED TOGETHER **TOO** LONG.

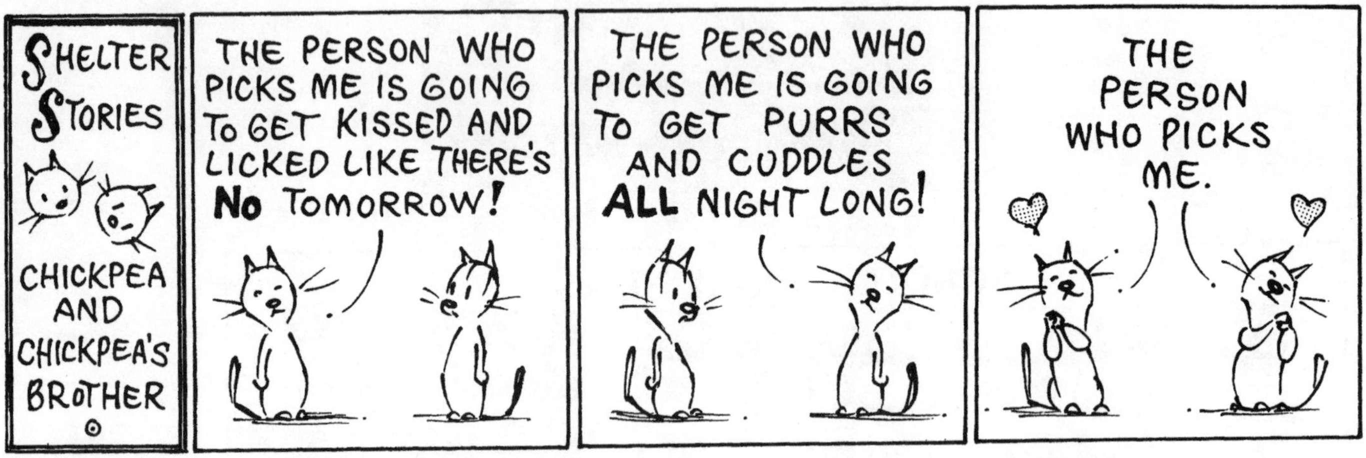
SHELTER STORIES
CHICKPEA AND CHICKPEA'S BROTHER
THE PERSON WHO PICKS ME IS GOING TO GET KISSED AND LICKED LIKE THERE'S **NO** TOMORROW!
THE PERSON WHO PICKS ME IS GOING TO GET PURRS AND CUDDLES **ALL** NIGHT LONG!
THE PERSON WHO PICKS ME.

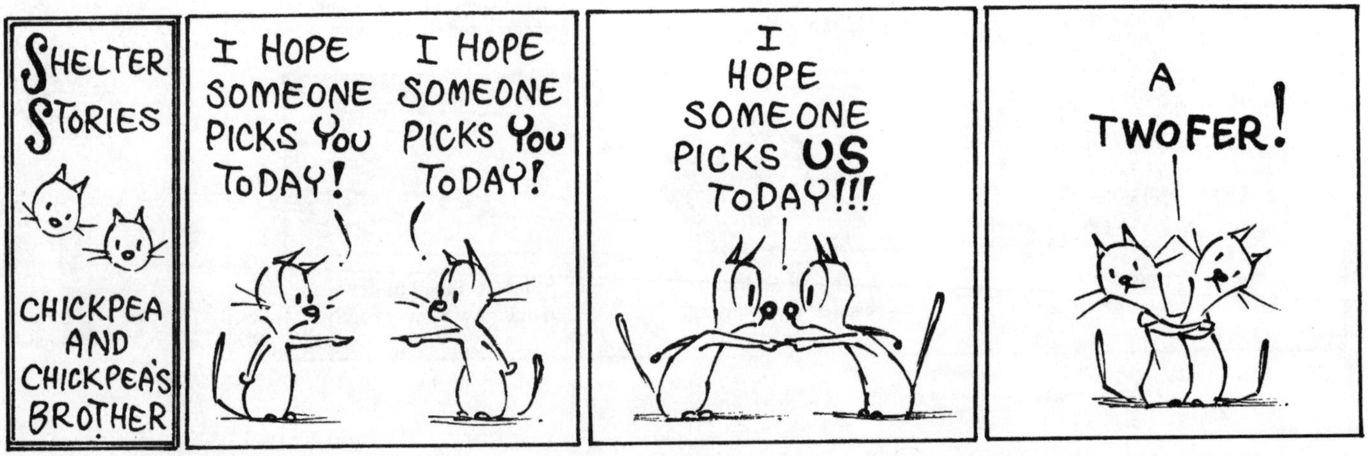
SHELTER STORIES
CHICKPEA AND CHICKPEA'S BROTHER
I HOPE SOMEONE PICKS **YOU** TODAY!
I HOPE SOMEONE PICKS **YOU** TODAY!
I HOPE SOMEONE PICKS **US** TODAY!!!
A **TWOFER**!

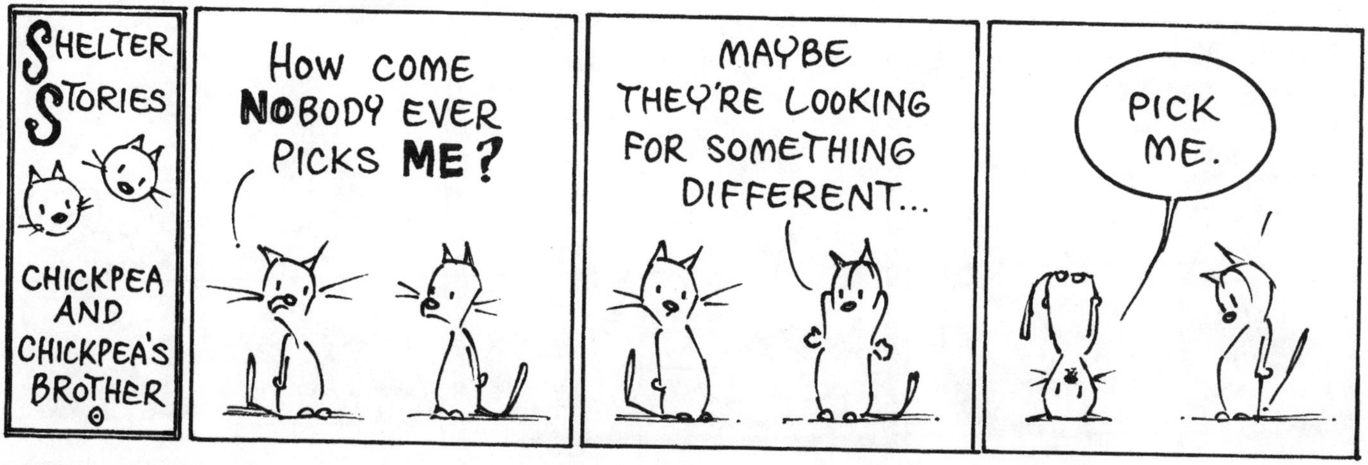
SHELTER STORIES
CHICKPEA AND CHICKPEA'S BROTHER
HOW COME NOBODY EVER PICKS ME?
MAYBE THEY'RE LOOKING FOR SOMETHING DIFFERENT...
PICK ME.

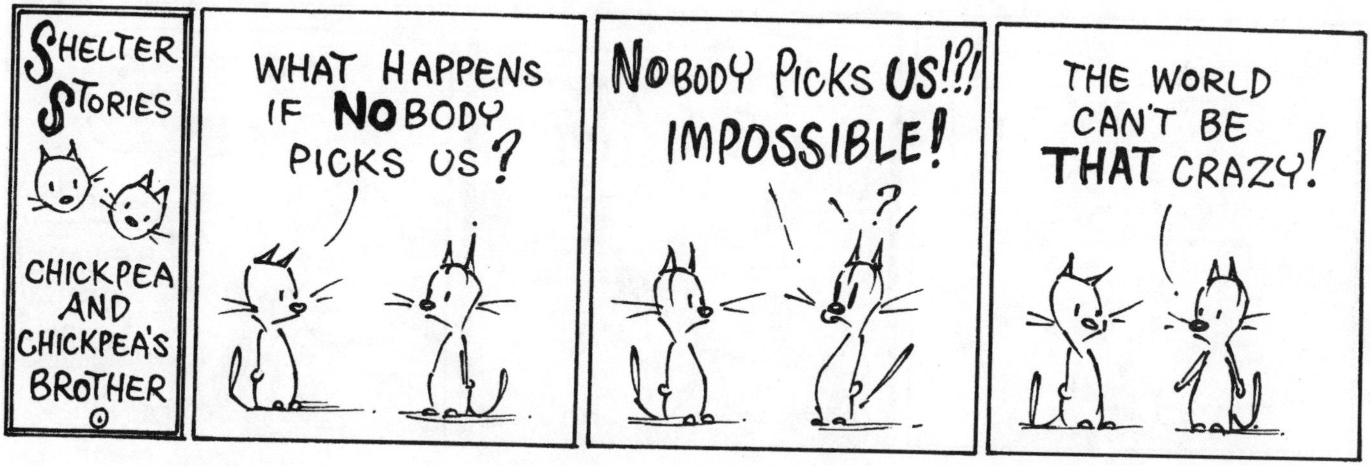
SHELTER STORIES
CHICKPEA AND CHICKPEA'S BROTHER
WHAT HAPPENS IF NOBODY PICKS US?
NOBODY PICKS US!?! IMPOSSIBLE!
THE WORLD CAN'T BE THAT CRAZY!

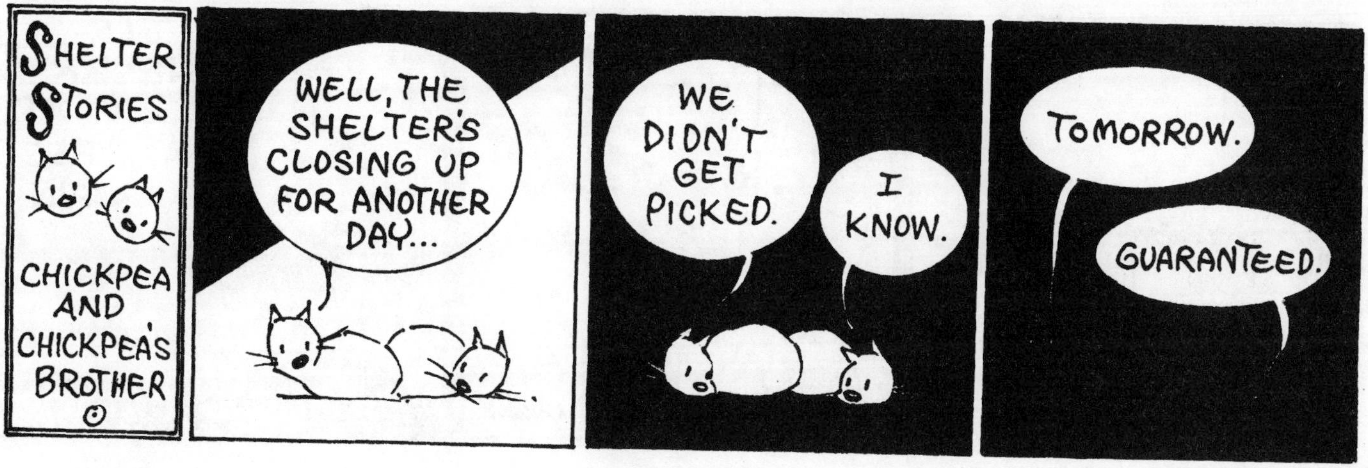
SHELTER STORIES
CHICKPEA AND CHICKPEA'S BROTHER
WELL, THE SHELTER'S CLOSING UP FOR ANOTHER DAY...
WE DIDN'T GET PICKED.
I KNOW.
TOMORROW.
GUARANTEED.

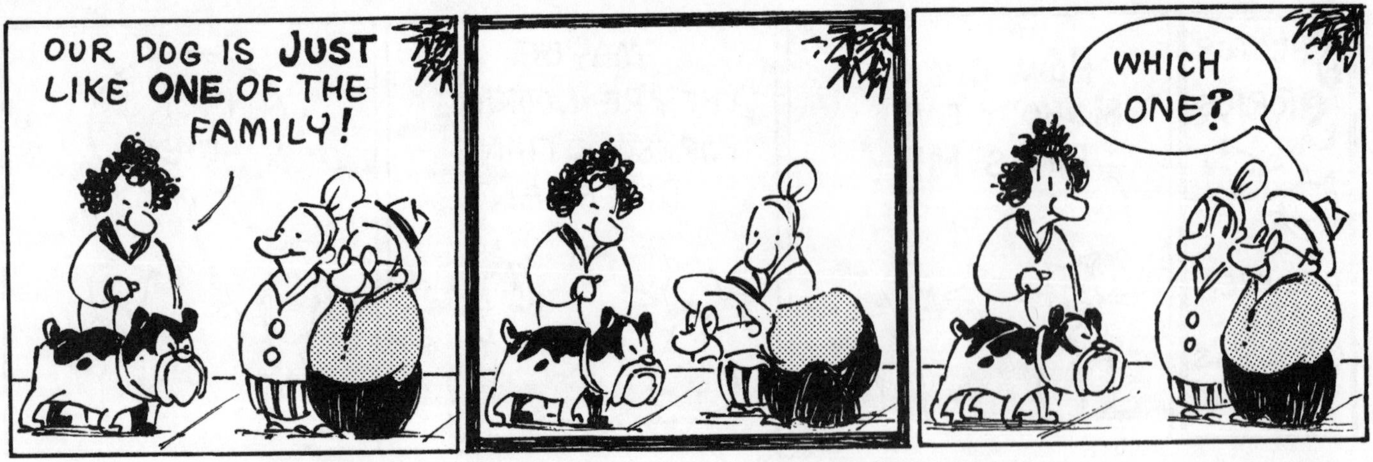
OUR DOG IS JUST LIKE ONE OF THE FAMILY!
WHICH ONE?

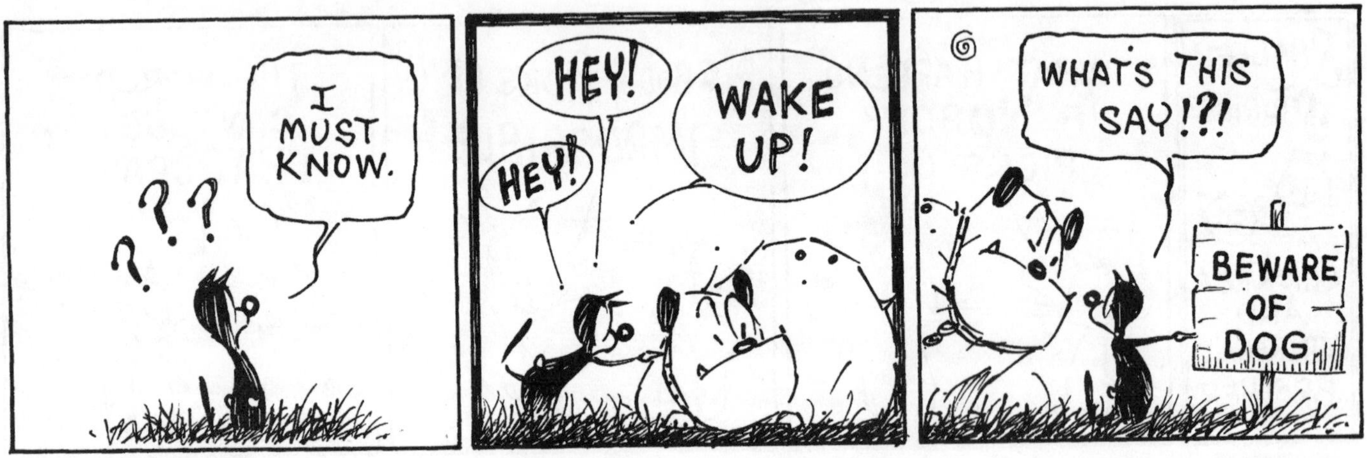
I MUST KNOW.
???
HEY!
HEY!
WAKE UP!
WHAT'S THIS SAY!?!
BEWARE OF DOG

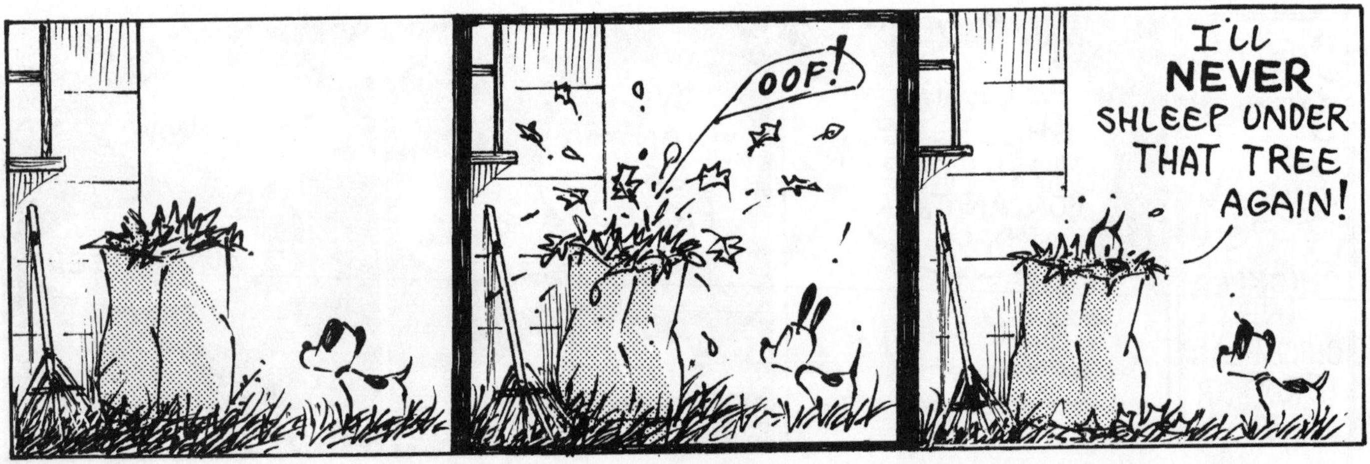
OOF!
I'LL NEVER SHLEEP UNDER THAT TREE AGAIN!

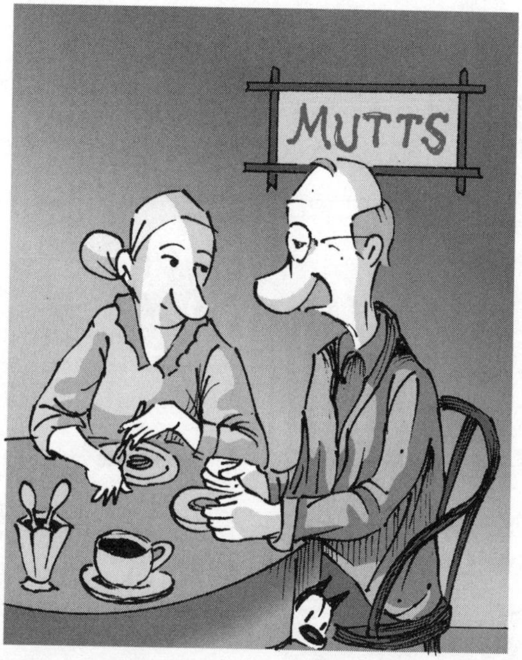
MUTTS

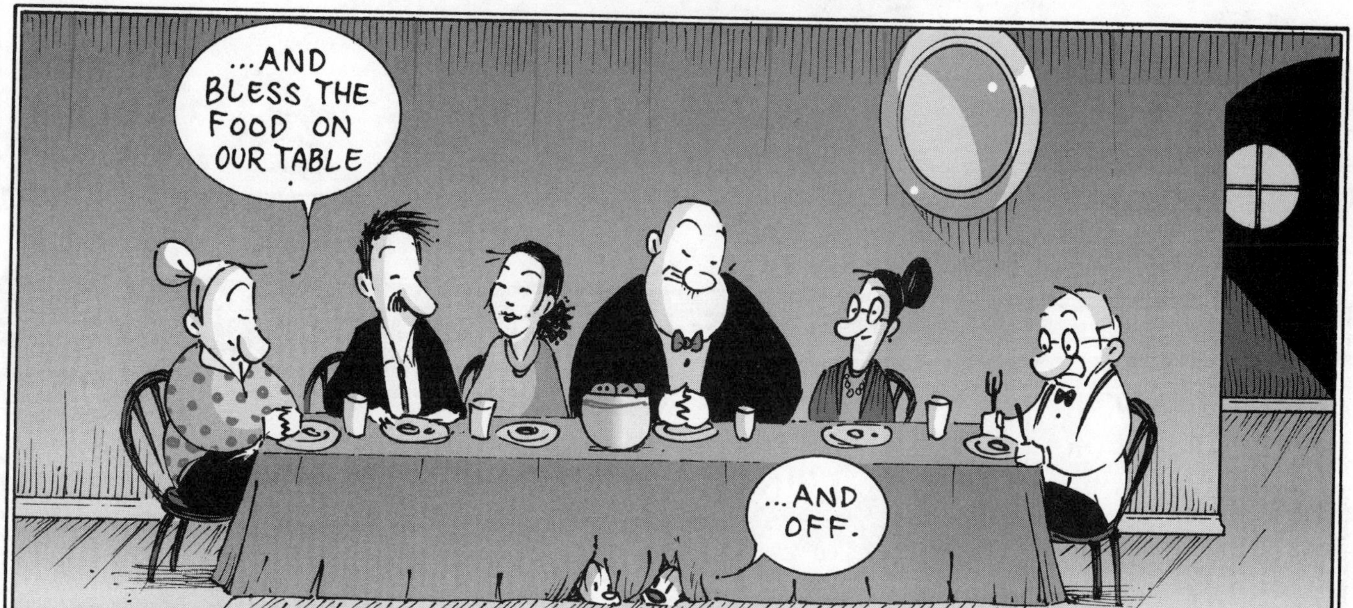
...AND BLESS THE FOOD ON OUR TABLE
...AND OFF.

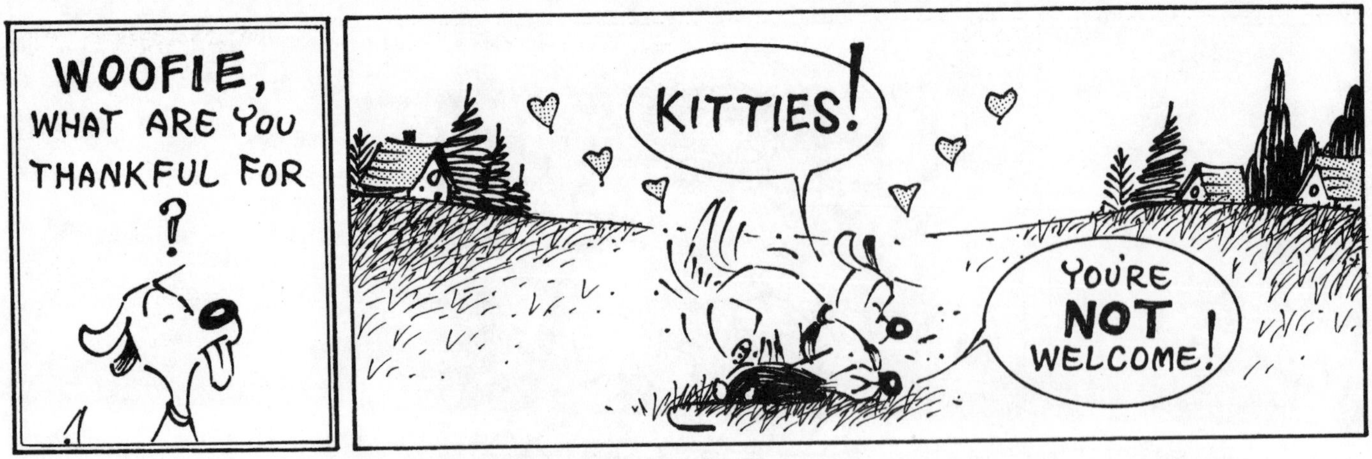
WOOFIE, WHAT ARE YOU THANKFUL FOR ?
KITTIES!
YOU'RE NOT WELCOME!

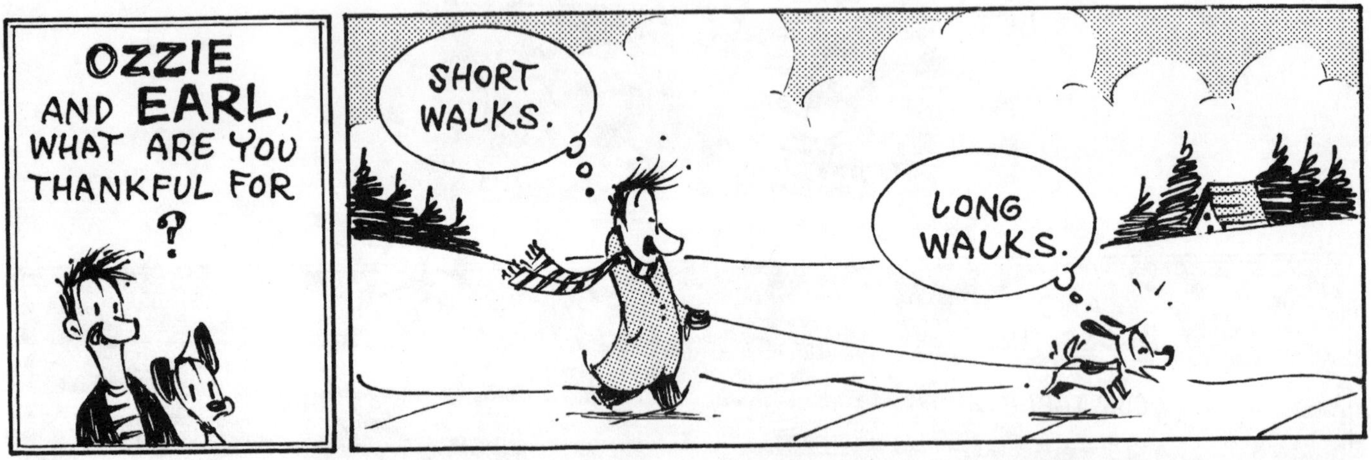
OZZIE AND EARL, WHAT ARE YOU THANKFUL FOR ?
SHORT WALKS.
LONG WALKS.

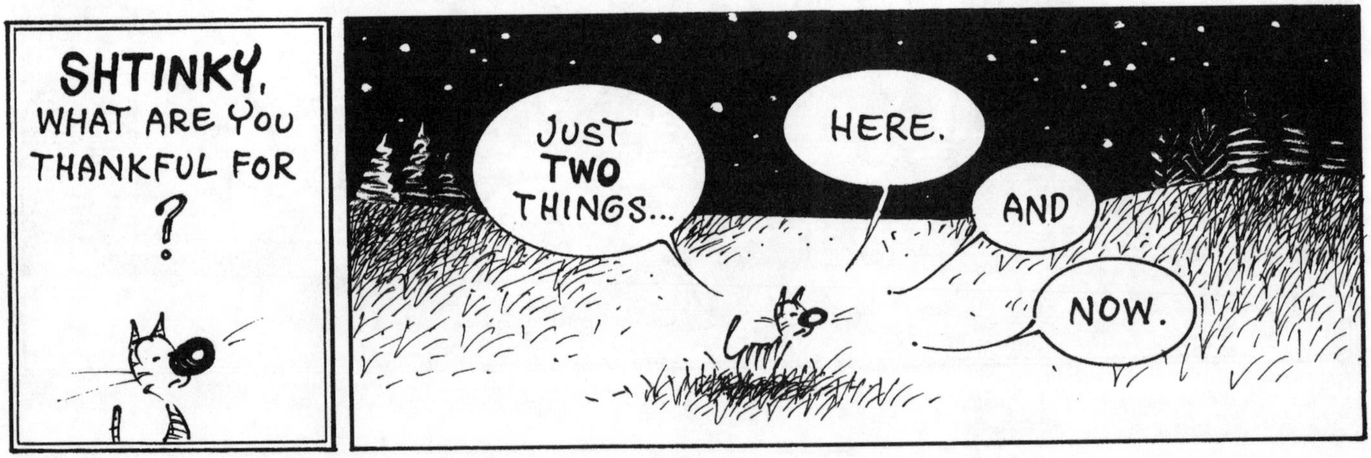
SHTINKY, WHAT ARE YOU THANKFUL FOR ?
JUST TWO THINGS...
HERE.
AND
NOW.

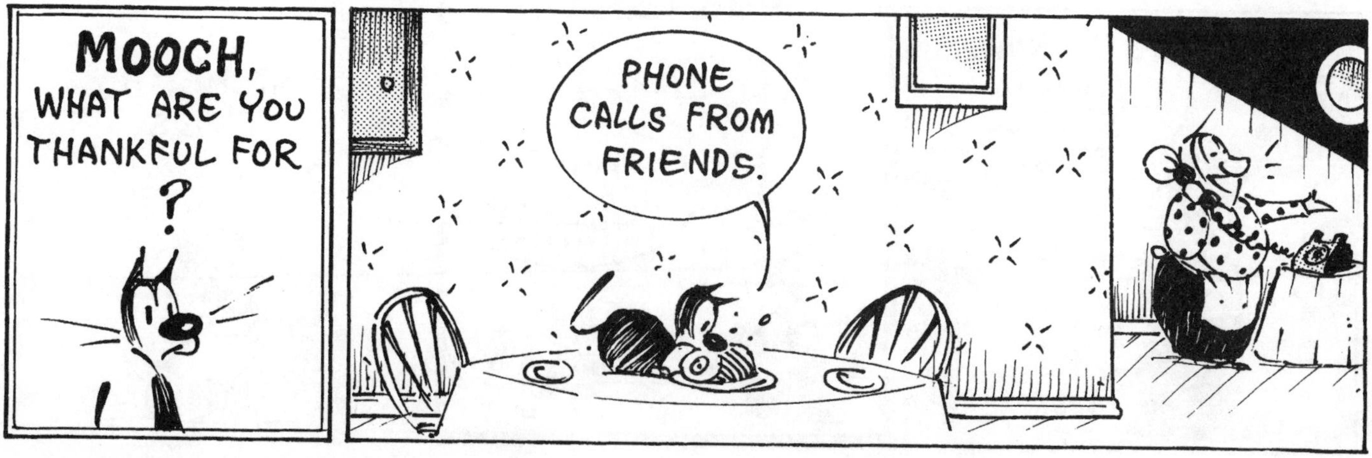
MOOCH, WHAT ARE YOU THANKFUL FOR ?
PHONE CALLS FROM FRIENDS.

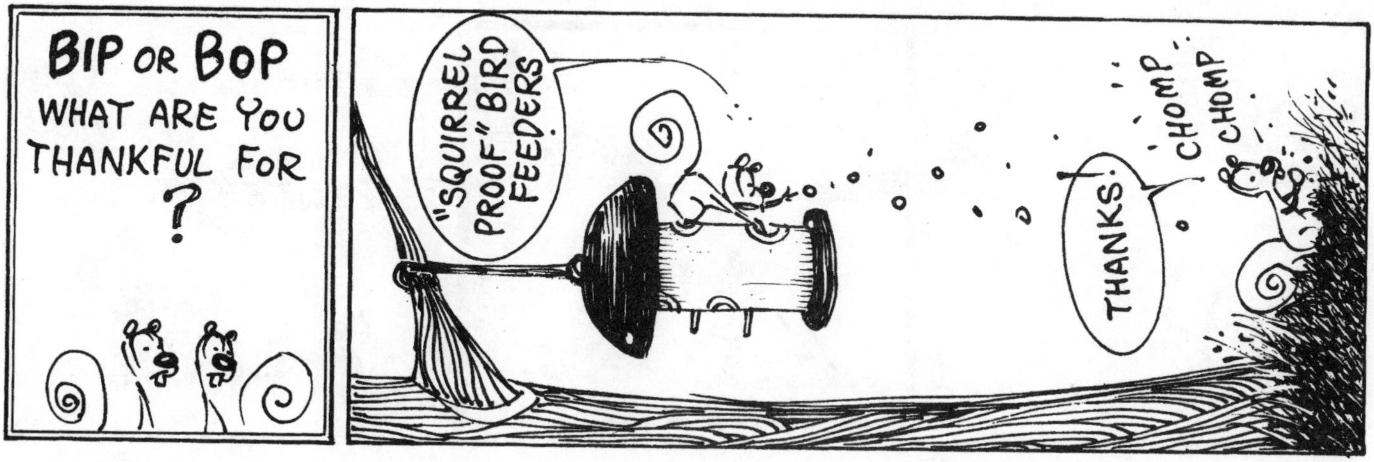
BIP OR BOP WHAT ARE YOU THANKFUL FOR ?
"SQUIRREL PROOF" BIRD FEEDERS.
THANKS.
CHOMP
CHOMP

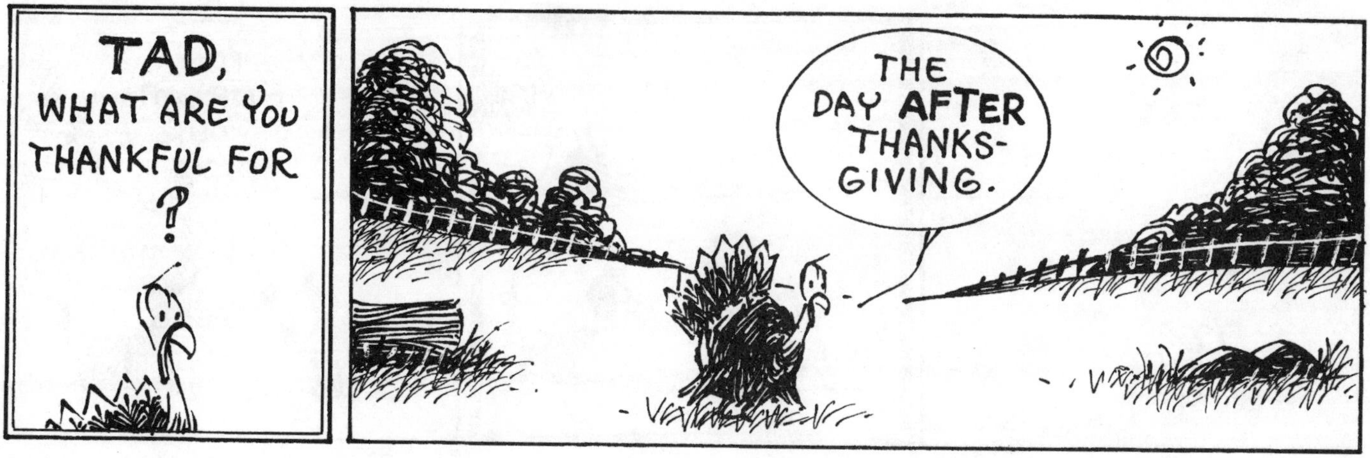
TAD, WHAT ARE YOU THANKFUL FOR ?
THE DAY AFTER THANKSGIVING.

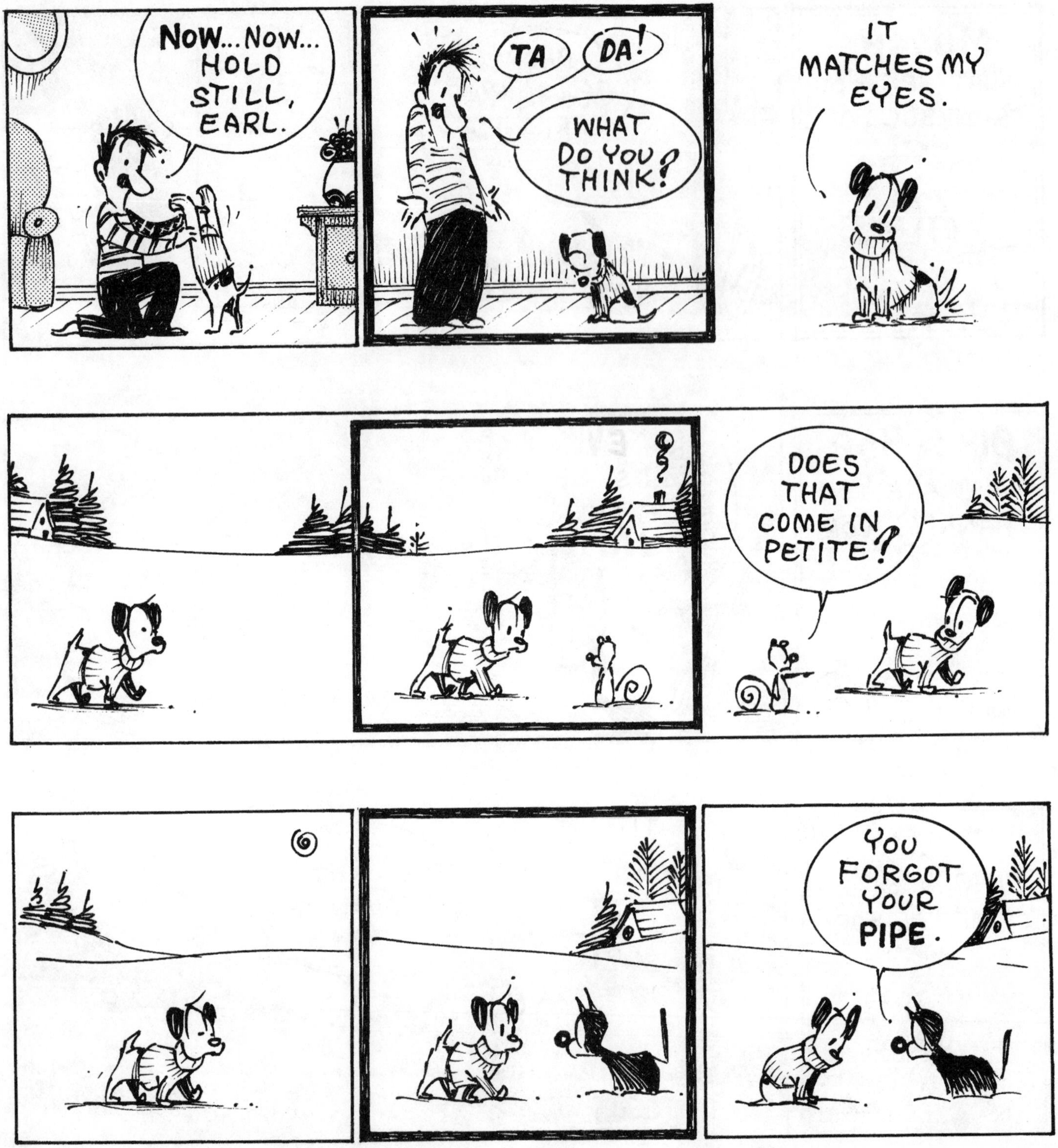
NOW... NOW... HOLD STILL, EARL.
TA
DA!
WHAT DO YOU THINK?
IT MATCHES MY EYES.
DOES THAT COME IN PETITE?
YOU FORGOT YOUR PIPE.

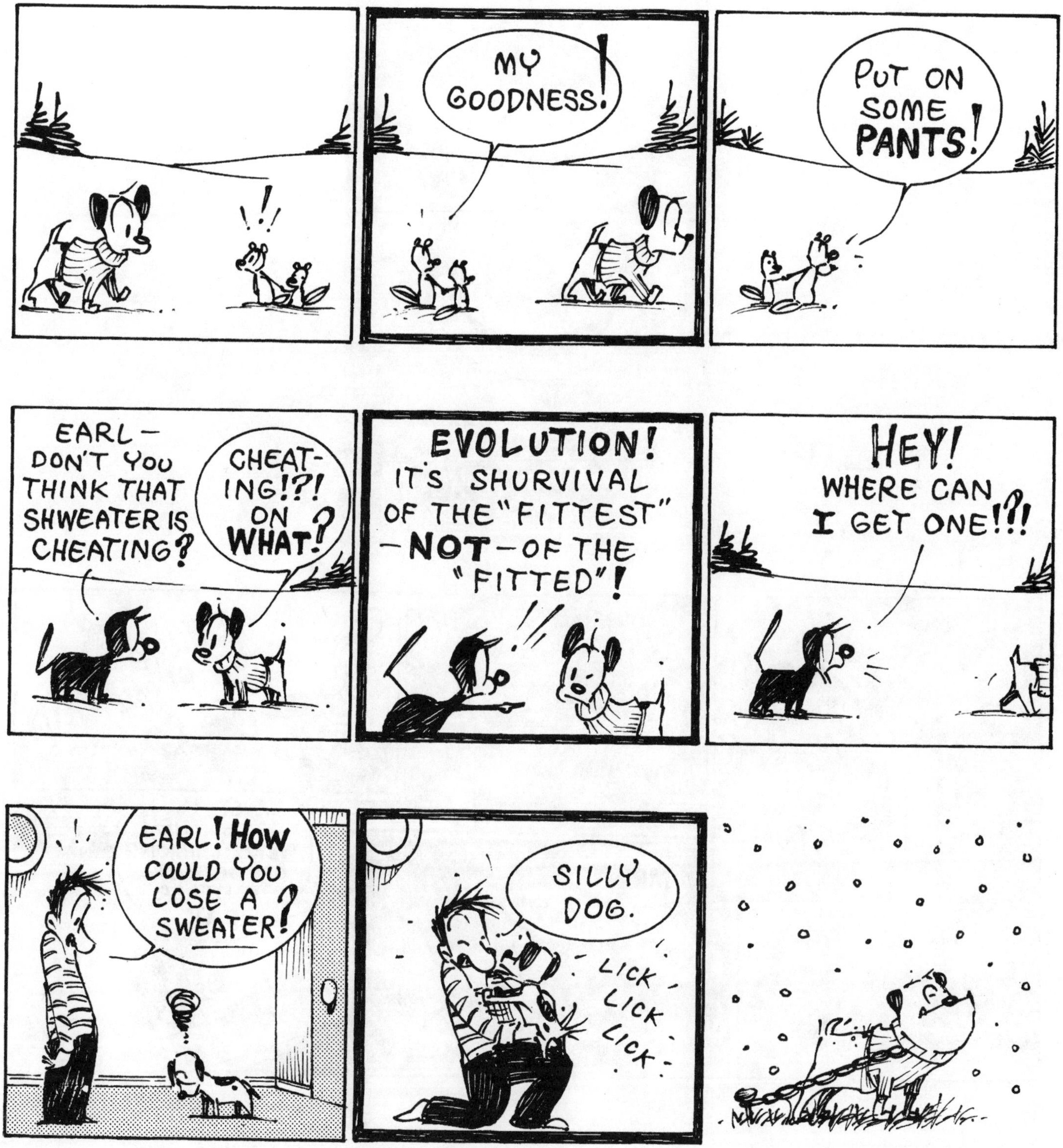
MY GOODNESS!
PUT ON SOME PANTS!
EARL- DON'T YOU THINK THAT SHWEATER IS CHEATING?
CHEAT-ING!?! ON WHAT?
EVOLUTION! IT'S SHURVIVAL OF THE "FITTEST" -NOT- OF THE "FITTED"!
HEY! WHERE CAN I GET ONE!?!
EARL! HOW COULD YOU LOSE A SWEATER?
SILLY DOG.
LICK LICK LICK

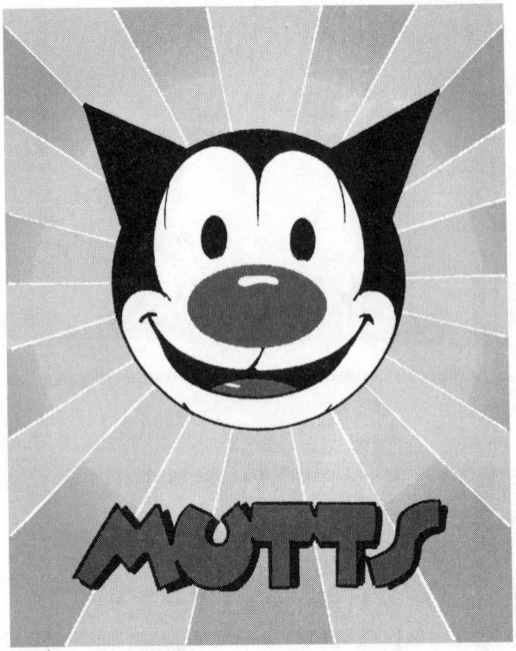
MUTTS

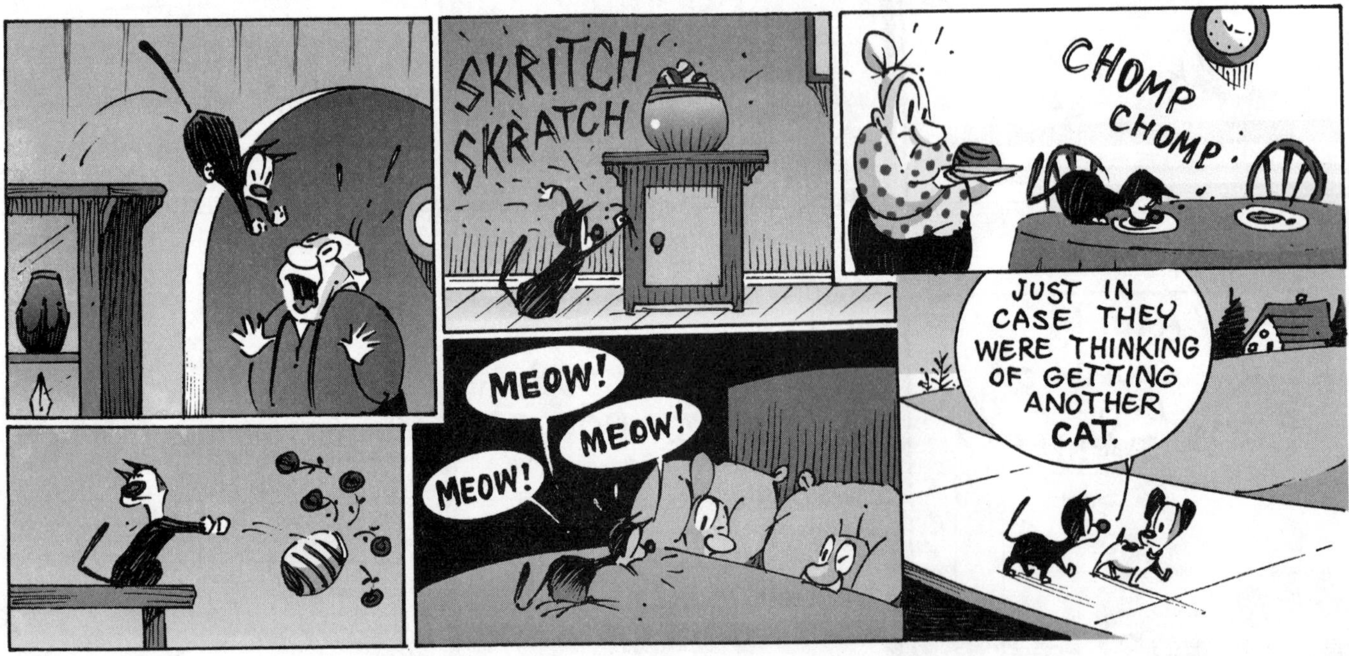
SKRITCH
SKRATCH
CHOMP
CHOMP
MEOW!
MEOW!
MEOW!
JUST IN CASE THEY WERE THINKING OF GETTING ANOTHER CAT.

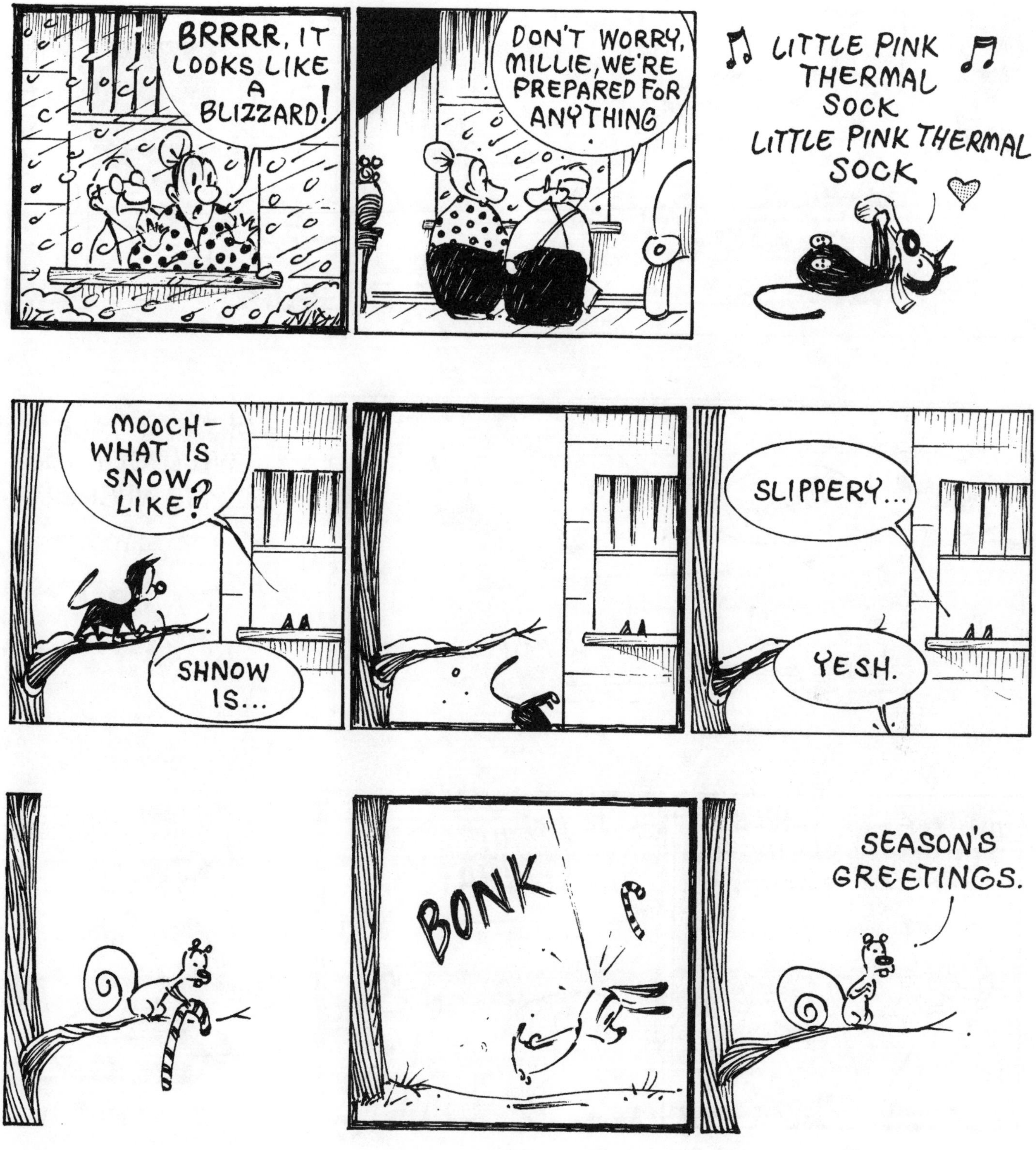
BRRRR, IT LOOKS LIKE A BLIZZARD!
DON'T WORRY, MILLIE, WE'RE PREPARED FOR ANYTHING
LITTLE PINK THERMAL SOCK LITTLE PINK THERMAL SOCK
MOOCH- WHAT IS SNOW LIKE?
SHNOW IS...
SLIPPERY...
YESH.
BONK
SEASON'S GREETINGS.

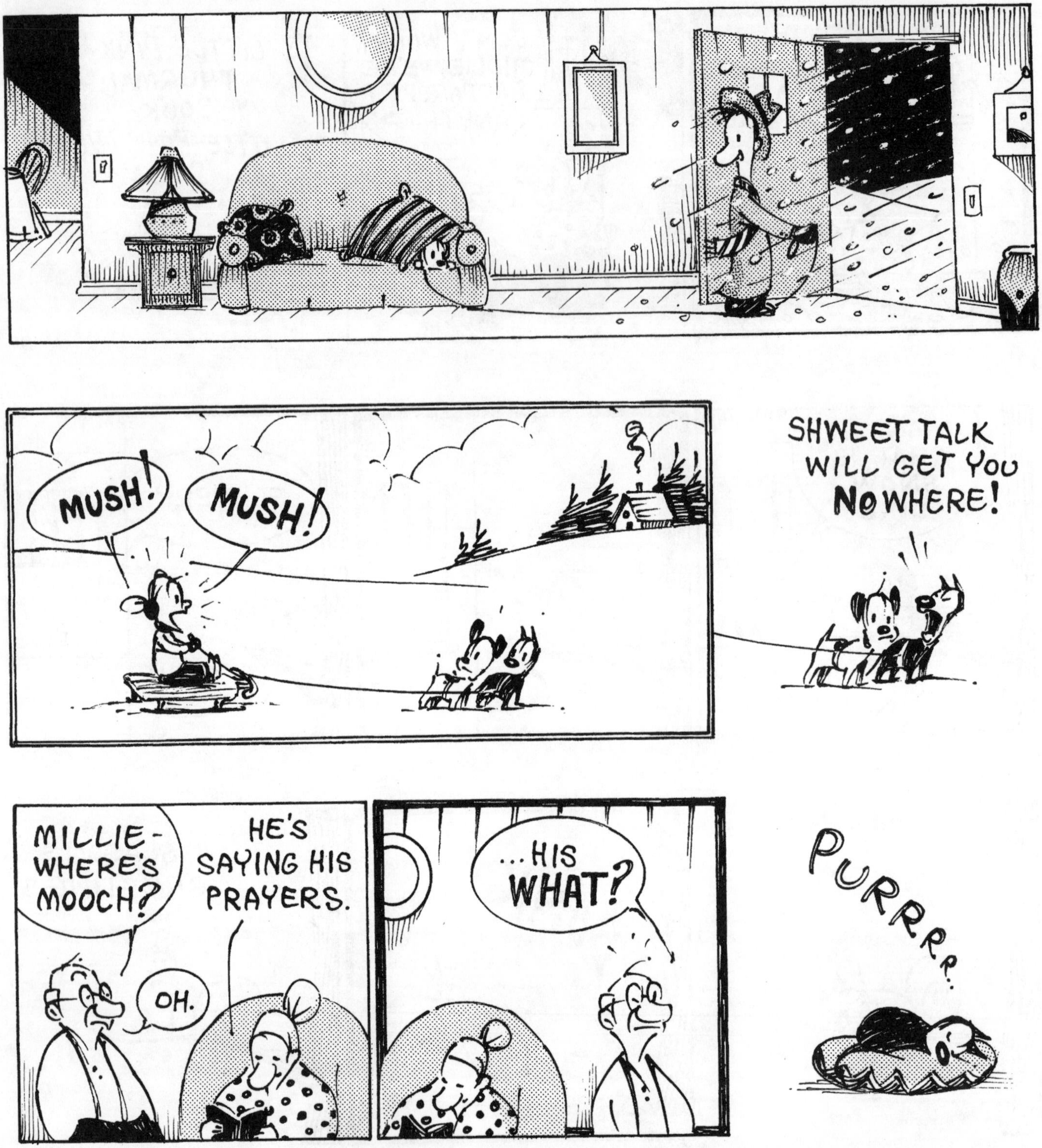
MUSH!
MUSH!
SHWEET TALK WILL GET YOU NOWHERE!
MILLIE- WHERE'S MOOCH?
HE'S SAYING HIS PRAYERS.
OH.
...HIS WHAT?
PURRRR..

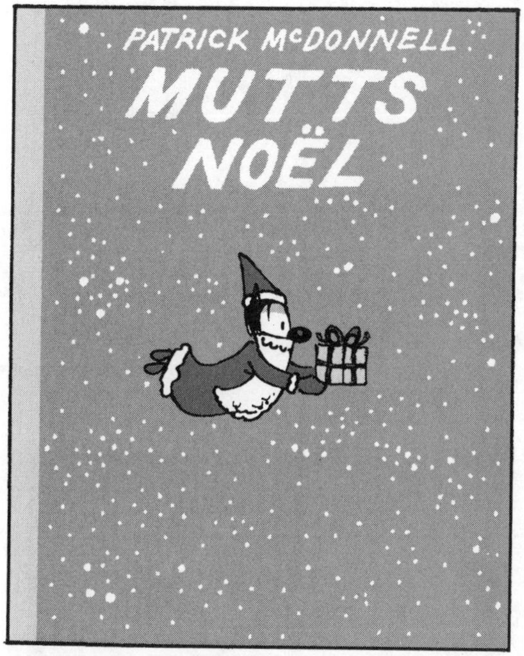
PATRICK McDONNELL
MUTTS
NOËL

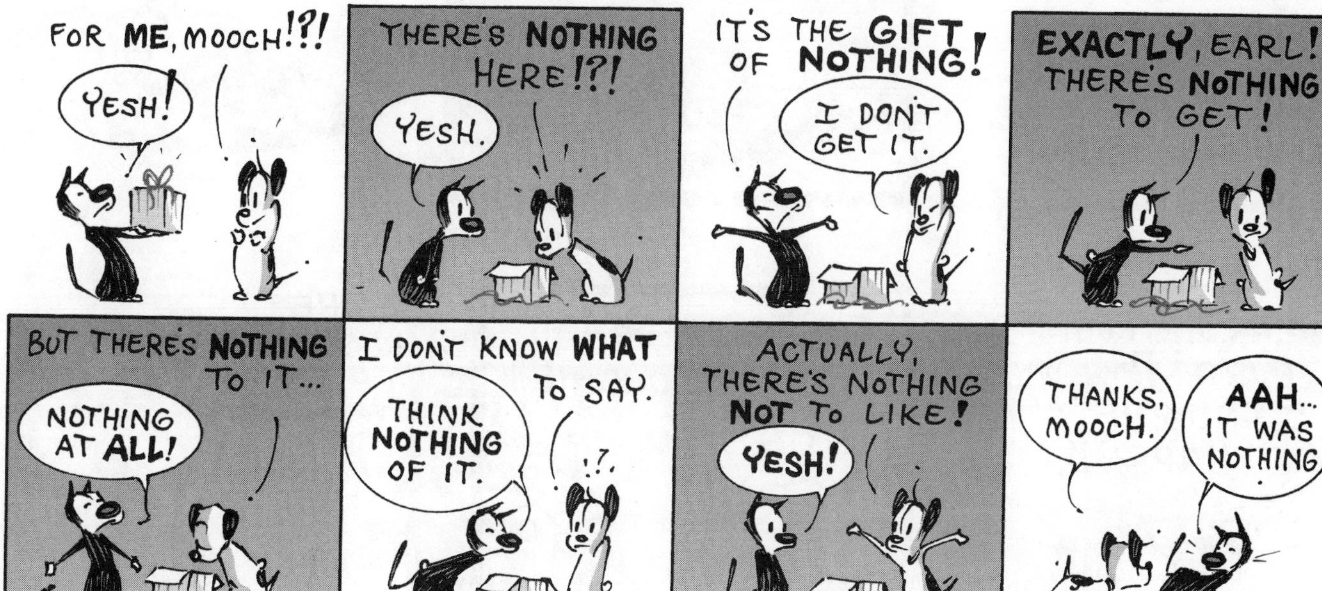
FOR ME, MOOCH!?!
YESH!
THERE'S NOTHING HERE!?!
YESH.
IT'S THE GIFT OF NOTHING!
I DON'T GET IT.
EXACTLY, EARL! THERE'S NOTHING TO GET!
BUT THERE'S NOTHING TO IT...
NOTHING AT ALL!
I DON'T KNOW WHAT TO SAY.
THINK NOTHING OF IT.
ACTUALLY, THERE'S NOTHING NOT TO LIKE!
YESH!
THANKS, MOOCH.
AAH... IT WAS NOTHING.

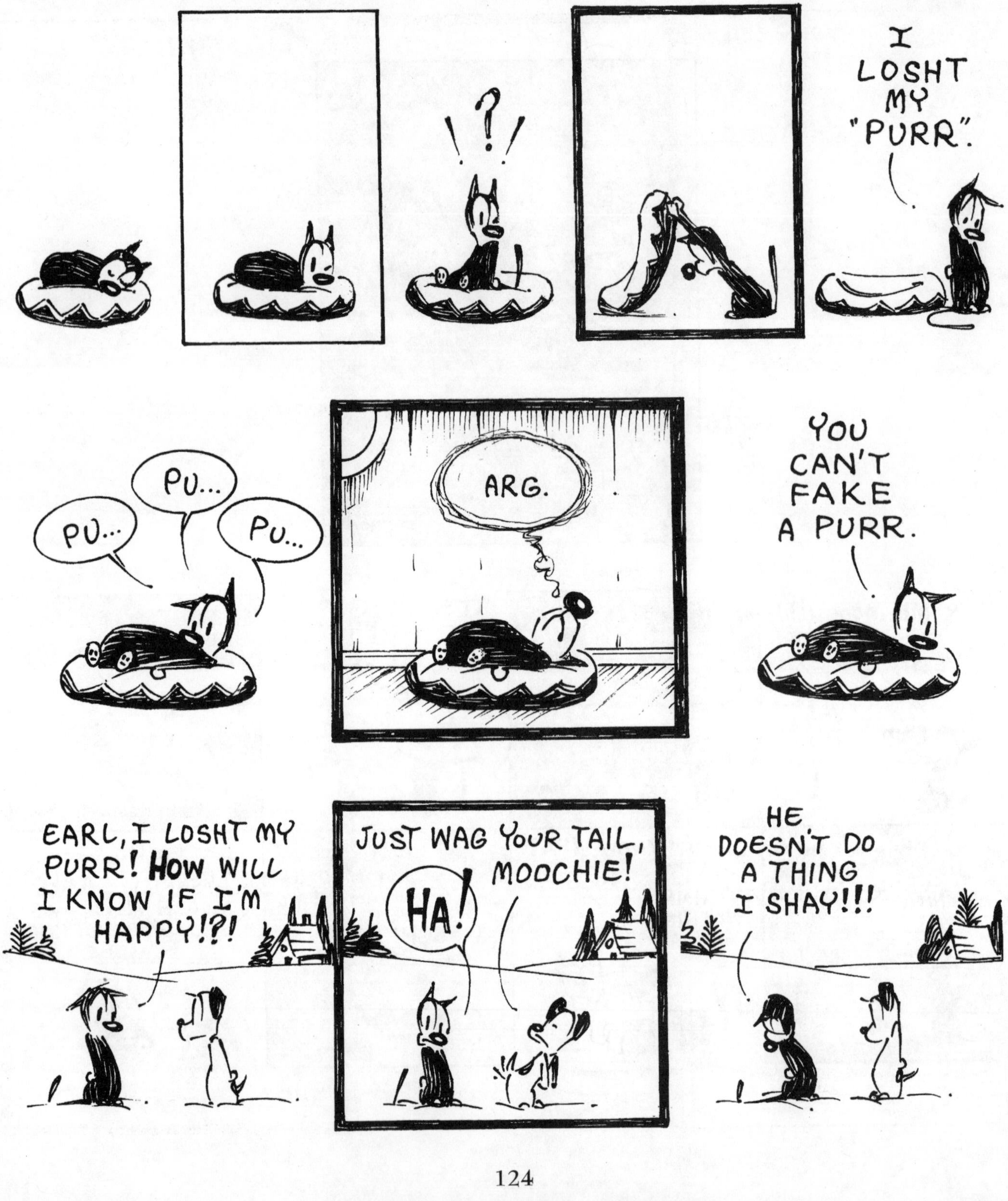

?
I LOSHT MY "PURR".
PU...
PU...
PU...
ARG.
YOU CAN'T FAKE A PURR.
EARL, I LOSHT MY PURR! HOW WILL I KNOW IF I'M HAPPY!?!
JUST WAG YOUR TAIL, MOOCHIE!
HA!
HE DOESN'T DO A THING I SHAY!!!

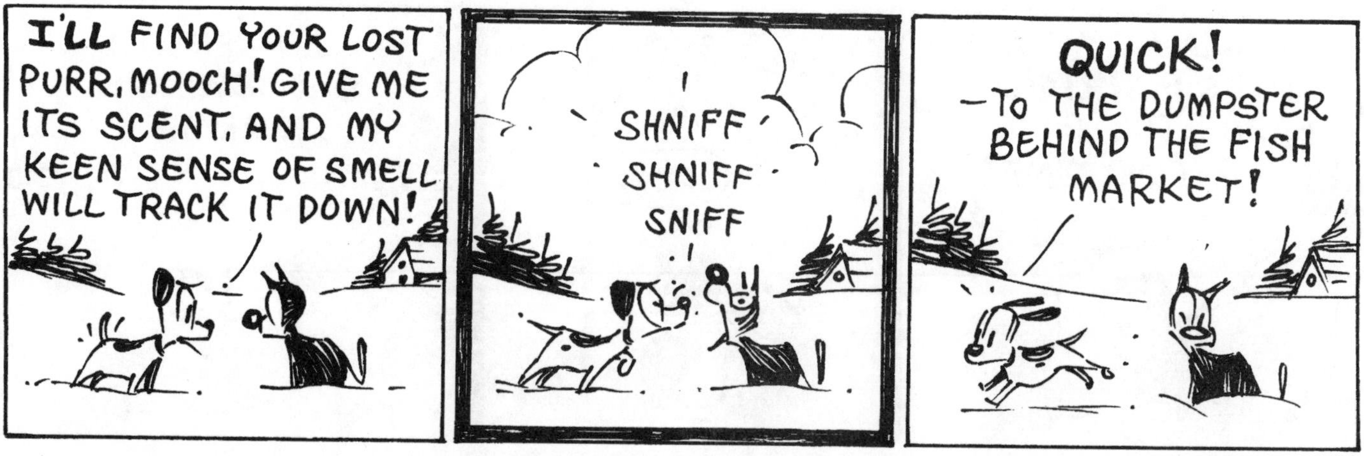
I'LL FIND YOUR LOST PURR, MOOCH! GIVE ME ITS SCENT, AND MY KEEN SENSE OF SMELL WILL TRACK IT DOWN!
SHNIFF
SHNIFF
SNIFF
QUICK!
–TO THE DUMPSTER BEHIND THE FISH MARKET!

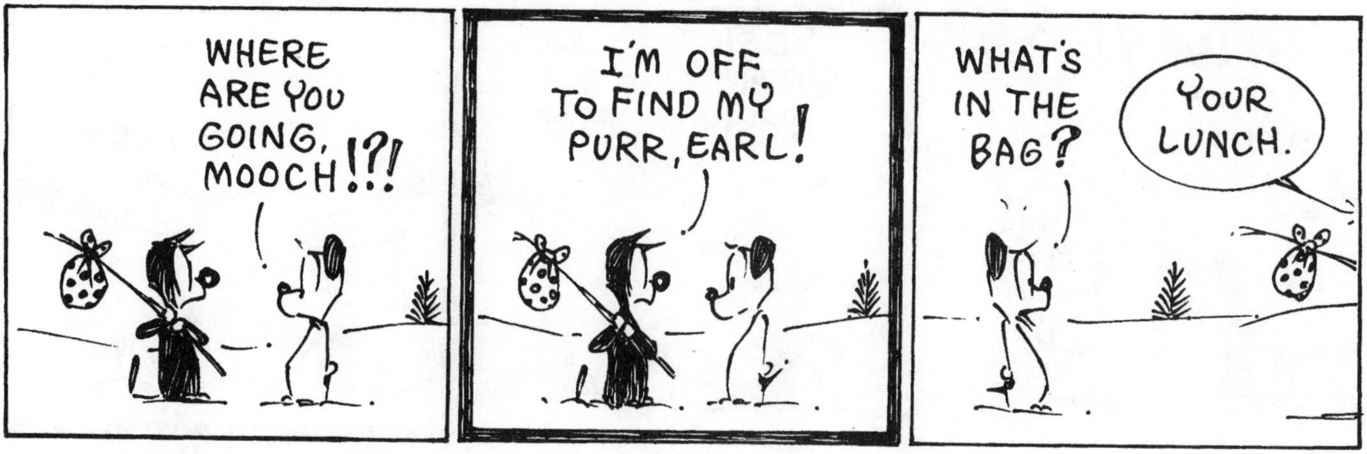
WHERE ARE YOU GOING, MOOCH!?!
I'M OFF TO FIND MY PURR, EARL!
WHAT'S IN THE BAG?
YOUR LUNCH.

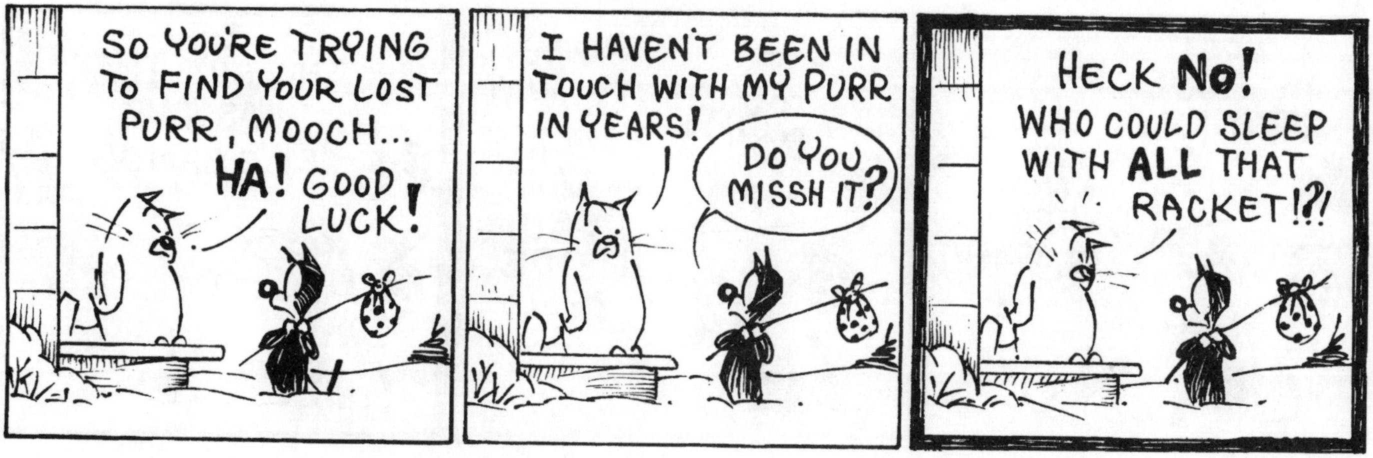
SO YOU'RE TRYING TO FIND YOUR LOST PURR, MOOCH...
HA! GOOD LUCK!
I HAVEN'T BEEN IN TOUCH WITH MY PURR IN YEARS!
DO YOU MISSH IT?
HECK NO!
WHO COULD SLEEP WITH ALL THAT RACKET!?!

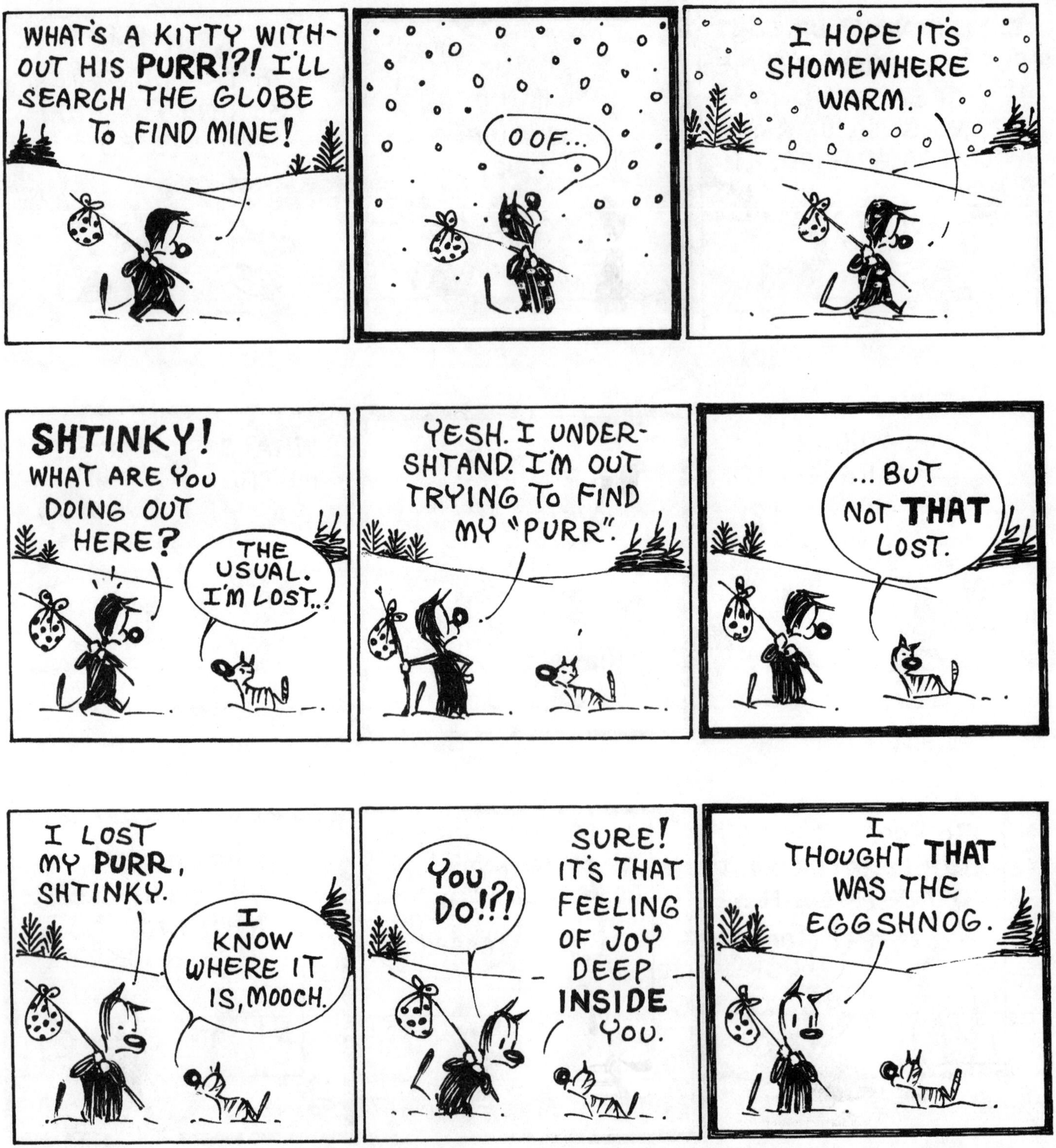
WHAT'S A KITTY WITHOUT HIS PURR!?! I'LL SEARCH THE GLOBE TO FIND MINE!
OOF...
I HOPE IT'S SHOMEWHERE WARM.
SHTINKY! WHAT ARE YOU DOING OUT HERE?
THE USUAL. I'M LOST...
YESH. I UNDERSHTAND. I'M OUT TRYING TO FIND MY "PURR".
...BUT NOT THAT LOST.
I LOST MY PURR, SHTINKY.
I KNOW WHERE IT IS, MOOCH.
YOU DO!?!
SURE! IT'S THAT FEELING OF JOY DEEP INSIDE YOU.
I THOUGHT THAT WAS THE EGGSHNOG.

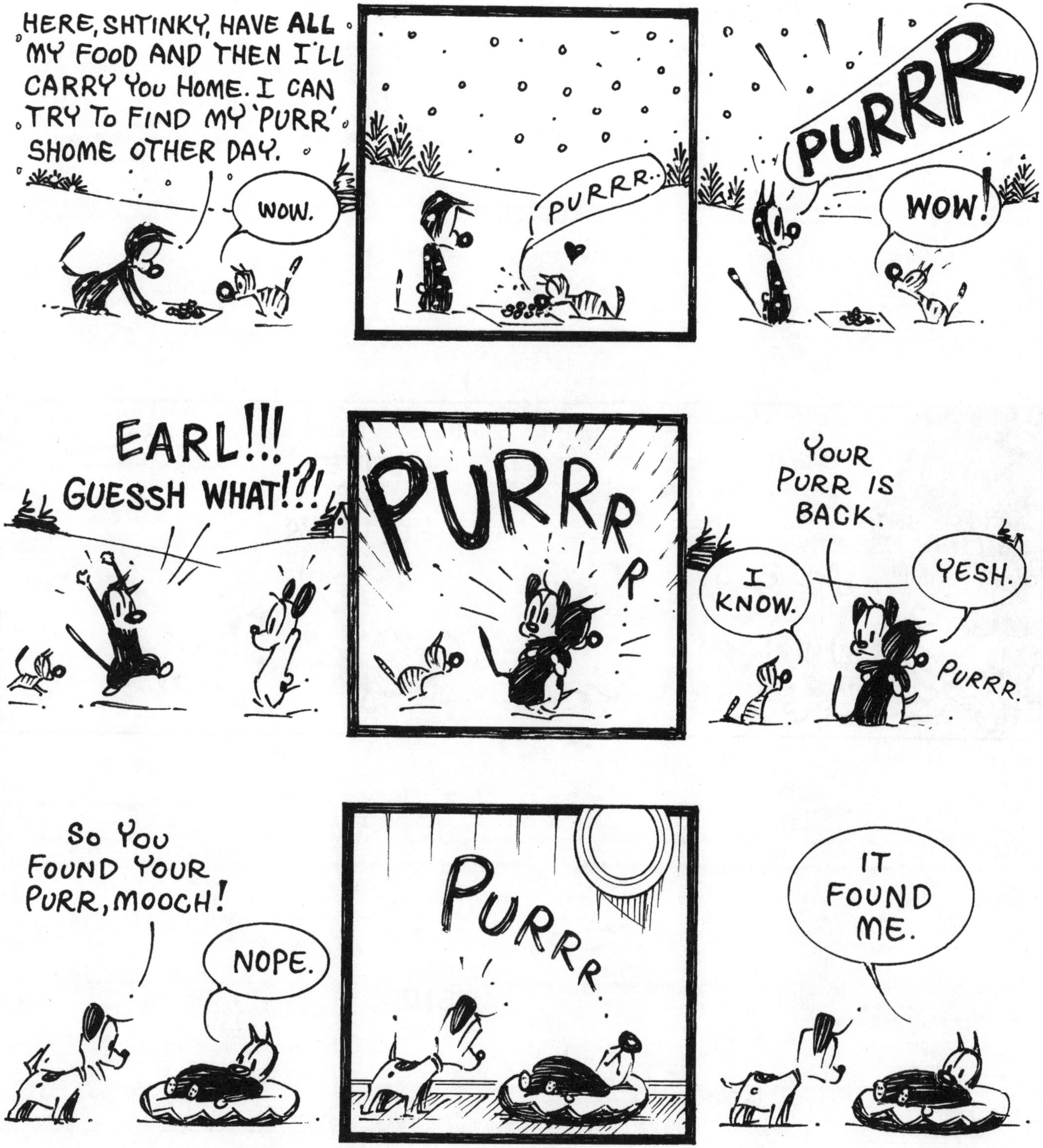
HERE, SHTINKY, HAVE **ALL** MY FOOD AND THEN I'LL CARRY YOU HOME. I CAN TRY TO FIND MY 'PURR' SHOME OTHER DAY.
WOW.
PURRR..
PURRR
WOW!
EARL!!! GUESSH WHAT!?!
PURRRR
YOUR PURR IS BACK.
I KNOW.
YESH.
PURRR.
SO YOU FOUND YOUR PURR, MOOCH!
NOPE.
PURRRR.
IT FOUND ME.

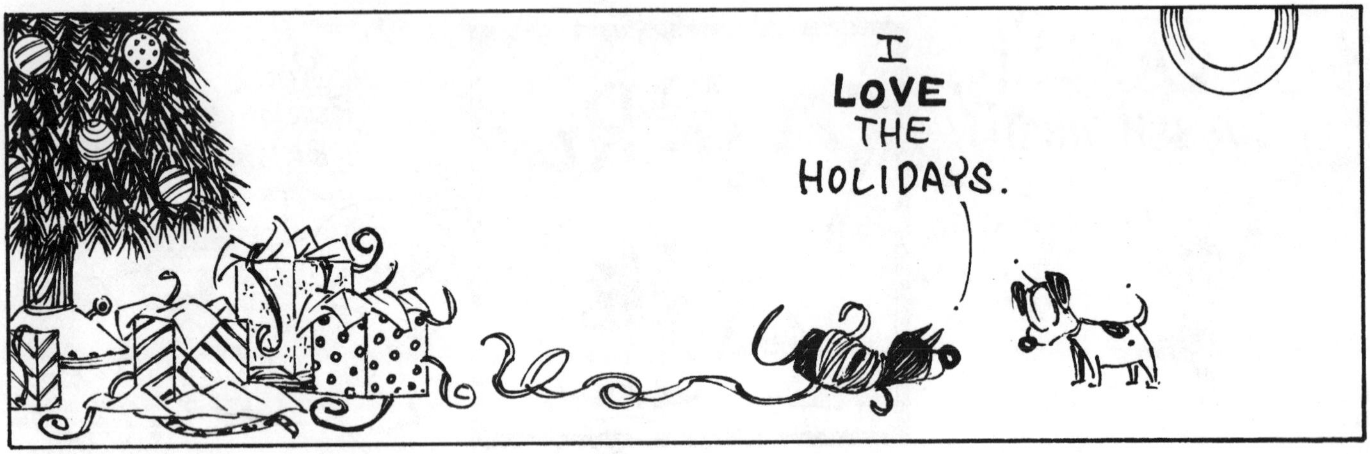
I LOVE THE HOLIDAYS.